The Psychology o

"As someone who has studied the impact of technology since the early 1980s I am appalled at how psychological principles are being used as part of the business model of many tech companies. More and more often I see behaviorism at work in attempting to lure brains to a site or app and to keep them coming back day after day. This book exposes these practices and offers readers a glimpse behind the "emotional scenes" as tech companies come out psychologically firing at their consumers. Unless these practices are exposed and made public, tech companies will continue to shape our brains and not in a good way."
—Larry D. Rosen, *Professor Emeritus of Psychology*, author of 7 books including
The Distracted Mind: Ancient Brains in a High Tech World

"*The Psychology of Silicon Valley* is a remarkable story of an industry's shift from idealism to narcissism and even sociopathy. But deep cracks are showing in the Valley's mantra of 'we know better than you.' Katy Cook's engaging read has a message that needs to be heard now."
—Richard Freed, author of *Wired Child*

"A welcome journey through the mind of the world's most influential industry at a time when understanding Silicon Valley's motivations, myths, and ethics are vitally important."
—Scott Galloway, *Professor of Marketing, NYU* and author of *The Algebra of Happiness* and *The Four*

Katy Cook

The Psychology of Silicon Valley

Ethical Threats and Emotional Unintelligence in the Tech Industry

palgrave
macmillan

1

Introduction

It is one of life's more amusing truths that we very rarely find what we set out in search of—nor do we usually end up exactly where we meant to go. That is the case with almost everything in my life and, thankfully, it holds true for this book as well.

Without realizing it, this work began taking shape in 2013. Like many people, I was becoming a little unnerved by the pace and scope of technology—how untested it seemed, how omnipresent and seductive. I would watch toddlers glued to iPads, parents glued to smartphones, and the rest of us chained to one device or another. I wondered what the effects would be, 20 years down the line, when it might be too late to do anything about it. A psychology nerd at heart, I was particularly worried about how these shiny little black boxes might affect our mental health and wellbeing, while the romantic in me wondered how they would change our relationships.

Two years later, my questions had snowballed dramatically. I ran a non-profit that looked at the effects of technology, co-founded awareness campaigns, and gave talks on any tech-related subject whenever I was able (despite a deep dislike of public speaking). I was probably the last person you'd want to get stuck talking to at a party, so precise was my

© The Author(s) 2020
K. Cook, *The Psychology of Silicon Valley*,
https://doi.org/10.1007/978-3-030-27364-4_1

ability to steer any conversation into a discussion about the human and social impacts of technology. What began as a concern about how technology impacts our wellbeing had evolved into a study of how tech affects society more broadly. I researched how technology was changing our institutions, our interactions, the way we work, our understanding of privacy, and the very notion of truth and information. But I knew I hadn't found what tied it all together.

After years of studying how tech was changing our world—and whether it was changing us—my questions circled back to psychology; but instead of wondering about the psychological effects technology was having on us, I started to wonder about the psychology that was creating technology itself. This book is a result of that question. It is an attempt to explore the thinking and behaviors present in Silicon Valley, how these are defining the world that is being built, how that is positive, and how it is not.

*   *   *

While many books have usefully outlined what is happening in Silicon Valley, fewer have attempted to explore why. The first part of this book looks at the psychology of the industry—its identity, culture, myths, and motivations. Each chapter begins with a short introduction to the psychological components of these terms, then explores how they are relevant to the mindset or behaviors of Silicon Valley. The second part explores some of the major social impacts linked to the spread of technology—misinformation, the decline of democracy, wealth and income inequality, changes to employment, and mental health, relationships, and cognition—and how the psychology of tech may have contributed to or enabled these. The third and final part looks at the psychological and leadership qualities that are either missing or socially maladaptive within Silicon Valley and what we can do to course-correct the industry.

A few caveats before we get started.

It is not the intention of this book to shame or cast blame, but to draw attention to behavioral norms within the industry that are unhealthy or harmful to society. When it comes to its beliefs, behaviors, and choices—the building blocks of its psychology—the tech industry could use some help, of the kind that cannot be engineered away. I hope this book fosters some useful discussions and positive changes towards that end.

Nor is it the intent of this study to 'diagnose' the whole of Silicon Valley, an exercise that is as impossible as it would be unhelpful. Rather, this book will borrow ideas and frameworks used to understand psychological processes and apply them to the tech industry. It will look at trends and behaviors that establish the standards and conventions of Silicon Valley. It will not aim to label, but to explore and shed light on the dynamics that inform the culture of the tech industry—its beliefs, values, and motivations. Unlike personal psychology, industrial, cultural, and organizational psychology each require generalizations, which capture systemic issues but often leave out the voices and nuance of individual experience. While I have attempted to retain personal accounts by including interviews, a broad range of research, and detailed analysis, I am conscious that at times these must give way to the larger themes and psychological commonalities of the industry, which are the focus of this study. Thus, this book will likely disappoint anyone searching for a panacea for all tech's problems. What I hope it can offer is a collection of observations about the psychology of the tech industry and a different way of thinking about how we might address the unique and urgent issues that mindset has created.

Defining the tech industry is another ambiguous starting point. While the field of technology was more contained when I first began researching its effects, it has since become a layer over everything. To help clarify the scope of what the following chapters explore, I borrow Jamie Bartlett's definition, which refers to the modern tech industry "specifically [as] the digital technologies associated with Silicon Valley—social media platforms, big data, mobile technology and artificial intelligence—that are increasingly dominating economic, political and social life."[1] There is also the issue of categorization. Azeem Azhar has rightfully pointed out that not all tech companies are created equal; when we talk about the tech industry, there is a danger of conflating the Facebooks, Googles, and Twitters of the world with "small-t technology." This risks the possibility that "[t]he real (and exaggerated) misbehaviour, stubbornness and obnoxiousness of... the Big-T Tech industry might spill over into a general diminution of faith in small-t technology."[2] To address this, Azhar has called for "two different strategies: one to tackle the power, where it distorts, of bigtech, and another to critically evaluate, steer and design the direction of small-t technology" in a way that is consistent with social values.[3] This book aims both to explore the power dynamics, attitudes, and behaviors of big tech, and consider the future direction of technology more broadly, with particular attention to the industry's ethics.

Despite the difficulties of definition and containment, it is my hope that the following pages foster a deeper understanding of the tech industry that allow us to begin answering important questions about the future. What types of thinking and beliefs define the industry? What voices and perspectives are missing? Is the leadership of the quality we expect? How can we build on what works and challenge what doesn't? And, most importantly, how can we ensure the products and platforms of Silicon Valley contribute to a world that ensures technology provides the best possible future for the greatest number of people?

The purpose of this book is not to suggest that we have a problem, but rather that we have a multitude of opportunities to shape the kind of future we imagine: a future grounded in awareness, responsible motivations, sound social values, and more ethical technology. I also hope to convey that these challenges are not Silicon Valley's alone to answer. The social and economic conditions that have enabled the challenges we face were realized and condoned collectively, and we are responsible for solving them together.

Like me, and perhaps like you, Silicon Valley has not ended up where it set out to go. It has certainly progressed, but perhaps not in the direction any of us imagined or in the way we would like to see it continue. Tim Berners-Lee, the creator of the World Wide Web, has called the current, centralized version of the internet "anti-human" and argued that it has failed humanity, rather than serving it.[4] MIT professor, internet activist, and tech pioneer Ethan Zuckerman has deemed the modern web a "fiasco."[5] Indeed, Silicon Valley's promise to make the world a better place seems increasingly hollow as it becomes clear that its values and intentions have been corrupted by a system that continues to prioritize the wrong things: profits, shareholders, consumption. Most compellingly, to my mind, it has undergone a profound shift from the thinking and psychological tenets on which it was founded, resulting in both an industry-wide identity crisis and a range of social impacts with which we are now grappling.

Strictly speaking, this book is a story about the psychology of an industry and the people who comprise it. It is also, however, a story about progress, about myths, philosophy, economics, and ethics. About how society is changing and how we keep up. It is a story about values. Above all, it is a story about the way things are, and an invitation to imagine how they might be different. I hope you enjoy reading it as much as I've enjoyed writing it.

Notes

1. Bartlett, J. (2018). *The People vs Tech: How the Internet is Killing Democracy (and How We Save It)* (p. 1). New York: Penguin.
2. Azhar, A. (2018, November 17). *Oh, Facebook! IQ, Speeding Evolution, Slowing Science; Designing Chatbots; Chomsky vs Piaget; Clothes Rental, Exoplanets, the Poop Catalogue++ #192.* Retrieved from https://mailchi.mp/exponentialview/ev192?e=4998896507
3. Ibid.
4. Brooker, K. (2018, August). "I was Devastated": The Man Who Created the World Wide Web has Some Regrets. Retrieved August 18, 2018, from *The Hive* website: https://www.vanityfair.com/news/2018/07/the-man-who-created-the-world-wide-web-has-some-regrets
5. Zuckerman, E. (2014, August 14). The Internet's Original Sin. Retrieved May 23, 2019, from *The Atlantic* website: https://www.theatlantic.com/technology/archive/2014/08/advertising-is-the-internets-original-sin/376041/

Part I

Psychology

observable behaviors, traits, or language that align with our fundamental definition of who we are. This has two important effects. First, demonstrating certain characteristics reinforces our own understanding of our identity. Second, these qualities project an image that communicates to others how we would like to be perceived. The last thing to know about our identities is that they can be incredibly inaccurate, particularly if we fail to honestly observe ourselves or don't possess the tools needed to accurately self-reflect.

The more accurate one's definition of oneself is, the better equipped we are to conduct and regulate ourselves in a healthy way, particularly in our relationships with other people. Psychoanalyst Edward Edinger describes the importance of personal identity—or ego,[1] as he calls it—in terms of how we affect the world around us:

> It's vitally important just considering the social aspect of the matter that the members of society have good, strong, reliable egos. That means they have to have an authentic sense of their own identity—they have to have acquired a responsible character structure that enables them to function responsibly in relation to other people. That's all a product of ego development…. Good ego development is good not only for the individual, it's good for the society that the individual's a part of.[2]

The story of who we are, in other words, should ideally be both consistent and grounded in reality, as the accuracy and congruence of our identity will invariably affect our relationships with others. A healthy identity is characterized by a robust awareness of oneself that is in accordance with reality; an unhealthy, or undifferentiated identity, by contrast, either (1) lacks an awareness of itself, or (2) is incompatible with others' experience of that person or group. In other words, if the way others see us is not aligned with how we see ourselves, it is possible our identity is not very fully integrated or we lack awareness about certain aspects of ourselves.

At both an individual and collective level, our identity is always the first and most visible element of our psychology. Our image of ourselves tends to be the first thing we offer up to others, for the simple reason that it is largely conscious and observable. When we interact with people, we extend or communicate our version of who we are, which others use in conjunction with other observable facts or behaviors to form an opinion of us. For example, I may tell you I am from Southern California, am an only child, love good coffee, modern art, and lived abroad for most of the last decade, where I worked for the National Health Service in London. This short description contains components of who I am, which I strongly identify with and want to communicate: I am from a liberal place; a bit of an independent loner; I'm interested in things like art and culture (and caffeine); and I spent time working for the U.K.'s single-payer health system. Embedded within this information, you could begin to piece together at least some of my interests, background, values, and perhaps even my political affiliation. If you spent more time with me and gathered a bit more information from whatever cues I dropped, you would be able to build out this picture more fully. You would also be able to corroborate whether what I told you was an accurate representation of who I claim to be, or if I'm a little bit full of crap.

It is not uncommon (or a criticism) that how we describe ourselves doesn't always line up with our actions or with others' experience of who we are. There are a variety of ways our identity can be misaligned with or unrepresentative of what we're like in reality. We might oversell an aspect of our behavior, such as telling others we're an advocate of volunteering, when in fact we volunteered once several years ago and haven't done it again since. We may want to believe something about ourselves so strongly that we maintain it is part of who we are, when in practice we do not demonstrate that quality at all. Someone might believe himself to be open-minded, for example, when in fact he is quite judgmental. In other cases, we may simply be unaware of our actions or how we come across. When elements of our identity do not ring true, or if there are demonstrable aspects of ourselves of which we are unaware, we can infer that there are components of our identity we have not fully integrated, and that building out a more cohesive and accurate identity may be a valuable piece of our psychological work.

Collective identity, like personal identity, consists of a set of ideas that inform how a group of individuals see themselves and behave. Companies, sports teams, countries, and political parties, for example, collectively agree on aspects of their identity that explain who they are and what distinguishes them from others, which may be a certain set of beliefs or qualities. Group identity can be highly adaptive in that it provides a sense of belonging or allegiance and can direct social behavior in more prosocial ways. At an organizational level, technology writer and venture capitalist Om Malik, describes this as the corporate DNA of an organization or industry. Malik explains that the products, services, and behaviors of a company are rooted in the commonalities of the people who work there, creating a cultural identity or "corporate psyche" that defines the organization.[3]

Whatever you think of Silicon Valley and the companies that comprise it, given technology's reach, scope, and influence on our lives, it's hard to argue that understanding the industry on a deeper level wouldn't prove a worthwhile endeavor. The first step to accomplish this is to expand our understanding of what the tech industry is and is not—which begins with an accurate understanding of its identity.

Silicon Valley in a Nutshell

When we consider the identity of Silicon Valley—by which I mean the set of ideas that informs how Silicon Valley sees itself—certain qualities and characteristics probably spring to mind. The Valley is, first and foremost, a geographical space, nestled between the San Francisco Bay and one of Northern California's many Redwood State Parks, stretching about 15 miles from end to end and a few miles across. It is home to some of the most iconic tech companies in the world, including Apple, Facebook, Netflix, LinkedIn, Google, Hewlett-Packard, Intel, Cisco, eBay, and many, many more. Despite its iconic inhabitants, however, Silicon Valley, as a space, is relatively nondescript. Its streets are clean, safe, and tidy, but more suburban than one would expect. There are more strip malls and Safeways than shiny, space-age campuses. Even Sand Hill Road, a stretch of several blocks that is home to some of the biggest venture capital offices in the Bay Area, is in no way glamorous or ostensibly interesting. The garages where Hewlett-Packard, Google, and Apple were born look like something out of an 80s film or, if you grew up in a middle-class neighborhood, maybe your childhood. Standing in the middle of Silicon Valley, you could be anywhere.

urban areas. A Lyft driver in Berkeley summed up the problem rather succinctly:

> There are a lot of people who are getting pushed out of their apartments in San Francisco. Landlords kick people out with no legitimate reason, then renovate their properties and rent them out for $4,000 or $6,000 a month. People are getting kicked out and have nowhere else to go. Their rent is four times what it was and they can't afford it, so a lot of people end up living in tents, going to work, and taking a shower at their gym.

"It's just so unrealistic how much you get paid when it costs this much to live here," the woman said, after telling me about past jobs at Airbnb, Zupper, and Apple, jobs which always had to be worked in pairs to allow her to make rent. As we drove from West Oakland to Berkeley, she told me about a former roommate who was so discouraged by the cost of living that he decided to move to Mount Diablo, a state park east of San Francisco, where he lived in a tent and commuted to the city to work. This is the new deal in the Bay Area for its shrinking middle class: either live outside the city and commute for hours,[16] or sleep in your car, in a tent, or on the street—all while potentially still working long hours and multiple jobs.[17]

The problem has led many to pack up for more affordable pastures. At the end of 2017, more residents moved out of San Francisco than any other city in the country,[18] and in 2018, the Edelman Trust Barometer reported that 49% of Bay Area residents were considering moving, a number that jumped to 58% amongst millennials.[19] The crux of the issue, as Farha and others have identified, is an increasingly unequal set of economic and social factors that no longer work for the average person. Of those Edelman surveyed, 74% said the socioeconomic system in the community favors the rich and powerful, particularly those in the tech industry, who respondents said should be doing more to combat the impact the industry has made on housing and living costs.[20]

While no one in tech would deny the extent of the homelessness crisis or rising inequality in the Bay Area, some are more likely than others to assume responsibility for driving the economic factors contributing to it. Certain tech companies and CEOs, such as Salesforce's Marc Benioff, have dedicated their energy and resources to initiatives that would increase social housing and shelters, such as San Francisco's Proposition C, which will tax the top 1% of corporations in order to generate funds to tackle the city's homelessness epidemic.[21] Others, such as Twitter CEO Jack Dorsey, openly opposed the bill and actively lobbied against it. The takeaway here is not that one of these CEOs is benevolent and the other immoral; they do, however, represent two competing versions of Silicon Valley's identity struggle. Benioff and his wife have campaigned for years to raise millions of dollars to combat economic dislocation, and have integrated the role of the tech community in addressing the systemic problems of inequality facing the Bay Area. Other tech execs, like Dorsey, employ a more hands-off approach, refusing to acknowledge their company's role either in contributing to or solving the problem.

Admitting we are in some way accountable for something is neither a welcome nor an easy task. Psychologically, it takes a great deal of awareness and maturity to accept that our identity is marked by both positive and negative traits. When told we are complicit or culpable of something, particularly when it is framed as blame, our knee-jerk reaction is often defensiveness, reactivity, and an inability to be open to alternative points of view. Silicon Valley's reluctance to acknowledge and integrate the economic side effects of its success and the stark inequality in the Bay Area remains an uncomfortable and largely unaccounted for element of its identity.

A Tale of Two Internets

To understand the identity of Silicon Valley, we must not only appreciate its historical and modern socioeconomic landscape, but also the values on which it was founded and how these have evolved over time. The internet we have come to know, love, and, at times, curse and bemoan, began as a U.S. government-funded project called the Advanced Research Projects Agency Networks, or ARPAnet. Historical writer Mary Bellis describes ARPAnet, which launched in 1969 for use in the U.S. military, as "the grandfather to the Internet."[22] The purpose of the project was to share information held on individual government computers across an interconnected network. In the late 80s and early 90s, a public version of the web, created by a team at CERN and led by Oxford physicist Tim Berners-Lee, began to take shape. Berners-Lee and the CERN team not only developed the World Wide Web, but also defined features central to the creation of the internet, such as hypertext markup language (HTML), HyperText Transfer Protocol (HTTP), and Universal Resource Locators (URLs), which even those of us who can't code to save our lives will recognize.

The internet, as envisioned by its founder, was a place that offered high-quality information, peer-to-peer sharing of such information, and a means to access useful services. Berners-Lee and others conceived of a "free, open, creative space"[23] that would serve human beings individually and humanity collectively. Internet culture journalist Jason Parham describes this era of the early internet as a turning point in history, which was underpinned by a collective expectation of human flourishing.

> In the dawning days of the millennium, a great harvest was promised. A new class of young revolutionists, who saw the world as not yet living up to its grandeur and thus felt the duty to order it in their vision, vowed a season of abundance and grand prosperity.[24]

This democratic, utopian vision of the web survived for a number of years, but began to break down with the commercialization of the internet in the early 2000s.

> The web that many connected to years ago is not what new users will find today. What was once a rich selection of blogs and websites has been compressed under the powerful weight of a few dominant platforms. This concentration of power creates a new set of gatekeepers, allowing a handful of platforms to control which ideas and opinions are seen and shared.[25]

Berners-Lee goes on to describe the centralization of power, the corruption of truth, and the weaponization of information that has become synonymous with the modern internet and its myriad problems and PR disasters. The competition-blocking practices, startup acquisition, and monopolization of talent by internet giants has led Berners-Lee to forecast not only that the next two decades will see a decline in innovation,[26] but also that the internet, if left in its current form, will exacerbate the problems of global inequality.[27]

While the road to the internet was paved with good intentions, it has not weathered the corporate onslaught against its original values very well. Berners-Lee argues that the root cause of this returns, again and again, to "companies that have been built to maximise profit more than to maximise social good."[28] So pervasive is this dynamic that understanding the implications of such motivations requires its own chapter.[29] It is equally important, however, to appreciate how this shift in values within Silicon Valley has impacted the identity of the industry. Douglass Rushkoff, lecturer, media theorist, and author of over a dozen books, including *Throwing Rocks at the Google Bus*, frames the transition of the tech industry's values in the following terms:

> There was a brief moment, in the early 1990s, when the digital future felt open-ended and up for our invention. Technology was becoming a playground for the counterculture, who saw in it the opportunity to create a more inclusive, distributed, and pro-human future. But established business interests only saw new potentials for the same old extraction, and too many technologists were seduced by unicorn IPOs. Digital futures became understood more like stock futures or cotton futures—something to predict and make bets on. So nearly every speech, article, study, documentary, or white paper was seen as relevant only insofar as it pointed to a ticker symbol. The future became less a thing we create through our present-day choices or hopes for humankind than a predestined scenario we bet on with our venture capital but arrive at passively.[30]

So began a process in which the original prosocial, democratic objectives of the web were co-opted by commercial interests. Jaron Lanier, author of *Who Owns the Future?* and *Ten Arguments for Deleting Your Social Media Accounts Right Now*, describes the fundamental contradiction that has plagued Silicon Valley ever since:

> [T]he fundamental mistake we made is that we set up the wrong financial incentives, and that's caused us to turn into jerks and screw around with people too much. Way back in the '80s, we wanted everything to be free

because we were hippie socialists. But we also loved entrepreneurs because we loved Steve Jobs. So you wanna be both a socialist and a libertarian at the same time, and it's absurd. But that's the kind of absurdity that Silicon Valley culture has to grapple with.[31]

Despite the profound shifts that have occurred in the industry as the web has been invaded by big tech, the image of the rebellious counterculture of underdogs has been preserved within the psyche of the industry and incorporated into the story of its identity. Such a picture is increasingly difficult to reconcile with the more modern, corporate objectives of most Silicon Valley companies, and has created a tension that strikes to the heart of the industry's confusion about what it truly is.

It is important to note that this misunderstanding tends not to be inauthentic so much as profoundly outdated. In the same way the Gold Rush lingers in the collective unconscious of the Bay Area, so does the rebellious, socially woke ideals on which the tech industry was founded. A more honest appraisal of the industry's values, an appreciation of how these have changed, and a willingness to reenvision the principles of Silicon Valley may help the industry as a whole synthesize two competing (though perhaps incompatible) elements of its character.

Let's Talk About Tech, Baby

A final element of the tech industry's somewhat disordered identity lies not in its history or the rocky journey of its principles, but in the mentality, attitudes, and behaviors of those who comprise it. The nature of any group of people—be it a business, team, religion, or family—is in many ways related to the qualities of the people in it. Do they tend to be more open-minded or a bit judgmental? If you have a problem, are they more likely to hold your hand and listen, or want to help you fix it? Are they, on the whole, humble and considerate of other points of view, or more unwavering or assertive in their opinions? Would you describe them as kind? Likeable? Socially aware? Self-aware? There is, of course, a huge variance of traits within any collection of people, particularly in large groups. But there are also salient features that, while they may not hold true for everyone, are common enough that they inform a significant feature of the group as a whole.

Understanding the commonalities of thinking and behavior in Silicon Valley, which inform a significant portion of the industry's image and identity, centers on looking at its dominant characteristics, both positive and negative. In a group setting, particularly when we find ourselves with like-minded people, the group's dominant qualities—such as what is most valued or how people behave—will be normalized, reinforced, and multiply. The remainder of this chapter will look at some of the most prominent values, attitudes, and ways of thinking that dominate the tech community.

Two of the most salient values found throughout Silicon Valley are a dedication to problem-solving and big ideas. Looking through my notes and hundreds of pages of transcribed interviews, there is rarely a conversation that doesn't, at some point, veer into the tech industry's desire to solve big problems. One woman I spoke to in San Francisco explained this drive in the following way: "People are always running here, they're always on, and they're always motivated to be ideas people. They're constantly asking themselves, 'how do we solve big problems?'" Another explained to me, over lunch at his company's rooftop patio, "engineers run this place, and their main value is solving a problem." Problem-solving is a refrain you'll hear over and over again as soon as you start asking what those in the tech community value.

In Silicon Valley, solving big problems most often comes in the form of technical solutions. Tom Goodwin describes the culture of tech as ideas-focused and "driven by people who make stuff. It's a very pragmatic, functional, and mathematic and engineering-driven culture."[32] Goodwin, who works in advertising, makes another good point: the products of Silicon Valley are mediated through a technical medium, and the creative instinct of the industry is primarily embodied through code, algorithms, and technical expertise. The drive to build and find technically elegant solutions to the problems Silicon Valley companies tend to tackle is often associated with a particular way of thinking, which Goodwin alludes to above; engineering work in particular is often associated with a mathematical and logical way of envisioning solutions. The prevalence of this type of thinking in tech, it seems, stems from both a natural affinity for technical programming by many who enter the field, and a historical depiction of the type of person psychologists believed would make a good computer engineer.

Just as the Gold Rush fostered the image of opportunity in Silicon Valley, the industry's analytical mindset is rooted in its history as well. Birgitta Böckeler explains the context in which the image of the programmer was born, which began with the birth of the tech industry in the 1960s and the rapid demand for computer engineers that followed.

> It was hard for companies to figure out what skills were needed for this totally new profession. They needed programmers to be really good, because they were panicking about errors. At the same time, they had no specific idea of the necessary skill set. Companies started to think programmers had to be "born, not made," and that programming was a "Black Art." This was fuelled by the fact that programming was a very idiosyncratic activity at the time, almost every computer operated differently. How do you recruit people for a profession like that, when at the same time the demand increases rapidly?[33]

In order to identify what kind of people they were looking for, the computer industry began using aptitude tests. Throughout the 1950s and 1960s, upwards of 80% of tech companies used measures such as the IBM Programmer Aptitude Test to screen millions of applicants and identify those they believed would be the most skilled. In the mid-1960s, in an attempt to define not just the skills, but the personalities of programmers, a software company called System Development Corporation hired two psychologists, William Cannon and Dallis Perry, to build a "vocational interest scale," which would profile computer engineers and assess them for common skills and interests. Their findings were published in a 1966 paper, which detailed two key profile traits characteristic of programmers: an interest in solving puzzles and a dislike of or disinterest in people.[34] In his book, *The Computer Boys Take Over*, Nathan Ensmenger explains that these tests were used to select engineers within the industry for decades, until eventually Cannon and Perry's recommendations proved something of a self-fulfilling prophecy.

The primary selection mechanism used by the industry selected for antisocial, mathematically inclined males, and therefore antisocial, mathematically inclined males were over-represented in the programmer population; this in turn reinforced the popular perception that programmers ought to be male, antisocial and mathematically inclined, and so on.[35]

Once hiring practices based on these guidelines were in place, the industry began to nurture, albeit largely unconsciously, roles and environments aimed at attracting men who were reserved, logical, detail-oriented, and antisocial.

It's hard to say what would have happened had Dallis and Perry never prescribed a representation of the "ideal" computer programmer. Many believe that regardless of the historical call for mathematically astute, logical thinkers, certain types of people may have been drawn to the industry anyway. Simon Baron-Cohen, a psychologist and researcher at the University of Cambridge, has researched the neurological characteristics endemic in certain fields, most notably in science, technology, engineering, and mathematics (STEM) professions. Baron-Cohen has repeatedly found that those with autism or autistic traits are over-represented in these disciplines, particularly in engineering and mathematics,[36,37,38] a finding that has been corroborated by different research teams.[39] (Over-represented is a key word here; not all engineers or tech employees demonstrate such characteristics, there is simply, according to these findings, a higher representation of those on the autistic spectrum in these fields.) There is much anecdotal evidence and growing research that points to a correlation between the type of work necessitated in tech and the analytical, highly intelligent, and cognitively-focused minds of "Aspies" who may be instinctively drawn to the engineering community.

Autism is a developmental disorder that is often characterized by delays in communication, difficulty relating to others, and restrictive patterns of behavior. Asperger's Syndrome falls under the umbrella of autistic spectrum disorders, but is considered a milder and more high-functioning form of autism. The most common symptoms of Asperger's typically manifest as subtle idiosyncrasies, such as a failure to make eye contact, a preoccupation with a narrow field of study, or pedantic methods of speech, but can also result in more pronounced social difficulties, such as trouble connecting with others conversationally, a failure to pick up on social cues, or a need for repetition and routine. Other diagnostic markers include trouble recognizing and interpreting emotion in others[40] and reduced levels of empathy.[41] It is estimated that one in every 59 children has some form of autism and the disorder is approximately four times more prevalent in males than females.

Baron-Cohen explains that those with Asperger's tend to demonstrate strong logical reasoning, rational thinking, and problem solving, and are particularly adept at work that focuses on "pick[ing] out patterns in information" and "discern[ing] the logical rules that govern systems."[42] The single most distinguishing symptom of Asperger's syndrome, according to the National Institute of Neurological Disorders, is an "obsessive interest in a single object or topic to the exclusion of any other."[43] In 2012, technology journalist Ryan Tate published an article in which he argued that this obsessiveness was in fact "a major asset in the field of computer programming, which rewards long hours spent immersed in a world of variables, data structures, nested loops and compiler errors."[44] Tate contended that the number of engineers with Asperger's was increasing in the Bay Area, given the skillset many tech positions demanded.[45] Entrepreneur and venture capitalist Peter Thiel similarly described the prevalence of Asperger's in Silicon Valley as "rampant."[46] Autism spokesperson Temple Grandin, a professor at Colorado State University who identifies as an Aspie, also echoes Tate, Thiel, and Baron-Cohen's conclusion:

> Is there a connection between Asperger's and IT? We wouldn't even have any computers if we didn't have Asperger's…. All these labels—'geek' and 'nerd' and 'mild Asperger's'—are all getting at the same thing. ….The Asperger's brain is interested in things rather than people, and people who are interested in things have given us the computer you're working on right now.[47]

According to the Summit State Recovery Center, a non-profit that supports people with autism, those with Asperger's often possess "great talents for creating and analyzing mechanical systems, such as engines, or abstract systems, like mathematics and computer programs."[48] It is

emotional intelligence across the industry, this was not necessarily the experience they had of their company or their co-workers. This may be an indication that the field is in the process of changing and diversifying in significant ways or that problems of emotional intelligence may be localized to specific companies. Across the industry, however, there remains an over-representation of cognitive rather than emotional intelligence, and technical rather than social skills.

The Hubris Bubble

In addition to the type of thinking that dominates the industry, there are also behaviors and attitudes that Silicon Valley does not recognize about itself. The two that will prove most consequential when we begin looking at the impacts of technology are the industry's insularity and its arrogance. Journalist Leslie Hook describes the Bay Area tech community as a place "of great earnestness," which "tends to be inwardly focused, with little interest in the rest of the world (except as a potential market)."[58] The result, Hook argues, is a type of insularity that has earned Silicon Valley a reputation as something of a "bubble," that is not only socioeconomically but ideologically isolated from the world around it. Jaron Lanier, author of *Who Owns the Future?* and *Ten Arguments for Deleting Your Social Media Accounts Right Now*, has lamented the insularity of the industry. In 2017, he told reporter Maureen Dowd "how out of touch Silicon Valley people [had] become,"[59] a dynamic that Lanier believes had been exacerbated by their monumental financial success.[60] M.G. Siegler, a general partner at Google Ventures and a long-time veteran of Silicon Valley, has also written extensively on the lack of awareness in tech and his fear that those in the industry "are losing touch with reality."[61]

Many believe the success of the industry, combined with its newfound cultural relevance and the glamorous pull of working for a top tech company, has reinforced not only Silicon Valley's insularity, but also driven what some describe as outright hubris. (Humility, incidentally, was not amongst the qualities anyone I spoke to associated with Silicon Valley.) A woman at one social media firm explained the industry's growing arrogance as stemming from a belief that no problem existed that tech could not solve. Such conceit becomes problematic, she explained, when lessons that could be learned from other industries, the past, or the experiences of others are ignored, which might potentially make the products and services of the industry better, safer, or more ethically informed. When I asked why this attitude was so prevalent, the woman described a systemic belief, particularly amongst executives, which held that those in the industry were the smartest and best suited to solve the problems they were tasked with, and therefore couldn't "really learn anything from anyone else." I asked what she believed informed this attitude, the woman replied the problem stemmed, in her experience, from a lack of awareness and emotional intelligence within Silicon Valley. When I posed a similar question to an engineer at a different company, his response illustrated her point: "I spend all day thinking," he explained, "and believe I've exhausted all possible scenarios in that thought process and tend to arrive at the right answer." The idea that there might be an alternate, let alone a better solution brought about by a different process or way of thinking was simply not a possibility that seemed particularly likely to him.

In addition to speaking to those who worked at tech companies, I also spent time with psychotherapists in the Bay Area, each of whom had clients who worked in tech. The arrogance exhibited by these clients was one of the more pronounced themes the therapists reported. One man, who worked in-house at a large tech company two days a week, described the attitude as one of "unaware exceptionalism." When I asked what he meant by this, he explained that the perception of doing something new and radical was often accompanied by a sense of hubris and, in extreme cases, almost an expectation of worship. Another psychotherapist in San Francisco described a similar dynamic among many of his clients, which he ascribed to the "positive feedback loop"—both within companies and from society more broadly—that "exalted" tech employees for the skills and service they provided.

Silicon Valley 2.0

Before we can meaningfully change anything—ourselves, our relationships, our institutions—we must first have a grounded understanding of what we seek to change. (It's much more difficult to fix something when no one agrees on who or what needs to be fixed.) Rectifying the more socially harmful elements of Silicon Valley's identity begins with a more accurate, conscious, and thorough understanding of what that identity is—both what the industry excels at, what it lacks, and the values, thinking, and attitudes that predominate. Jessi Hempel has argued that the greatest danger the tech community faces is that it "cling[s] to an outdated" identity of itself, which is no longer accurate or helpful. In order to move forward, "the Valley itself must evolve" and re-examine the ideas that underlie its conception of itself, a process Hempel acknowledges will require "a severe and sudden-feeling identity shift."[62]

The outdated, unconscious, and, at times, inaccurate view of what it is, suggests that Silicon Valley is an industry that does not understand itself in a variety of important ways. As we outline regulatory guidelines, adopt ethical frameworks for development, and reimagine the standards and values we want to instill in future technologies, it is important we understand both the conscious and the unacknowledged aspects of the industry's identity. This must include the tech industry's less positive characteristics, including its insularity, lack of emotional intelligence, and abdication of responsibility for the social problems it has helped create. It must also include a realistic understanding of its culture and environment, which is the subject of the following chapter.

Notes

1. Ego derives from the Greek word meaning "I".
2. *Edward F. Edinger—Social Implications.* (1997). Retrieved from http://www.jungstudycenter.org/Edward-F-Edinger
3. Malik, O. (2011, February 11). Change is Good, But It's also Really Hard. Retrieved August 28, 2018, from *OnmyOm* website: https://om.co/2011/02/11/change-is-good-but-its-also-really-hard/
4. Hook, L. (2018, February 28). In Search of the Real Silicon Valley. Retrieved August 22, 2018, from *Financial Times* website: https://www.ft.com/content/17a90c88-1c0e-11e8-aaca-4574d7dabfb6
5. Bass, A. S. (2018, August 30). Why Startups are Leaving Silicon Valley. *The Economist.* Retrieved from https://www.economist.com/leaders/2018/08/30/why-startups-are-leaving-silicon-valley
6. Ibid.

7. Walker, R. (2018). *Pictures of a Gone City: Tech and the Dark Side of Prosperity in the San Francisco Bay Area* (p. 76). Oakland: PM Press.

8. Thurm, S. (2019, May 21). What Tech Companies Pay Employees in 2019. *Wired*. Retrieved from https://www.wired.com/story/what-tech-companies-pay-employees-2019/

9. Goodwin, T. (2017, August 3). *Interview with Tom Goodwin* (K. Cook, Interviewer).

10. Walker, R. (2018). *Pictures of a Gone City: Tech and the Dark Side of Prosperity in the San Francisco Bay Area* (p. 77). Oakland: PM Press.

11. Graff, A. (2018, January 24). UN Expert on San Francisco Homelessness: "I Couldn't Help but be Completely Shocked". *SFGate*. Retrieved August 18, 2018, from https://www.sfgate.com/bayarea/article/Leilani-Farah-UN-rapporteur-homelessness-SF-CA-12519117.php

12. Ibid.

13. Shaban, B., Campos, R., Rutanooshedech, T., & Horn, M. (2018, February 18). San Francisco Spends $30 Million Cleaning Feces, Needles. Retrieved August 18, 2018, from *NBC Bay Area* website: http://www.nbcbayarea.com/news/local/Diseased-Streets-472430013.html

14. Ibid.

15. Graff, A. (2018, January 24). UN expert on San Francisco Homelessness: "I Couldn't Help but be Completely Shocked". *SFGate*. Retrieved August 18, 2018, from https://www.sfgate.com/bayarea/article/Leilani-Farah-UN-rapporteur-homelessness-SF-CA-12519117.php

16. Gee, A. (2016, December 28). More than One-Third of Schoolchildren are Homeless in Shadow of Silicon Valley. *The Guardian*. Retrieved from https://www.theguardian.com/society/2016/dec/28/silicon-valley-homeless-east-palo-alto-california-schools

17. To appreciate the scale of income required to live in the Bay Area, consider the average monthly housing cost in San Francisco, which is a whopping $8,330, compared to the national average of $1,270; or the median house price in San Francisco, $1,610,000, compared to the national average of $245,000; or the minimum annual income needed to purchase a home: $333,270 in San Francisco, compared to the national average of $50,820. It's little wonder that normal people, with normal jobs, can no longer afford the city.

18. Real-Time, R. (2018, February 7). Affordable Inland Metros Drew Migration from Coastal Metros at Year End. Retrieved August 19, 2018, from *Redfin Real-Time* website: https://www.redfin.com/blog/2018/02/q4-migration-report.html

http://gawker.com/5885196/the-tech-industrys-asperger-problem-affliction-or-insult

45. Tate, R. (2010, September 13). Facebook CEO Admits to Calling Users "Dumb Fucks". Retrieved August 24, 2018, from *Gawker* website: http://gawker.com/5636765/facebook-ceo-admits-to-calling-users-dumb-fucks

46. Packer, G. (2011, November 21). *No Death, No Taxes: The Libertarian Futurism of a Silicon Valley Billionaire.* Retrieved from https://www.newyorker.com/magazine/2011/11/28/no-death-no-taxes

47. Mayor, T. (2008, June 22). Asperger's: The IT industry's Dark Secret. Retrieved August 19, 2018, from *Computerworld New Zealand* website: https://www.computerworld.co.nz/article/494907/asperger_it_industry_dark_secret/

48. Summit Estate Recovery Center. (2018, April 19). Autism, Asperger's and Addiction in the High-Tech Industry. Retrieved August 19, 2018, from *Summit Estate* website: https://www.summitestate.com/blog/autism-aspergers-addiction-high-tech-industry/

49. Bazalgette, P. (2017). *The Empathy Instinct: How to Create a More Civil Society* (p. 5). London: John Murray.

50. Ibid., p. 63.

51. The structures of the empathy circuit include: The anterior cingulate cortex, anterior insula, medial prefrontal cortex, temporoparietal junction, and the orbitofrontal cortex.

52. Bazalgette, P. (2017). *The Empathy Instinct: How to Create a More Civil Society* (pp. 56–57). London: John Murray.

53. Ibid., pp. 57–58.

54. Brewer, R., & Murphy, J. (2016, July 13). People with Autism can Read Emotions, Feel Empathy. *Scientific American.* Retrieved from https://www.scientificamerican.com/article/people-with-autism-can-read-emotions-feel-empathy1/

55. Mul, C., Stagg, S. D., Herbelin, B., & Aspell, J. E. (2018). The Feeling of Me Feeling for You: Interoception, Alexithymia and Empathy in Autism. *Journal of Autism and Developmental Disorders, 48*(9), 2953–2967. https://doi.org/10.1007/s10803-018-3564-3

56. Stamos, A. (2017). *Black Hat Keynote: Stepping Up Our Game: Re-focusing the Security Community on Defense and Making Security Work for Everyone.* Retrieved from https://www.youtube.com/watch?v=YJOMTAREFtY

57. Wakefield, J. (2018, September 27). Linus Torvalds: I'm Trying to be Polite. *BBC News.* Retrieved from https://www.bbc.com/news/technology-45664640

58. Hook, L. (2018, February 27). In Search of the Real Silicon Valley. *Financial Times*. Retrieved from https://www.ft.com/content/17a90c88-1c0e-11e8-aaca-4574d7dabfb6

59. Dowd, M. (2018, January 20). Soothsayer in the Hills Sees Silicon Valley's Sinister Side. *The New York Times*. Retrieved from https://www.nytimes.com/2017/11/08/style/jaron-lanier-new-memoir.html

60. Lanier, J. (2018, April 17). *We Won, and We Turned into Assholes* (N. Kulwin, Interviewer) [*New York Magazine*]. Retrieved from http://nymag.com/selectall/2018/04/jaron-lanier-interview-on-what-went-wrong-with-the-internet.html

61. Siegler, M. G. (2018, April 18). Arrogance Peaks in Silicon Valley. Retrieved August 19, 2018, from *500ish Words* website: https://500ish.com/arrogance-peaks-in-silicon-valley-b3020f542e5e

62. Hempel, J. (2018, January 21). The Spin Master Behind Facebook, Airbnb, and Silicon Valley as You Know It. *Wired*. Retrieved from https://www.wired.com/story/margit-wennmachers-is-andreessen-horowitzs-secret-weapon/

environment, psychologists might study the makeup of the community: who comprises it? Is it a diverse or homogenous group? Is it inclusive, welcoming, and connected, or exclusive, inhospitable, and isolated? They would also observe the quality of the relationships: are the interactions between members of the group healthy or unhealthy? Do members of the group support each other and treat each other with respect? Finally, we might ask more about the cultural norms: What is permissible? Do all members of the community feel psychologically safe? Answering these questions would not only help us to better understand different environments, but also provide an indication of the relative health of a group's culture.

At an individual level, the quality of our environment can profoundly impact both our physical and mental health.[1,2] Collectively, the culture of an organization informs the broader psychosocial health of its workforce. At an even higher level, the psychological health of an industry—its behavioral norms, group dynamics, and in-group relationships—can have profound social consequences as these bleed beyond the confines of the industry. If the psychology and values of an industry are sound, or at least not grossly negligent or unhealthy, we may never notice or even think about an industry's culture. When group psychological health is in some way compromised, however, its effects may be observable or experienced beyond the industry itself. A thorough study of pre-2008 Wall Street culture, for example, might have uncovered a male-dominated, risk-oriented, and profit-hungry industry focused on short-term returns. The financial typhoon that resulted from specific behaviors and priorities was, to a large degree, the result of the culture of the industry at that time.

Cupertino, We Have a Problem

My time in Silicon Valley can generally be divided into two categories: things I felt privileged to see and things I wished I could un-see. The former was almost always a result of products shown or described to me: apps that laid out non-partisan local voting information, impact investing platforms, phones designed to reduce specific absorption rates[3] to protect users from radiation, early warning indicators for medical imaging, drones that tracked and predicted poaching patterns. The things I wanted to un-see were almost always social: the way people spoke to each other, venture capitalists (VCs) bullying young CEOs, women feeling unwelcome in their jobs, sexual harassment, a lack of awareness of others' feelings, and a staggering amount of unconscious bias. As the months passed, I realized everything I wanted to un-see came back to a problem of culture, of what was permissible within the working relationships of the industry that elsewhere would not have been acceptable.

A number of unflattering realities, including skewed hiring practices, rampant bias, and a shocking degree of insularity have led to what engineer Erica Joy Baker calls a "catastrophic failure in [the] culture"[4] of Silicon Valley. Perpetuated by what Tom Goodwin describes as a "tribe of people that have come together and reinforce questionable values with each other,"[5] the cultural problems in Silicon Valley tend to come back to three primary issues, from which a variety of other complications arise. First, tech tends to be an uncommonly homogenous culture, marked by a lack of diversity and an unwillingness to embrace pluralism; second, it is rife with discrimination, including sexism, ageism, and racism, as well as harassment; and third, there is a disturbing level of immaturity that permeates many corporations, often emanating from the highest levels of the company. You can probably already see these issues are interrelated: a homogenous culture is more likely to exhibit discriminatory behaviors; discrimination is more likely to run rampant and unchallenged in an immature organization. Without the awareness necessary to recognize such behaviors as inappropriate, tendencies become patterns, which become increasingly embedded not only in the industry's culture, but also in its products.

One dynamic that perpetuates the homogeny of the industry is what companies in Silicon Valley refer to as "culture fit," which is the idea that to be a good addition to the organization, you must possess the same qualities as those already employed within it. Author and venture capitalist Brad Feld explains that culture fit is essentially the practice of "hiring people like everyone else in the company," and has become the norm in many Silicon Valley companies.[6] The result is an industry that has a great deal in common with itself and is comprised primarily of people with similar backgrounds, perspectives, and experiences. The idea of culture fit is so deeply embedded within the vocabulary of Silicon Valley that Google famously has its own word for it: Googley.[7] There are two primary problems with Googleyness, aside from the cringe factor. The first is the lack of transparency about what the term encompasses. There is no list of qualities that spell out what would make someone Googley or un-Googley, and therefore there is little insight into whether the qualities Google prioritizes promote a fair and nondiscriminatory work environment. The main problem, however, is the suggestion that there is a single mold of the ideal Google employee, which encourages fitting in rather than standing out, prioritizes homogeny over diversity, and puts pressure on employees, according to former employee Justin Maxwell, to act in a "Googley way."[8]

A focus on preserving its existing culture has led many to charge that Googleyness is a vehicle for discrimination. Norman Matloff, who studies age discrimination in tech, explains that unlike gender and racial discrimination, which are captured in annual diversity reports, "the magic word 'diversity' doesn't seem to apply to age in Silicon Valley,"[9] despite the fact that age discrimination lawsuits and investigations have plagued Google and other tech giants for years. In 2004, Google fired 52-year-old manager Brian Reid just over a week before the company went public. Reid filed a discrimination suit, citing comments from "his supervisors, including the company's vice president for engineering operations, allegedly called him a poor 'cultural fit,' an 'old guy' and a 'fuddy-duddy' with ideas 'too old to matter.'"[10] (The suit settled out of court for an undisclosed amount.) A more recent case charged that "Googleyness or culture fit are euphemisms for youth and Google interviewers use these to intentionally discriminate on the basis of age."[11] While Google continues to deny charges of ageism and discrimination, the Department of Labor found the company guilty of repeatedly engaging in "extreme" age discrimination.[12]

The problem of ageism, unfortunately, is not Google's alone, but an industry-wide bias. Matloff explains that prioritizing younger workers began largely as a cost-cutting exercise, wherein older staff were increasingly replaced with younger and cheaper employees willing to do the same work for less money.[13] Yiren Lu has suggested that if tech is "not ageist, then at least increasingly youth-fetishizing," noting the average age at Facebook is 26 (at the more mature Hewlett-Packard, by contrast, the median age is 39).[14] However we label it, the prioritization of youth has resulted not only in destructive patterns of age-related complaints and lawsuits, but the perpetuation of uniformity in an already highly uniform culture.

99 Problems and Diversity's Just One

In addition to prioritizing youthful employees, tech has historically failed to welcome women and people of color into its ranks across a variety of roles. Year-on-year, diversity reports at tech companies reflect the abysmal demographics of Silicon Valley's workforce, which remains largely white and predominantly male. While such reports may not capture the complex dynamics behind the industry's failure of diversity, they remain a useful tool to understand the scale of the problem.

When it comes to gender, recent diversity reports at Google, Facebook, and Microsoft show men make up 70%,[15] 65%,[16] and 74% of all staff,[17] respectively, statistics which are broadly reflective of gender demographics across the industry. In technical roles, the numbers skew even higher: at all three companies, men make up approximately 80% of engineering roles. In leadership roles across tech firms in the Bay Area, over 72% of positions are held by men.[18] A joint study conducted by Wired and Element AI, for example, found only 12 percent of leading machine learning researchers were women,[19] a statistic that has profound implications for future bias embedded in systems that rely on AI. When it comes to ethnic diversity, the numbers are even worse. At Google, Facebook, and Microsoft, white and Asian staff make up 87%, 89%,[20] and 90% of all roles, respectively,[21] and in technical and leadership roles, the numbers again increase dramatically. For women and people of color who do make it into these roles, data suggests their pay is typically far less than that of their white and Asian male colleagues.[22]

The problem with focusing on diversity statistics alone is that numbers fail to offer insight into the attitudes, behaviors, and cultural norms of the industry that drive these dynamics. Diversity reports provide quantitative data—which the tech industry loves—but they do not provide qualitative information about why the numbers are the way they are or how to make them better. While some have suggested there are simply not enough women and people of color applying for engineering jobs, research shows that even when under-represented employees are appointed to technical or leadership roles, many tech companies have difficulty retaining them. In a survey of 716 women who had worked in tech, over a quarter cited an "overtly or implicitly discriminatory" environment as their primary reason for leaving the industry.[23]

Attrition rates in tech are indeed much higher for women and people of color, particularly black and Latin American employees,[24] suggesting it is likely the industry's culture, rather than its pipeline, that makes many tech corporations unwelcoming, unfair, and unhealthy environments for those not in the majority. The suggestion that there should be more women and people of color in tech is not wrong—there should be—but embarking on a hiring spree of non-white, non-male employees will not alone change the culture of the industry, which is deeply embedded in its social and organizational psychology. Social change can be a slow and often painful process and it may take years to effectively modify the norms of a large group or an entire industry. Thankfully, there are many people stepping up to the challenge.

In her book *Reset: My Fight for Inclusion and Lasting Change*, Ellen Pao describes her experience working in the white, male dominated world of venture capital at Kleiner Perkins. Pao's account of Silicon Valley portrays an industry that is not only unwelcoming, but "*designed* to keep people out who aren't white men."

> You can't always get ahead by working hard if you're not part of the 'in' crowd. You will be ostracized no matter how smart you are, how bone-crushingly hard you work, how much money you make for the firm, or even how many times they insist they run a meritocracy. Year after year, we hear the same empty promises about inclusion, and year after year we see the same pitiful results.[25]

Reset chronicles years of discrimination against both Pao and her female colleagues, including pay disparities and promotions that were repeatedly reserved for male colleagues. Women were consistently driven out of the firm; few lasted more than two to three years. The world Pao portrays in *Reset* is one of homogeny perpetuated by bias and favoritism. She recalls her former boss speaking to the National Venture Capital Association, describing ideal tech founders as "white, male, nerds who've dropped out of Harvard or Stanford" and have absolutely "no social life,"[26] perpetuating the false narrative of the consummate engineer: young, Caucasian, and socially skill-less.

Pao eventually filed a discrimination lawsuit against Kleiner Perkins, which she lost, but not before bearing an onslaught of abuse, harassment, and retaliation in her final weeks at the firm. Following her departure, Pao founded Project Include, an initiative that advocates for diversity and inclusion in tech. Both Project Include and *Reset* make strong cases for amending the psychosocial norms of the tech industry such that they are open to and inclusive of everyone, regardless of gender, race, ethnicity, disability, or age. "To make tech truly diverse," Pao argues, "we need to make all sorts of people feel welcome and set them up to succeed."[27]

Erica Joy Baker, a founding advisor at Project Include, is an engineer who has worked in tech for over a decade. She recounts a similar environment and dynamic within her Silicon Valley engineering teams, each of which Baker describes as comprised predominantly of young, white men. As an African-American woman, Baker recalls feeling that she stuck "out like a sore thumb" in what she soon realized were consistently homogenous surroundings, where she was often neither welcomed nor recognized as an engineer.[28]

> I have been mistaken for an administrative assistant more than once. I have been asked if I was physical security (despite security wearing very distinctive uniforms). I've gotten passed over for roles I know I could not only perform in, but that I could excel in. Most recently, one such role was hired out to a contractor who needed to learn the language the project was in (which happened to be my strongest language).[29]

Baker describes her time in the Bay Area as great for her career but bad for her as a person, noting the cultural dynamics that were, at best, inhospitable, at worst, sexist, racist, and discriminatory.[30] The psychological scars such treatment can inflict, particularly if sustained over a period of time, is what led many of the women I spoke to not only to leave the industry, but to do so with the knowledge they would never return.

The environment Pao and Baker describe is emblematic of a pattern in Silicon Valley that has been largely ignored and, in many cases, condoned. The homogeny, bias, and, at times, hostile culture towards those who don't "fit" have forced Silicon Valley companies to acknowledge an industry-wide working environment that is fundamentally broken and unhealthy, and which no amount of free lunches or company perks can fix. It also illustrates an industry that fails to understand the distinction between diversity and pluralism. Where the former implies a culture or group that is mixed, pluralism is defined by a sense of inclusion, engagement, and power-sharing. Diversity is measured in numbers; pluralism is demonstrated in environments that value inclusion, equality, and respect. Facebook can hire as many women and people of color as their HR department will allow, but without engaging with the voices, talents, and experiences different people bring, diversity in itself remains a rather meaningless aim that ends with quotas and hiring targets. There are perfectly diverse populations where discrimination and harassment are still alive and well. While diversity should continue to be fought for—particularly as a first step towards a more inclusive environment—diversity on its own is not enough, and the complex problems in Silicon Valley's environment will not be fixed without examining the culture that allows such homogeny to thrive.

The discrimination Pao and Baker depict quietly communicates the belief that women and people of color cannot perform engineering and leadership roles to the same standard as their young, white, male counterparts. In 2017, Google employee James Damore published an internal memo outlining his belief that the "abilities of men and women differ in part due to biological causes and that these differences may explain why we don't see equal representation of women in tech and leadership."[31] Damore suggested companies should "stop assuming that gender gaps imply sexism," and that women were simply more prone to choose different career paths.[32] The memo received criticism both within and outside Google and Damore was soon fired for what CEO Sundar Pichai called "advancing harmful gender stereotypes" in the workplace by suggesting "a group of our colleagues have traits that make them less biologically suited to" their work.[33] Damore's memo is at once awful and illuminating; perhaps without intending to, Damore illustrated precisely the type of discrimination that runs rampant, unchecked, and unspoken within many Silicon Valley tech companies, and has thus pushed the problem of discrimination in tech to the fore.

The question of how men and women are different, and if these differences might affect their work, is actually an interesting one—though the research does not point in the direction people like Damore might like. A 2015 study from Iowa State University found that the psychological differences between men and women were far less pronounced than most people assume. In 75 percent of the psychological qualities that were measured, including morality, risk taking, and occupational stress, men and women's responses overlapped approximately 80 percent of the time. The study's researchers explain these results suggest that men and women are actually "more similar than most people think, and the majority of perceived differences can be attributed to gendered stereotypes."[34] A separate study found that where there are measureable psychometric differences between men and women, these tend to be constellated around characteristics such as empathy, compassion, problem-solving, psychological awareness, and social sensitivity, which women collectively are inclined to demonstrate more frequently.[35] A separate study on gender differences found men were more than twice as likely as women to engage in behaviors regarded as unethical.[36] (Whether these are learned or innate qualities the studies do not say.) Other researchers have mirrored these results, and shown that qualities such as collaboration,[37] empathy,[38] open-mindedness and maturity,[39] and social and emotional skills,[40] tend to be more prevalent amongst women than men. When we consider the value that more gender diversity may bring to the tech industry, the very skills research suggests may be more common in female employees are precisely those that would benefit the industry as it enters the third year of its identity crisis.[41]

Yonatan Zunger, a former Google engineer has argued that the skills women bring to tech are a welcome addition to the field. "It's true that women are socialized to be better at paying attention to people's emotional needs and so on—this is something that makes them *better* engineers, not worse ones."[42] Bob Wyman, who has worked in the industry for over forty years, has written that while men and women may differ in some respects, any purported differences "which are relevant to 'software' are culturally imposed."[43] Where woman are often different, Wyman suggests, is in their refusal to celebrate and adhere to the distinctly "dysfunctional" male culture that encourages working "ridiculously hard for stupidly long hours… while exhibiting no cultural awareness or social skills."[44] Zunger and Wyman's accounts are the exact opposite of Damore's: where Damore believes women are biologically less equipped to work as engineers, Zunger and Wyman recognize not only that such beliefs are unfounded, but also that the qualities women do bring to the industry are exactly those it needs most.

There is strong evidence that increasing diversity in the industry would not only elevate the psychological and emotional skillsets that are lacking in tech, but also increase profitability. Studies show companies perform better when they have at least one female executive on the board[45,46] and companies with a more diverse workforce across all demographic measures tend to have higher profits and earnings. Both racial and gender diversity are associated with "increased sales revenue, more customers, greater market share, and greater relative profits."[47] A report by McKinsey similarly found that gender diversity positively impacted profitability and value creation and that the most ethnically diverse executive teams were on average 33 percent more profitable.[48] Not only, then, could the inclusion of more women and people of color in tech help shift the mindset and social priorities of Silicon Valley that are so desperately needed, but could also increase financial returns in the process.

This is not only true of gender and ethnicity, of course; increasing diversity across the industry is important in less obvious ways as well. People with different backgrounds and experiences have the capacity to consider Silicon Valley's issues from a different perspective, which may encourage greater empathy for those using the industry's products and more effectively consider the long-term impacts of those products on society. In a 2017 TED talk, Harvard psychologist Susan David reminds her listeners that "diversity isn't just people, it's also what's inside people." David persuasively contends that this includes thinking of diversity in terms of how we experience emotion. A greater capacity for emotional intelligence, according to David, will result in organizational dynamics that are more agile and resilient across the board. Those capable of asking questions such as "What is my emotion telling me?" "Which action will bring me towards my values?" "Which will take me away from my values?" encourages greater self-awareness and emotional agility, which tend to lead to what David describes as more "values-connected" behaviors.[49]

Attitudes that have allowed beliefs such as Damore's to proliferate in the tech community are largely the result of unconscious bias, rather than conscious malicious intent. Howard J. Ross, author of *Everyday Bias*, compares the unconscious assumptions we accumulate throughout our lives to a "polluted river"[50] that runs through our conscious mind, silently informing what we believe about ourselves or others, often based on false information and mistaken ideas. Ross explains that no one is exempt: we all draw on conscious bias, unconscious bias, "and stereotypes, all of the time… without realizing we are doing it."[51] The process of stereotyping is actually a result of evolution. Stereotypes, Ross explains, "provide a shortcut that helps us navigate through our world more quickly, more efficiently, and, our minds believe, more safely,"[52] and keep us from having to reassess each situation from scratch every time we encounter something or someone new. The downside, of course, is that the same beliefs that ease our decision-making also cause a proliferation of biases, particularly in relation to people who we consider to be in some way different from us.

When left unchecked, discrimination is the inevitable precursor to a host of other issues. Not only does bias influence hiring, interviews, job assignments, and promotions,[53] it can also drive harassment, bullying, and dysfunctional cultures. Combined with the imbalance of power in Silicon Valley, which generally sits in the hands of white male executives, discrimination has led to intimidation, gross abuses of power, and inappropriate behavior throughout the industry and has given birth to what Caroline McCarthy, a former Google engineer, calls the "rampant and well-documented sexism and sexual harassment"[54] endemic in Silicon Valley.

One of the first and most famous examples of discrimination and harassment in Silicon Valley is Susan Fowler's account of her time working at Uber. Her first day at the company, Fowler was sexually propositioned by her manager on Uber's internal chat system. She took screenshots and brought them to HR, but was told it was the man's first offense and, given his status as a "high performer," the company was unwilling to punish him. Instead, he received a warning. Soon after, the same high performer was reported again; HR reiterated to his new accuser that it was his first offense. The situation was escalated to upper management, but no action was taken. When Fowler attempted to transfer to a different team, despite her excellent performance reviews, a book contract with O'Reilly publishing, and multiple speaking engagements, she was blocked from moving within the company. When she attempted to transfer again, she was told her performance reviews had been changed; it was now noted that she showed no signs of "an upward career trajectory." The wide-spread sexist attitudes at Uber ran deeply throughout the organization, resulting in an exodus of female employees, including Fowler, who left after a year, calling it "an organization in complete, unrelenting chaos."[55] When she joined the company, Fowler's department was over 25% female; when she attempted to transfer, that number had dropped to 6%; by the time she left, only 3% of the SRE engineers in the company were women. Before her departure, Fowler attended an all-hands meeting, where she asked a director what was being done to address the depleted numbers of women in the organization: "his reply was, in a nutshell, that the women of Uber just needed to step up and be better engineers."[56] At the time of this writing, the company is being investigated by the EEOC over charges of gender inequity,[57] and has also been accused of attempting to silence not only its own employees, but female riders who have reported harassment and rape by the company's driver partners.[58]

Fowler's case may be one of the most notable, but her experience is hardly an anomaly. For every Ellen Pao, Erica Joy Baker, and Susan Fowler, there are countless cases of discrimination, bullying, and harassment that go unreported or which tech companies keep out of the public eye. A 2017 survey found that 60 percent of female employees working in tech in Silicon Valley had experienced unwanted sexual advances.[59] Thanks to women like Pao, Baker, and Fowler, as well as the #metoo movement, more cases than ever have been reported in the past several years. Some of the most prominent inquiries and investigations of gender and racial harassment and discrimination include:

- Justin Caldbeck, a Venture Capitalist and founder of Binary Capital, was accused of multiple charges of sexual harassment in a suit brought against him by 6 women. While he immediately denied the claims, he soon took a leave of absence and later resigned.[60]
- Mike Cagney, CEO of SoFi, stepped down following accusations of harassment and a lawsuit by former employee Brandon Charles, who was fired after reporting the harassment of female co-workers and "alleging a toxic culture of gender-related discrimination and harassment."[61]
- Elizabeth Scott filed a suit against VR company Upload in 2017, after she was fired for issuing a complaint about the inappropriate and "hostile atmosphere" of the company, which Scott alleged included a room in the office with a bed "to encourage sexual intercourse at the workplace," colloquially known as the "kink room."[62]
- A number of charges have been leveled against Tesla, including lawsuits filed on the basis of harassment, racism, discrimination, and homophobia.[63] One example includes an 11-count suit filed by California Civil Rights Law Group on behalf of DeWitt Lambert that alleges instances of "Race Harassment, Race Discrimination, Sexual Harassment, Retaliation, Failure to Prevent Harassment, Discrimination and Retaliation, Threats of Violence in Violation of the Ralph Act, Violation of the Bane Act, Failure to Accommodate, Failure to Engage in the Interactive Process, and Assault and Battery."[64] In addition to refuting the claims, Tesla has criticized those who bring charges or complaints against the company, including engineer AJ Vandermeyden, who sued Tesla for harassment and discrimination,[65] and Tesla factory workers who have complained about working conditions and safety concerns.[66]
- Software engineer Kelly Ellis, accused her senior male colleagues at Google of harassment in 2015, including one manager telling her during a company trip to Hawaii that it was "taking all of [his] self control not to grab" her.[67]

- Whitney Wolfe sued Tinder in 2014, after she alleged the company's Chief Marketing Officer, Justin Mateen, referred to her as a "slut" and "whore." Wolfe also alleged she was not given the co-founder title she deserved because she was female.[68]
- Tom Preston-Werner, founder of GitHub, resigned in 2014 following sexual harassment charges and an investigation into his behavior toward female colleagues. The company found there to be no "legal wrongdoing" on Preston-Werner's part, but "evidence of mistakes and errors of judgement."[69]

In some of the above cases, the accused were found guilty, in others they were not; some left their companies voluntarily, while others were forced out; some cases were found not to have sufficient evidence, while many settled with the plaintiffs out of court. The sheer volume of harassment lawsuits in tech have thrown light onto a culture one case described as "male bravado" combined with "unchecked arrogance" and "a laser focus on growth and financial success while ignoring workplace regulations." The lawsuit explained how the attitudes of the organization had "filter[ed] down from the leadership team... throughout the company, empowering other managers to engage in sexual conduct in the workplace." The result was an environment in which sexual harassment was not only condoned, but those who spoke out against it were punished.[70] Even the most for-giving employees of one tech organization under investigation described it as "a company run by young, immature men who were flush with cash and did not know how to handle their power."[71]

Research has demonstrated, somewhat unsurprisingly, that bullying and harassment lead to a low-quality work environment, not only for those who are victimized, but also for those who witness inappropriate behaviors, which may take the form of "insulting remarks and ridicule, verbal abuse, offensive teasing, isolation, and social exclusion, or the constant degrading of one's work and efforts."[72] Decreased job satisfaction, decreased productivity, and high turnover are among the most common organizational consequences, to say nothing of the psychological effects on those involved, which can include depression, anxiety, and post-traumatic stress.

How Bias Is Encoded

When sexism, racism, and ageism are written into the cultural norms of an industry, it is naïve to think these would somehow not be coded into the products and services that industry produces. Given the homogeny and dysfunctional behavior of an appreciable cohort of Silicon Valley, we shouldn't be surprised when Google's photo service tags black people as gorillas[73]; when predatory loans are targeted at racial minorities[74]; when research photo collections supported by Facebook and Microsoft associate women with cooking and men with sports[75]; when parole decisions and risk scores used by courts are grossly biased against black people[76]; when hostile online communities target, harass, and threaten women and minorities[77]; when video games called RapeLay go viral[78]; or when algorithms automatically produce and sell t-shirts with the words "Keep Calm and Rape A Lot," "Keep Calm and Grope A Lot," and "Keep Calm and Knife Her."[79] We should be outraged, but we shouldn't be surprised.

Though they can be incredibly complex and inexplicable even to their creators, algorithms are, at their core, machines that employ a "set of steps that can be used to make calculations, resolve problems and reach decisions."[80] And because humans program algorithms, algorithms are encoded with human biases. Cathy O'Neil, author of *Weapons of Math Destruction: How Big Data Increases Inequality and Threatens Democracy*, explains that the danger of training computers using existing data is that our existing data is littered with our own biases. "Algorithms are opinions embedded in code. It's really different from what most people think of algorithms. They think algorithms are objective and true and scientific. That's a marketing trick."[81] O'Neil also points out that once bias is built into a system, it is incredibly difficult to remove, making it harder to correct our previous stereotypes and assumptions down the road. Instead of making things more fair, as we assume they should, O'Neil argues algorithms "automate the status quo" and encourage us to "repeat our past practices, [and] our patterns."[82] Imagine yourself in high school. Would you act the same way, hold the same beliefs, or even use the same phrases you did back then? There's every chance you've changed and matured quite a bit since your teens, given the opportunity to grow and expand your understanding of the world around you. When we take a snapshot of our values and beliefs and freeze them in time, we limit our ability to progress beyond them. When this happens individually, it's a shame; when we freeze our prejudices, beliefs, and biases in time collectively, it may limit our capacity to grow and advance as a species.

A 2018 study in the journal *Nature* explains how using large data sets to program algorithms—whether they are social, research, or legal systems—will naturally perpetuate the biases, both conscious and unconscious, that we hold as a society.

> A major driver of bias in AI is the training data. Most machine-learning tasks are trained on large, annotated data sets. Deep neural networks for image classification, for instance, are often trained on ImageNet, a set of more than 14 million labelled images. In natural-language processing, standard algorithms are trained on corpora consisting of billions of words. Researchers typically construct such data sets by scraping websites, such as Google Images and Google News, using specific query terms, or by aggregating easy-to-access information from sources such as Wikipedia. These data sets are then annotated, often by graduate students or through crowd-sourcing platforms such as Amazon Mechanical Turk.[83]

When a small subset of individuals are responsible for programming algorithms that are used throughout the world, there are bound to be disparities between the world represented in such systems and the world as it actually is. The researchers explain that in the majority of data sets used to program systems and inform research, certain groups are over-represented, while others are under-represented.

> More than 45% of ImageNet data, which fuels research in computer vision, comes from the United States, home to only 4% of the world's population. By contrast, China and India together contribute just 3% of ImageNet data, even though these countries represent 36% of the world's population. This lack of geodiversity partly explains why computer vision algorithms label a photograph of a traditional US bride dressed in white as 'bride', 'dress', 'woman', 'wedding', but a photograph of a North Indian bride as 'performance art' and 'costume.'[84]

The result of having predominantly Western, white, male input into systems such as ImageNet, Google Images, and Mechanical Turk is the assumption of white, male dominance and the proliferation of racial and gendered stereotypes. When converting Spanish articles written by women into English, for example, Google Translate often defaults to "he said/wrote," assuming the writer is male.[85] Software developed for Nikon cameras, meant to warn when subjects are blinking, routinely tag Asian subjects as blinking. Algorithms designed to process naming data tend to classify Caucasian names as "pleasant" and African American names as "unpleasant."[86] A 2013 study by Harvard researcher Latanya Sweeney found that a greater number of ads on Google and Reuters mentioning "arrest" appeared beside searches for black identifying names than white identifying names.[87] A 2016 study by Boston University and Microsoft found that software "trained on Google News articles exhibit female/male gender stereotypes to a disturbing extent," yielding responses such as "Man is to computer programmer as woman is to homemaker."[88]

As algorithms increasingly take on ever more significant jobs, they will not only perpetuate grossly racist and sexist stereotypes, but will also have profound, tangible effects on peoples' lives. This is particularly problematic in cases where automated systems are used to assist judges in parole decisions, predict areas of future crime, help employers find job candidates, and negotiate contracts.[89] Because bias is hardwired in the data set, the decisions algorithms hand down are unlikely to be fair or just, as multiple investigations have already demonstrated. In 2014, former U.S. Attorney General Eric Holder requested the U.S. Sentencing Commission to review its use of risk scores, fearing they may be furthering prejudicial behavior in the court system.

> Although these measures were crafted with the best of intentions, I am concerned that they inadvertently undermine our efforts to ensure individualized and equal justice… [and] may exacerbate unwarranted and unjust disparities that are already far too common in our criminal justice system and in our society.[90]

When the Sentencing Commission failed to capitulate to Holder's suggestion, ProPublica launched an investigation. After analyzing over 7,000 risk scores, ProPublica's findings corroborated Holder's concerns: algorithmic risk scores were extremely unreliable in their ability to forecast crime (only 20 percent of those predicted to commit violent crimes actually did so). ProPublica also demonstrated that the algorithm was more likely to label white defendants as low-risk and "falsely flag black defendants as future criminals, wrongly labeling them this way at almost twice the rate as white defendants."[91]

Em'bot'iments of Bias

We are only starting to witness the impacts of our prejudices embedded in the machines and systems we create. If we take a moment to extrapolate these trends to future creations, we can easily imagine a world in which our most appalling impulses and reprehensible ideas are built into the fabric of everyday technologies. As they become more widespread, there is particular concern that physical robots, automated bots, and other anthropomorphized tools will continue to be programed or designed without appropriate oversight and ethical considerations. Without meaningful civic discussion and appropriate governmental regulation, the machines we employ to do the work we relegate to them may amplify rather than alleviate current social problems, such as the inequality and discrimination uncovered by ProPublica and others.

Some of the most obvious examples of technological bias are the personas of bots and digital assistants, which have been fashioned almost exclusively to mimic women. In an article titled "We Don't Need Robots That Resemble Humans," Professor Evan Selinger points out that the names bestowed upon most bots "ring gendered bells" and the services they perform are "historically associated with stereotypes of women's work and women's emotional labor."[92] By assigning female rather than male voices and personas to popular digital assistants such as Amazon's Alexa, Apple's Siri, Microsoft's Cortana, Google's OK Google, and Facebook's now defunct M, there is an implicit correlation between women and helping and administrative positions. As Adrienne LaFrance points out, "the whole point of having a digital assistant is to have it do stuff for you. You're supposed to boss it around."[93] There are conflicting opinions about and rationales for using a female versus a male or gender-neutral bot as an assistant, but there is little conclusive evidence to suggest a reason for their prevalence that does not involve prejudice, objectification, and uneven power dynamics.[94,95]

In the same way assigning a gender to machines "risks amplifying social prejudices and incentivizing objectification,"[96] the decision to anthropomorphize robots can take on a racial dimension as well. A quick online image search will confirm that the majority of domestic robots are white, while more menacing, Terminator-like robots, such as those developed by Boston Dynamics, tend to be darker. A 2018 study found "people perceive robots with anthropomorphic features to have race, and as a result, the same race-related prejudices that humans experience extend to robots."[97] One group of researchers found that when a robot "has the physical appearance of a member of another race [it] is treated as a member of an outgroup and perceived as less human-like by people with racial prejudices."[98] A second study found that when robots were perceived to be of the same group, participants were more likely to interact with and evaluate them positively.[99] The phenomenon illustrated by the research above is known as ingroup-outgroup bias, which is a form of social classification in which people identify with and favor those they perceive as similar. In the same way developers should be aware of the implications of humanizing or assigning gender to robots, care must also be taken to avoid perpetuating racial or ethnic bias as the field of robotics becomes more prevalent in our everyday lives. While it may seem inconsequential to some that Alexa the digital assistant is a woman and Pepper the mall robot is white, it is useful to question why these are the default options engineers and roboticists have collectively deemed most appropriate. The problem is not that the individual developers and entrepreneurs in Silicon Valley are horribly racist, sexist people, but that we all exhibit subtle biases of which we are unaware. "We are all biased. We're all racist and bigoted in ways that we wish we weren't, in ways that we don't even know," explains O'Neil, "and we are injecting those biases into the algorithms."[100]

* * *

When we consider the environment of Silicon Valley, we can safely observe that there remains work to be done. Beyond the effects of exclusion, discrimination, and algorithmic bias, the tech industry as a whole suffers as a result of the attitudes and prejudices it condones. The lack of women and people of color in engineering and leadership roles raises—or should raise—the question of what is lost because of their absence and what kind of environment and culture the industry would like to prioritize moving forward.

Notes

1. Stansfeld, S., & Candy, B. (2006). Psychosocial Work Environment and Mental Health—A Meta-Analytic Review. *Scandinavian Journal of Work, Environment & Health, 32*(6), 443–462.
2. Taylor, S. E., Repetti, R. L., & Seeman, T. (1997). Health Psychology: What is an Unhealthy Environment and How Does It Get Under the Skin? *Annual Review of Psychology, 48*(1), 411–447. https://doi.org/10.1146/annurev.psych.48.1.411
3. Specific absorption rate, or SAR, is a measurement of the energy that is absorbed by the human body when it is exposed to radio frequency electromagnetic fields. It is used as a measurement for the radio wave power emitted by mobile phones and MRI machines. Both the U.S. Federal Communications Commission (FCC) and the E.U.'s European Committee for Electrotechnical Standardization (CENELEC) both limit the SAR level of mobile phones to 1.6 w/kg and 2.0 w/kg, respectively.
4. Baker, E. J. (2017, August 5). I Am Disappointed but Unsurprised by the News that an Anti-diversity, Sexist, Manifesto is Making.... Retrieved August 20, 2018, from *Medium* website: https://medium.com/projectinclude/i-am-disappointed-but-unsurprised-by-the-news-that-an-anti-diversity-sexist-racist-manifesto-is-5fdafbe19352
5. Goodwin, T. (2017, August 3). *Interview with Tom Goodwin* (K. Cook, Interviewer).
6. Feld, B. (2017, June 12). Go for Culture Add, Not Culture Fit. Retrieved August 21, 2018, from *Feld Thoughts* website: https://www.feld.com/archives/2017/06/go-culture-add-not-culture-fit.html

7. Googleyness is assessed both during a job candidate's interview process and also in quarterly reviews, where employees receive a "Googleyness score."

8. Solon, O. (2018, March 16). 'They'll Squash You like a Bug': How Silicon Valley Keeps a Lid on Leakers. *The Guardian.* Retrieved from https://www.theguardian.com/technology/2018/mar/16/silicon-valley-internal-work-spying-surveillance-leakers

9. Baron, E. (2016, July 5). Federal Investigators Probe Google over Age-Discrimination Complaints. Retrieved October 26, 2018, from *The Mercury News* website: https://www.mercurynews.com/2016/07/05/federal-investigators-probe-google-over-age-discrimination-complaints/

10. Glantz, A. (2012, January 28). Bay Area Technology Professionals Can't Get Hired as Industry Moves On. *The New York Times.* Retrieved from https://www.nytimes.com/2012/01/29/us/bay-area-technology-professionals-cant-get-hired-as-industry-moves-on.html

11. Baron, E. (2018, September 12). 'Googley' Does Not Mean 'Young,' Google Claims in Age-Bias Lawsuit. Retrieved October 26, 2018, from *The Mercury News* website: https://www.mercurynews.com/2018/09/12/googley-does-not-mean-young-google-claims-in-age-bias-lawsuit/

12. Ibid.

13. Ibid.

14. Lu, Y. (2018, January 19). Silicon Valley's Youth Problem. *The New York Times.* Retrieved from https://www.nytimes.com/2014/03/16/magazine/silicon-valleys-youth-problem.html

15. Google. (2018). *Google Diversity Annual Report 2018.* Retrieved from https://diversity.google/annual-report/

16. Facebook. (2017). *Facebook Diversity Update: Building a More Diverse, Inclusive Workforce.* Retrieved from https://fbnewsroomus.files.wordpress.com/2017/08/fb_diversity_2017_final.pdf

17. Microsoft. (2018). *Inside Microsoft.* Retrieved August 21, 2018, from http://www.microsoft.com/en-us/diversity/inside-microsoft/default.aspx

18. U.S. Equal Employment Opportunity Commission. (2014). *Diversity in High Tech.* Retrieved from https://www1.eeoc.gov/eeoc/statistics/reports/hightech/index.cfm?renderforprint=1

19. Williams, M. (2018). *Facebook 2018 Diversity Report: Reflecting on Our Journey* [*Facebook Newsroom*]. Retrieved from *Facebook* website: https://newsroom.fb.com/news/2018/07/diversity-report/

20. Microsoft. (2018). *Inside Microsoft*. Retrieved August 21, 2018, from http://www.microsoft.com/en-us/diversity/inside-microsoft/default.aspx

21. Google. (2018). *Google Diversity Annual Report 2018*. Retrieved from https://diversity.google/annual-report/

22. Tiku, N. (2019, January 18). Oracle Paid Women $13,000 Less Than Men, Analysis Finds. *Wired*. Retrieved from https://www.wired.com/story/analysis-finds-oracle-paid-women-13000-less-than-men/

23. Snyder, K. (2014, October 2). Why Women Leave Tech: It's the Culture, Not because "Math is Hard." Retrieved August 20, 2018, from *Fortune* website: http://fortune.com/2014/10/02/women-leave-tech-culture/

24. Google. (2018). *Google Diversity Annual Report 2018*. Retrieved from https://diversity.google/annual-report/

25. Pao, E. K. (2017). *Reset: My Fight for Inclusion and Lasting Change* (p. 8). New York: Spiegel & Grau.

26. Ibid.

27. Ibid., p. 254.

28. Baker, E. J. (2014, November 4). The Other Side of Diversity. Retrieved August 20, 2018, from This is *Hard* website: https://medium.com/this-is-hard/the-other-side-of-diversity-1bb3de2f053e

29. Ibid.

30. Ibid.

31. Lee, D. (2017, August 8). Google Fires Diversity Memo Author. *BBC News*. Retrieved from https://www.bbc.com/news/technology-40859004

32. Ibid.

33. Ibid.

34. Zell, E., Krizan, Z., & Teeter, S. R. (2015). Evaluating Gender Similarities and Differences Using Metasynthesis. *American Psychologist, 70*(1), 10–20. https://doi.org/10.1037/a0038208

35. Schulte-Rüther, M., Markowitsch, H. J., Shah, N. J., Fink, G. R., & Piefke, M. (2008). Gender Differences in Brain Networks Supporting Empathy. *NeuroImage, 42*(1), 393–403. https://doi.org/10.1016/j.neuroimage.2008.04.180

36. Betz, M., O'Connell, L., & Shepard, J. M. (1989). Gender Differences in Proclivity for Unethical Behavior. *Journal of Business Ethics, 8*(5), 321–324. https://doi.org/10.1007/BF00381722

37. Bear, J. B., & Woolley, A. W. (2011). The Role of Gender in Team Collaboration and Performance. *Interdisciplinary Science Reviews, 36*(2), 146–153. https://doi.org/10.1179/030801811X13013181961473

38. Farrell, W., Seager, M. J., & Barry, J. A. (2016). The Male Gender Empathy Gap: Time for Psychology to Take Action. *New Male Studies, 5*, 6–16.

39. Walsh, C. M., & Hardy, R. C. (1999). Dispositional Differences in Critical Thinking Related to Gender and Academic Major. *Journal of Nursing Education, 38*(4), 149–155. https://doi.org/10.3928/0148-4834-19990401-04

40. Groves, K. S. (2005). Gender Differences in Social and Emotional Skills and Charismatic Leadership. *Journal of Leadership & Organizational Studies, 11*(3), 30–46. https://doi.org/10.1177/107179190501100303

41. Unfortunately, a report by Davos has found the opposite to be the case: Progress for women in fields such as IT and biotech have stagnated, reversing a decades-long trend towards greater equality. Unfortunately, just as they are needed the most, women—along with their ideas, perspectives, and skills—are being lost. Based on diversity reports and research on underrepresented minorities in tech, this appears to be the case for other minorities as well. In all cases, unless the homogeny in tech is reversed—and quickly—the trends of inequality already associated with tech will continue to increase.

42. Zunger, Y. (2017, August 6). So, about this Googler's Manifesto. Retrieved August 20, 2018, from *Yonatan Zunger* website: https://medium.com/@yonatanzunger/so-about-this-googlers-manifesto-1e3773ed1788

43. Wyman, B. (2017, August 6). Back in the 1970's, When I First Got in the Software Business, I Remember there being a Much Higher…. Retrieved August 21, 2018, from *Medium* website: https://medium.com/@bobwyman/back-in-the-1970s-when-i-first-got-in-the-software-business-i-remember-there-being-a-much-higher-f70e8197fbd9

44. Ibid.

45. Lagerberg, F. (2015). *Women in Business: The Value of Diversity* (pp. 1–4). Retrieved from *Grant Thornton* website: https://www.grant-thornton.global/globalassets/wib_value_of_diversity.pdf

46. Campbell, K., & Mínguez-Vera, A. (2008). Gender Diversity in the Boardroom and Firm Financial Performance. *Journal of Business Ethics, 83*(3), 435–451. https://doi.org/10.1007/s10551-007-9630-y

47. Herring, C. (2009). Does Diversity Pay?: Race, Gender, and the Business Case for Diversity. *American Sociological Review, 74*(2), 208–224. https://doi.org/10.1177/000312240907400203

48. Hunt, V., Yee, L., Prince, S., & Dixon-Fyle, S. (2018). Delivering Growth Through Diversity in the Workplace. Retrieved August 21, 2018, from *McKinsey* website: https://www.mckinsey.com/business-functions/organization/our-insights/delivering-through-diversity

49. David, S. (2017). *The Gift and Power of Emotional Courage*. Retrieved from https://www.ted.com/talks/susan_david_the_gift_and_power_of_emotional_courage/

50. Ross, H. J. (2014). *Everyday Bias: Identifying and Navigating Unconscious Judgments in Our Daily Lives* (p. 3). Rowman & Littlefield.

51. Ibid., p. 4.

52. Ibid., p. 6.

53. Ibid., p. xxi.

54. McCarthy, C. (2017, September 25). Confessions of a Failed Female Coder. Retrieved August 20, 2018, from *Hacker Noon* website: https://hackernoon.com/confessions-of-a-failed-female-coder-956cbe138c69

55. Fowler, S. (2017, February 19). Reflecting on One Very, Very Strange Year at Uber. Retrieved August 20, 2018, from *Susan Fowler* website: https://www.susanjfowler.com/blog/2017/2/19/reflecting-on-one-very-strange-year-at-uber

56. Ibid.

57. Bensinger, G. (2018, July 16). Uber Faces Federal Investigation Over Alleged Gender Discrimination. *The Wall Street Journal*. Retrieved from https://www.marketwatch.com/story/uber-faces-federal-investigation-over-alleged-gender-discrimination-2018-07-16-171034149

58. Levin, S. (2018, March 16). Uber Accused of Silencing Women Who Claim Sexual Assault by Drivers. *The Guardian*. Retrieved from https://www.theguardian.com/technology/2018/mar/15/uber-class-action-lawsuit-sexual-assault-rape-arbitration

59. Vassallo, T., Levy, E., Madansky, M., Mickell, H., Porter, B., Leas, M., & Oberweis, J. (2017). *The Elephant in the Valley*. Retrieved from Women in Tech website: https://www.elephantinthevalley.com/

60. Lee, D. (2017, July 1). Silicon Valley's Women have Spoken. Now What? *BBC News*. Retrieved from https://www.bbc.com/news/technology-40465519

61. O'Connor, C. (2017, September 15). SoFi CEO Mike Cagney Out Immediately Amid Sexual Harassment Investigation. Retrieved August 21, 2018, from *Forbes* website: https://www.forbes.com/sites/clareoconnor/2017/09/15/sofi-ceo-mike-cagney-out-immediately-amid-sexual-harassment-investigation/

62. Streitfeld, D. (2017, September 15). Lurid Lawsuit's Quiet End Leaves Silicon Valley Start-Up Barely Dented. *The New York Times*. Retrieved from https://www.nytimes.com/2017/09/15/technology/lurid-lawsuits-quiet-end-leaves-silicon-valley-start-up-barely-dented.html

63. Wong, J. C. (2018, June 14). Tesla Workers Say they Pay the Price for Elon Musk's Big Promises. *The Guardian*. Retrieved from https://www.theguardian.com/technology/2018/jun/13/tesla-workers-pay-price-elon-musk-failed-promises

64. California Civil Rights Law Group files lawsuit against Tesla Motors Inc. after Oakland man endured months of racial discrimination, sexual harassment and violent threats from co-workers. (2017, March 27). Retrieved August 28, 2018, from *PR Newswire* website: https://www.prnewswire.com/news-releases/california-civil-rights-law-group-files-lawsuit-against-tesla-motors-inc-after-oakland-man-endured-months-of-racial-discrimination-sexual-harassment-and-violent-threats-from-co-workers-300430149.html

65. Levin, S. (2017, February 28). Female Engineer Sues Tesla, Describing a Culture of "Pervasive Harassment." *The Guardian*. Retrieved from https://www.theguardian.com/technology/2017/feb/28/tesla-female-engineer-lawsuit-harassment-discrimination

66. Wong, J. C. (2017, May 18). Tesla Factory Workers Reveal Pain, Injury and Stress: "Everything Feels like the Future But Us." *The Guardian*. Retrieved from https://www.theguardian.com/technology/2017/may/18/tesla-workers-factory-conditions-elon-musk

67. Does Silicon Valley have a sexism problem? (2017, February 21). *BBC News*. Retrieved from https://www.bbc.com/news/world-us-canada-39025288

68. Ibid.

69. Ibid.

70. O'Connor, C. (2017, September 15). SoFi CEO Mike Cagney Out Immediately Amid Sexual Harassment Investigation. Retrieved August 21, 2018, from *Forbes* website: https://www.forbes.com/sites/clareoconnor/2017/09/15/sofi-ceo-mike-cagney-out-immediately-amid-sexual-harassment-investigation/

71. Streitfeld, D. (2017, September 15). Lurid Lawsuit's Quiet End Leaves Silicon Valley Start-Up Barely Dented. *The New York Times*. Retrieved from https://www.nytimes.com/2017/09/15/technology/lurid-lawsuits-quiet-end-leaves-silicon-valley-start-up-barely-dented.html
72. Einarsen, S., Raknes, B. I., & Matthiesen, S. B. (1994). Bullying and Harassment at Work and their Relationships to Work Environment Quality: An Exploratory Study. *European Work and Organizational Psychologist, 4*(4), 381–401. https://doi.org/10.1080/13594329408410497
73. Simonite, T. (2017, August 21). Machines Taught by Photos Learn a Sexist View of Women. *Wired*. Retrieved from https://www.wired.com/story/machines-taught-by-photos-learn-a-sexist-view-of-women/
74. Kun, J. (2015, July 13). What does It Mean for an Algorithm to be Fair? Retrieved September 12, 2018, from Math ∩ Programming website: https://jeremykun.com/2015/07/13/what-does-it-mean-for-an-algorithm-to-be-fair/
75. Simonite, T. (2017, August 21). Machines Taught by Photos Learn a Sexist View of Women. *Wired*. Retrieved from https://www.wired.com/story/machines-taught-by-photos-learn-a-sexist-view-of-women/
76. Angwin, J., Larson, J., Mattu, S., & Kirchner, L. (2016, May 23). Machine Bias. Retrieved August 31, 2018, from *ProPublica* website: https://www.propublica.org/article/machine-bias-risk-assessments-in-criminal-sentencing
77. United Nations Broadband Commission. (2015). *Cyber Violence Report Press Release*. Retrieved from http://www.unwomen.org/en/news/stories/2015/9/cyber-violence-report-press-release
78. Lah, K. (2010, March 31). "RapeLay" Video Game Goes Viral Amid Outrage. Retrieved June 18, 2019, from *CNN* website: http://www.cnn.com/2010/WORLD/asiapcf/03/30/japan.video.game.rape/index.html
79. Row over Amazon "rape" T-shirt. (2013, March 2). *BBC News*. Retrieved from https://www.bbc.com/news/business-21640347
80. Harari, Y. N. (2017). *Homo Deus: A Brief History of Tomorrow* (p. 97). London: Vintage.
81. O'Neil, C. (2017). *The Era of Blind Faith in Big Data Must End*. Retrieved from https://www.ted.com/talks/cathy_o_neil_the_era_of_blind_faith_in_big_data_must_end/transcript
82. Ibid.

83. Zou, J., & Schiebinger, L. (2018). AI can be Sexist and Racist—It's Time to Make It Fair. *Nature, 559*(7714), 324. https://doi.org/10.1038/d41586-018-05707-8

84. Ibid.

85. Ibid.

86. Ibid.

87. Sweeney, L. (2013). Discrimination in Online Ad Delivery. *Queue, 11*(3), 10:10–10:29. https://doi.org/10.1145/2460276.2460278

88. Bolukbasi, T., Chang, K.-W., Zou, J., Saligrama, V., & Kalai, A. (2016). Man is to Computer Programmer as Woman is to Homemaker? Debiasing Word Embeddings. *Advances in Neural Information Processing Systems* (pp. 4349–4357).

89. Miller, C. (2018, August 21). The Terrifying, Hidden Reality of Ridiculously Complicated Algorithms. *Times Literary Supplement.* Retrieved from https://www.the-tls.co.uk/articles/public/ridiculously-complicated-algorithms/

90. Angwin, J., Larson, J., Mattu, S., & Kirchner, L. (2016, May 23). Machine Bias. Retrieved August 31, 2018, from *ProPublica* website: https://www.propublica.org/article/machine-bias-risk-assessments-in-criminal-sentencing

91. Ibid.

92. Selinger, E. (2018, March 1). We Don't Need Robots that Resemble Humans. *Medium.* Retrieved from https://medium.com/s/when-robots-rule-the-world/we-dont-need-robots-that-resemble-humans-37bc79484f18

93. LaFrance, A. (2016, March 30). Why Do so Many Digital Assistants have Feminine Names? *The Atlantic.* Retrieved from https://www.the-atlantic.com/technology/archive/2016/03/why-do-so-many-digital-assistants-have-feminine-names/475884/

94. Selinger, E. (2018, March 1). We Don't Need Robots that Resemble Humans. *Medium.* Retrieved from https://medium.com/s/when-robots-rule-the-world/we-dont-need-robots-that-resemble-humans-37bc79484f18

95. LaFrance, A. (2016, March 30). Why Do so Many Digital Assistants have Feminine Names? *The Atlantic.* Retrieved from https://www.theatlantic.com/technology/archive/2016/03/why-do-so-many-digital-assistants-have-feminine-names/475884/

96. Selinger, E. (2018, March 1). We Don't Need Robots that Resemble Humans. *Medium*. Retrieved from https://medium.com/s/when-robots-rule-the-world/we-dont-need-robots-that-resemble-humans-37bc79484f18

97. Ackerman, E. (2018, July 18). Humans Show Racial Bias Towards Robots of Different Colors: Study. *IEEE Spectrum*. Retrieved from https://spectrum.ieee.org/automaton/robotics/humanoids/robots-and-racism

98. Złotowski, J., Proudfoot, D., Yogeeswaran, K., & Bartneck, C. (2015). Anthropomorphism: Opportunities and Challenges in Human–Robot Interaction. *International Journal of Social Robotics, 7*(3), 347–360. https://doi.org/10.1007/s12369-014-0267-6

99. Kuchenbrandt, D., Eyssel, F., Bobinger, S., & Neufeld, M. (2013). When a Robot's Group Membership Matters. *International Journal of Social Robotics, 5*(3), 409–417. https://doi.org/10.1007/s12369-013-0197-8

100. O'Neil, C. (2017). *The Era of Blind Faith in Big Data Must End*. Retrieved from https://www.ted.com/talks/cathy_o_neil_the_era_of_blind_faith_in_big_data_must_end/transcript

4

Myths & Stories

Words are, of course, the most powerful drug used by mankind.
–Rudyard Kipling

Humans love stories. We have been telling and listening to stories for as long as we have had language, and putting stories to paper (or scrolls, or the inside of caves) for as long as we've had the ability to record them. Our brains are predisposed to respond to, remember, and attach ourselves to narratives above facts, allegories above reality. While our identity can help us understand ourselves, and our culture helps us understand our environment, stories help us understand our place in the world.

Our actions, beliefs, and behaviors are informed, in large part, by the narratives we believe to be true about the world around us. These stories, which vary greatly between different groups and cultures, help us explain and interpret the world in a way that is consistent with our existing beliefs. Yuval Harari explains how our ability to create and propagate myths has not only enabled human cooperation, but also the dominance of our species.

© The Author(s) 2020
K. Cook, *The Psychology of Silicon Valley*,
https://doi.org/10.1007/978-3-030-27364-4_4

> *Homo sapiens* conquered this planet thanks above all to the unique human ability to create and spread fictions. We are the only mammals that can cooperate with numerous strangers because only we can invent fictional stories, spread them around, and convince millions of others to believe in them. As long as everybody believes in the same fictions, we all obey the same laws, and can thereby cooperate effectively.[1]

In addition to providing a shared sense of reality, narratives serve a variety of purposes: they act as expressions of our culture's values, encourage us to act in certain ways, and position our beliefs in accordance with the beliefs of others, such that we share a common reality. If our identity tells the story of who we are, our narratives inform how we act and what we believe to be true.

The stories we choose to adopt and accept as credible not only provide a rationale for our thinking and behaviors, they also give us the sense that we understand and are in control of our environment.

> As a species, humans prefer power to truth. We spend far more time and effort on trying to control the world than on trying to understand it—and even when we try to understand it, we usually do so in the hope that understanding the world will make it easier to control.[2]

Evolutionarily, myth-making is a hugely beneficial psychological mechanism. Narratives help us fill in the gaps of our knowledge and experience the world as more controllable and coherent.[3] By putting our faith in a variety of cultural narratives—whether religious, political, or social—we give intelligibility and structure to our experience, which feels far more comfortable than trying (and often failing) to piece together disparate bits of information about the world. Because narratives are developed not necessarily to inform, but to ensure psychological cohesion and social cooperation, our stories often come at a price and there is often a tension between the stories we tell and the facts we encounter.

The use of myths to structure our understanding of the world and our place in it goes back tens of thousands of years, to the religious myths dating back to Neanderthal burial rituals some 120,000–35,000 years ago. Before we understood things like rainfall, thunder, earthquakes, and other natural phenomena, such events were attributed to supernatural forces or the gods, which functioned to explain what scientific knowledge at the time could not. Myths were historically passed down as oral stories within individual communities, at a slow, generational pace. In our current world, however, myths have an unprecedented opportunity to insert themselves into modern discourse in a variety of ways. Enabled by the rise of digital media and the range of storytelling outlets we have access to—television, films, social media, online and print news, video games—modern culture's working mythology can be found everywhere we turn. Despite the changes to the mythic landscape, our cultural stories still help orient us in terms of our beliefs, values, and ambitions, though perhaps in more innocuous ways. Our stories are an expression not only of what we believe, but also what we fear, aspire to, and who we are.

While myths may help us do many things—order our experience, set behavioral expectations, better understand the world around us—they cannot act as a barometer of truth. Many ancient and religious myths, for example, we now recognize as socially constructed to illustrate moral precepts or reflect cultural values, rather than convey facts. You may not literally believe the story of Moses's journey to Mount Sinai, but you might still orient your life around the principles of the Ten Commandments. You probably still say "bless you" when someone sneezes even though you know their soul is not in danger of escaping from their body. Stories, if they are socially valuable, "survive as receptacles of important cultural values," even if "a culture no longer believes that its myths are true explanations" of events.[4] But what happens when a myth is neither true nor culturally beneficial? When stories neither hold up to scrutiny nor serve a valid purpose in society? Identifying current myths that may be patently false allows us not only to deconstruct them, but also to uncover what may be concealed beneath them and what impulses may have created them.

When Narratives Crumble

Silicon Valley is full of myths. Some of which are true, many of which are not. Unless you happen to live there or work in tech, you probably never thought much about Silicon Valley until the past decade. The tech industry has historically not been a group of people inclined to scream and shout about what they do. You are more likely to find an engineer building something, head down, deep in code, than marketing his or her latest app. As technology began to become more culturally and financially relevant, a handful of people recognized an opportunity to fill this gap and author the industry's as-yet-undefined narrative. Margit Wennmachers, an operating partner at VC firm Andreessen Horowitz, is largely credited with harnessing that narrative. In 1997, Wennmachers founded OutCast, a communication and marketing firm that now represents Facebook, Amazon, and numerous other tech giants. Since 2010, she has been tasked with creating and pushing a set of stories that, in the words of Andreessen Horowitz founder Marc Andreessen, "tie the disparate stories in the basket of startups into a cohesive narrative about tech's broader impact on business." She has been called the "spin master,"[5] "guru," and "godfather"[6] of the narratives that define tech. While Wennmachers is by no means solely responsible for the narrative of Silicon Valley, she is a good example of how and why modern myths function in the tech industry.

When Wennmachers was hired by Andreessen Horowitz, her purpose was largely to attract business to the company by communicating to engineers and entrepreneurs that the firm understood both their genius and their plight. It was also to help Andreessen Horowitz "set the agenda for tech's future."[7] Wennmachers recognized early that "the best way to defend oneself in the world of ideas is to shape those ideas, to author them. To play offense."[8] And so she helped shape the narratives of Silicon Valley in a way that advanced certain stories and diminished others. Jessi Hempel explains how Wennmachers and other marketing experts have "quietly advanced a narrative that has shaped how the world sees Silicon Valley and how the Valley perceives itself,"[9] promoting stories of nerdy but well-intentioned founders, "brainy outcasts upending the limits of the status quo,"[10] and the increasingly suspect "tech-for-good" narrative.

As more and more of Silicon Valley's myths are exposed as hollow and insincere, the industry has faced a growing identity crisis. There are some—the PR architects and corporate leaders across the industry—who we must assume knew the stories they were spinning were, to various degrees, false. And then there are the rest of us, who believed the slogans and promises of an industry that marketed itself as patently different to corporate cultures of the past. The reality, of course—and the disappointment for those of us who believed the shiny, PR version of Silicon Valley—is that the narratives these companies would like us to believe are largely formed of half-truths and outright lies. As the brands, slogans, and mission statements of some of tech's most influential companies fall apart, there is an opportunity to learn where certain leaders in the industry have gone wrong and how the effects of these false narratives might be redressed. The remainder of this chapter will explore the most prominent narratives we've been told about Silicon Valley, where they fail to hold up under scrutiny, and the consequences of building an industry on myth and pretense.

Silicon Valley Mythology

Don't be evil. (Google, scrapped in 2015.)
Bring the world closer together. (Facebook.)
Put a dent in the universe. (Steve Jobs, Apple.)
Move fast and break things. (Facebook.)
Organize the world's information. (Google.)
Broadcast yourself. (YouTube.)
Give everyone a voice. (Mark Zuckerberg, Facebook.)
Make tools that advance humankind. (Apple.)
Improve communities around the world. (Salesforce.)
Create a world where you can belong anywhere. (AirBnB.)
Communicate with the full range of human emotion. (Snapchat.)
Connect people to their passions, communities, and the world's knowledge. (Yahoo!)
Give everyone the power to create and share ideas and information instantly, without barriers. (Twitter.)
Simplify life for people around the world. (Dropbox.)
Empower every person and every organization on the planet to achieve more. (Microsoft.)
Solve intelligence, use it to make the world a better place. (Deepmind.)
Work hard. Have fun. Make history. (Amazon.)
Do the right thing. (Google, current.)

The sound bites of the Bay Area echo far and wide. Reminiscent of the inspirational, disruptive mentality Silicon Valley is known for, they serve to reflect the lofty aspirations and benevolent ideals of the world's most influential companies. They are also, to varying degrees, false and toxic aphorisms designed to mask the true intentions of the companies who craft them. Jeff Hauser, executive director of the Revolving Door Project, calls the mottos and propaganda of industry-leading companies in Silicon Valley "a public relations effort to make people think of technology very differently than they do Wall Street.... That's how they maintain the illusion that they are cutting-edge nerds who are toiling for the good of humanity."[11] Georges Abi-Heila, Head of Acquisition & Product Growth at Paris-based tech company Station, warns against being fooled by the corporate slogans of internet behemoths like Facebook, Google, and Amazon. The slogans, Abi-Heila explains, are a distraction from the true corporate aims of the industry, which are to bring in "the largest amount of users, for the longest period possible, at the most frequent rate."[12]

Thanks to the marketing efforts of people like Wennmachers and her former business partner Caryn Marooney, who now heads PR and communications at Facebook, the industry has managed to paint a self-serving picture of itself that fails to reflect the reality of its priorities and intentions. As journalist Olivia Solon explains, the mottos and missions of tech giants serve primarily as a diversion from their actual aims.

> Facebook has gone to great lengths to convince members of the public that it's all about "connecting people" and "building a global community". This pseudo-uplifting marketing speak is much easier for employees and users to stomach than the mission of "guzzling personal data so we can microtarget you with advertising".[13]

The branding of Silicon Valley, which focuses on warm, fuzzy catchlines, mottos, and clichés conceived of and cultivated by people like Wennmachers and Marooney, have distracted users from the fact that they are, indeed, corporations, designed to turn a profit—not to make your life better, and not to be your friend. This is the primary and most fundamental narrative of tech, which is worth deconstructing further: the myth that technology can not only change the world but, in the process, make it a better place.

Making the World a Better Place?

The benevolence of the tech industry is a common thread in many of the narratives that emanate from the PR teams of Silicon Valley. The idea that technology can change the world by acting as a tool for the advancement of the human species is baked into every carefully crafted advertising campaign we're bombarded with from morning till night. *Buy an iPhone: it will change your life! Broadcast yourself on YouTube: your cat videos will change the world! Connect your digital persona to every person you've ever met: it will bring us closer together!* The promises of digital technology companies sound ludicrous when we stop to consider what they're actually selling, and even more shocking when we realize how they've accomplished it. Anand Giridharadas, author of *Winners Take All: The Elite Charade of Changing the World*, explains how corporations have capitalized on what was traditionally a liberal and progressive idea:

> "Change the world" has long been the cry of the oppressed. But in recent years world-changing has been co-opted by the rich and the powerful.... At first, you think: Rich people making a difference—so generous! Until you consider that America might not be in the fix it's in had we not fallen for the kind of change these winners have been selling: fake change.[14]

Giridharadas explains that the "elite-led, market-friendly, winner-safe social change"[15] that companies pedal does not, in practice, make the world a better place, but instead multiplies the returns and financial dominance of those who already enjoy immense power. The collection of stories we are told by corporate giants such as Facebook, Twitter, and Google are, in fact, "myths that have fostered an age of extraordinary power concentration; that have allowed the elite's private, partial, and self-preservational deeds to pass for real change."[16] The industry has orchestrated a magic show of sorts, in which we are told the multitude of shiny objects we now enjoy (smartphones, Alexas, social media with endless scrolls, next day shipping), really have made the world a patently better place. The success of the show rests on the promulgation of a culture that is distracted, such that its customer base is unable to see through the barrage of myths, half-truths, and lies that mask the intentions behind the taglines and slogans.

The illusion of positive social change promised by the tech industry is flimsily guarded by myths and vague promises of innovation. As we wait on the world to change, many have begun to notice that things do appear to be shifting—but in the wrong direction. In his 2019 keynote speech at SXSW, T-Bone Burnett suggests that the "leaders of Google and Facebook may seem to some like benevolent plutocrats, but, in fact, they are malevolent and without ethics. On top of that," Burnett argues, "the time for plutocracy is over."[17] Noam Cohen, author of *The Know-It-Alls: The Rise of Silicon Valley as a Political Powerhouse and Social Wrecking Ball*, compares the deception of Silicon Valley's myths to "abuse" and "a form of gaslighting," in which tech companies continue to harm us while claiming "how great they are and how much they are helping [us]."[18] Umair Haque, who argues persuasively for reexamining modern, hypercapitalist business practices, particularly in the space of tech companies, explains that Silicon Valley "gives us the illusion that it's solving big problems—while in fact addressing utterly trivial ones. Consider Facebook. Friends are not exactly an existential threat to humanity. We've had them throughout history."[19]

Let's look at the products of the big four: Amazon, Facebook, Google, and Apple. Amazon sells you stuff. Its game is not profit but market dominance. Facebook allows you to see an ever-diminishing sliver of the lives of people you know in exchange for your attention, in order to sell you stuff. Google gives you search, email, maps, and a host of other conveniences for "free," in order to harvest data and serve ads. To sell you stuff. Apple is perhaps the only one of the four with an up-front business model: Apple sells you quality stuff for a significant price. All in all, there is very little world-changing going on. There is, however, a lot of selling stuff.

Along Came Capitalism

The myth that these companies exist to make your life better, your connections more meaningful, or the information you get more reliable may have been true when Google and Facebook were in their infancy, but time has collapsed the original intentions of many leading tech organizations.

Technology journalist Ben Tarnoff explains that the altruistic sentiments that underpin Silicon Valley's original myth arises from sincere origins of the tech counterculture of the 60s and 70s, which tried to imagine technology as an instrument of human liberation. Tarnoff points to examples such as Stewart Brand's Whole Earth Catalog and acknowledges that although "much of the culture, ethos, and self-image of the tech industry are still largely driven from those forces," there is now a growing incongruence between what tech says and what it does.[20] Increasingly, Tarnoff views the majority of Silicon Valley's "rhetoric as a cynical attempt to divert attention from what they're actually doing."

> They pretend to have altruistic motives when in fact this is an industry that is driven by capitalist imperatives, just as any other industry is. The culture of the tech industry is distinct—certainly—but the reason that a company like Google behaves the way it does is for the same reasons as Exxon-Mobile or Walmart. These are capitalist firms that are subject to the pressures of the market; they're beholden to shareholders, they're trying to build a large monopoly that can dominate markets. So in terms of how the techno-utopian rhetoric fits into that, I think that frankly at this point it seems to have just been weaponized in the service of profit maximization.[21]

Profit, in and of itself, is nothing to be ashamed of; companies need to make money in order to survive. What becomes problematic is the pretense—the dishonesty about what is being sold and how.

The need for fables of changed lives and technological benevolence arose during the transition from the internet's original intentions to its more recent ambitions, which center less on human liberation and more on revenue and shareholder value. The original aims and ideals of the tech community still linger on in company mottos and slidedecks, but they have been corrupted and misaligned from their original intent. Unfortunately for those who believed in the original vision of connectivity and the power of information, according to Noah Kulwin, the ideas "envisioned by Silicon Valley's early hippies turned out to be as well suited for making money as they were for saving the world."[22] The promises of utopian sharing and free information were ultimately, as anyone who has read Marx or has a Facebook account may have already guessed, seduced and co-opted by the market, whose invisible hand seems to be every-where these days. As one employee of a prominent Silicon Valley com-pany put it to me, "change the world. Sounds cool right? But in order to change the world you need capital. Capital doesn't want to change the world. Capital wants to make more capital." When it became clear the spoils of tech could extend beyond the social benefits of information sharing and networked collaboration, a different set of priorities material-ized. Ellen Pao ascribes this change, in part, to the meteoric success of companies like Facebook and Google and the rapid influx of investment capital in the Bay Area after the 2008 financial crash.

> [A]ll of a sudden you have these instant billionaires. No longer did you have to toil for decades. So in 2008, when the markets crashed, all those people from Wall Street who were motivated by money ended up coming out to Silicon Valley and going into tech. That's when values shifted even more. The early, unfounded optimism about good coming out of the inter-net ended up getting completely distorted in the 2000s, when you had these people coming in with a different set of goals.[23]

As the products and services of tech proved, again and again, to be money-spinners, the type of attention the industry received began to change, from both the public and investors. As the affluence of Silicon Valley grew, so did its enmeshment in the world of markets and venture capital. By the early twenty-first century, the birth of technocapitalism had begun.

There's an App for That

As money and interest flooded the Bay Area, the shift in values Pao describes began to affect the quality, aims, and social usefulness of the products and services that emerged from Silicon Valley. What began as genuine aspirations to solve legitimate problems, slowly devolved into an ethos that believed technology could solve any problem, an idea Evgeny Morozov has labelled techno-solutionism. In his 2014 book, *To Save Everything, Click Here: The Folly of Technological Solutionism*, Morozov explains that many founders and organizations in the Valley suffer from the misguided tendency to recast "all complex social situations either as neat problems with definite, computable solutions or as transparent and self-evident processes that can be easily optimized—if only the right algorithms are in place."[24] Amongst the many problems arising from solutionist thinking, Morozov argues, is a disregard for the scale and complexity of long-standing human and social issues, alongside a presumptive arrogance that the right code can fix any problem.

Armed with the belief that technology could solve any problem and propped up by the free-flowing capital of VCs, an unprecedented number of tech companies were born, each operating under the belief that their app or platform would change the world. In 2014, $48bn made its way into U.S. tech start-ups, with Silicon Valley and San Francisco companies receiving half the total.[25] Let loose with more money than sense, writer and software engineer Yiren Lu explains how it became less and less "necessary to have particularly deep domain knowledge before founding your own start-up," due to "the willingness of venture capitalists to finance Mark Zuckerberg look-alikes" in the hopes of betting on the right product or founder.[26] This, in turn, encouraged an influx of ideas—both good and bad, but largely unnecessary—that Lu argues changed the landscape of Silicon Valley's products.

> There are more platforms, more websites, more pat solutions to serious problems—here's an app that can fix drug addiction! promote fiscal responsibility! advance childhood literacy! Companies like Meraki that build enterprise-grade hardware and leverage years of research tend to be anomalies among the new guard. Even as the pool of founders has grown and diversified, the products themselves seem more homogeneous, more pedestrian.[27]

As some of the brightest minds in engineering flocked to the Bay Area— some to change the world, others to make millions and retire—Silicon Valley found itself with a very peculiar problem: a surplus of talent, comprised largely of young, Ivy League educated engineers, and a shortage of meaningful work for them to do. What followed has been a slew of mostly prosaic products that fail to solve real-world problems like economic inequality, climate change, or job displacement or which make the most of the engineering talent in the tech community.

In addition to the homogeneity of the products that began to emerge, Silicon Valley's onslaught of investment had another curious side effect: it encouraged the creation of problems. In an effort to make something—anything—that might prove to be the next big thing, entrepreneurs and tech founders began to scramble for problems they could fix. Professor Don Norman, head of the Design Lab at University of California, San Diego and author of *The Design of Future Things* and *Living with Complexity*, explains that, recently a lot of design energy has been spent finding problems that aren't problems. The first response of most designers and technologists, Norman laments, is "let's make an app."[28] With this mentality, Norman explains, comes a tendency to prioritize the application of technology without paying attention to the actual, underlying problem:

> A lot of the companies don't think much of the implications of what they're doing—they're often very excited by the technology, it's all about the technology and what the technology can do. In the design field, we try to train our students to find out what the fundamental need is for people is first, then decide how to deal with that and what they should do. The technology comes last.[29]

One famous example of the "technology first" phenomenon Norman describes is the Juicero, perhaps the most notorious example of over-engineering in Silicon Valley's history.

> The Juicero was always a contentious product. It launched in 2016 as a $700 Wi-Fi connected juicer designed to squeeze subscription-purchased, pre-cut veggies from a pouch into your cup—at a moment when the average American had less than a grand in their bank account. To many, it was a symbol of the Silicon Valley class designing for its own, insular problems. In Juicero's case, that problem was, "I'm rich, but I can't drive thru to get a morning juice." Juicero is basically a mini trash compactor that connects to the internet to squeeze bags of juice, and auto-replenish them as they run out. But it wasn't until we tried Juicero for ourselves that we faced the real silliness of some of its user experience design.[30]

The Juicero is completely unnecessary, as the packets can be squeezed easily by hand. Mark Wilson argues that the product epitomizes "everything wrong with Silicon Valley design today. It's a solution for rich people that's worse than the problem."[31] Juicero is something of a running joke now, a cautionary tale of over-designing products. It is also illustrative of a larger trend in tech in which products are not built to serve a real world need or a global audience, but made for those in its own, elite backyard.

In an article entitled, "The Shut-in Economy," tech journalist Lauren Smiley details how a growing majority of products emerging from Silicon Valley "are created by the urban young for the needs of urban young," many of which are born of the ubiquitous "on-demand economy."[32] Examples range from suitcases that follow you from the airport check-in desk to your gate; smart underwear; smart salt shakers; toothbrushes equipped with AI; virtual candles, lighters, and fireplaces; and more food delivery and laundry apps than you could ever hope to use in a lifetime. There really is something for everyone. And by everyone, I mean predominantly the people who envision and fund these products. Tom Goodwin describes how Silicon Valley's more recent products appear to be increasingly designed for a smaller subset of people.

> There's an app where you can order another car to come and fill your car with petrol. The target audience for a lot of these things appears to be the founders themselves, because it's normally something for a 26-year-old, privileged white guy who isn't very social. When you consider the products that they make and the way that they do things, it's as if they've never really met a normal human being.[33]

This is not to say there aren't a number of companies in the Bay Area working on socially responsible, civically-minded applications of technology. (The woman sitting next to me as I write works for a company that develops new technologies for libraries, which aim to increase accessibility of educational materials and improve literacy.) Overall, however, there is a disturbing lack of cohesion between the grand pronouncements of social change the industry promises, and the real-world effects of its most venerated, utilized, and well-financed products and platforms.

Tech's rallying cry to "change the world," then, proves not so much false as misleading. The world is indeed changing, but not in the ways we thought were being sold. The devil, in this case, is in the lack of details. No one asked exactly what kind of change we were being promised. Nor did anyone think to ask how we would pay for it or what the long-term impacts and side-effects might be. Instead, most of us swallowed whole the narrative spun by the marketers and PR experts charged with ensuring we explicitly trusted the industry and its products. As media journalist John Herrman explains, this masterful marketing spin allowed dominant tech companies to settle "into a sort of permanent revolution."

> If they were founded to address an easy question, that question has either been answered and forgotten or repeated enough times to convert it into an odd, self-justifying ideology. (See: Facebook's "Connecting the world.") The questions became companies, which then, mostly without explicitly deciding to, became institutions. And now, for anyone affected by the tech industry, the most obvious and important questions are about the world that these companies are making.[34]

And this is perhaps the most pressing, and interesting, contradiction: while promising one world that offers "happiness, peace, prosperity and even eternal life,"[35] tech has delivered another, fraught with problems and challenges none of us could have envisioned. The bargain we've made is beginning to feel rather Faustian, and the effects—broken democracies, mental health problems, economic dislocation—are rather more serious than we realized. Morozov's early recognition—that the solutionist thinking of the tech industry would "have unexpected consequences that could eventually cause more damage than the problems they seek to address"[36]— now seems eerily prophetic and disquieting. It should also make us question what might be broken next.

Move Fast and Break ~~Things~~ Civility, Truth & Democracy

The myth of speed and fast failure has dominated Silicon Valley's mythological landscape since Facebook's dorm room mentality went mainstream in 2006. "Move fast and break things" remained one of the company's mottos until 2014, when the phrase changed to a slightly more mature and less sexy, "Move fast with stable infra." But the standard of innovating first and asking permission later had been set, and with it a dangerous precedent. The intention that informed the thinking behind Facebook's well-known slogan arose innocently enough, as political economist and journalist Angus Hervey explains:

> Facebook's classic mantra represented a philosophy of trying out new ideas quickly so you could see if they survived in the marketplace. If they did, you refined them; if they didn't, you could throw them away without blowing more time and money on development.[37]

On a small scale—Harvard's 2004 student body, for example—the repercussions of innovating without consent were relatively benign, if a bit immature and indicative of poor values. On a global scale, however, the mentality that enabled the rise of Facebook and its contemporaries has come at a substantial price that only now, over a decade later, have begun to come to light.

The practical applications of agility and testing are hardly sinister. William Edward Deming's model, which is used throughout healthcare, is one of many theories of leadership and management that encourages improvement, testing, and iterative learning in a controlled and safe environment. Deming's theory of innovation is grounded in the idea of testing on a small scale to determine both methods of success and areas of potential harm. Where Deming's model balances innovation with a healthy respect for the environment in which it operates, Silicon Valley's philosophy prioritizes aggressive change and growth at scale, often without the safety net of controlled testing. As Andrew McCollum, one of Facebook's co-founders explains,

> ["Move fast and break things"] encapsulate[s] a philosophy of rapid development, constant iteration and the courage to leave the past behind. Of course, some might wonder why you couldn't just stop at the "move fast" part. The truth is that breaking things is unavoidable.... A billion people will pretty quickly try every possible way to interact with your code, so features will be used in ways you never expected,

and sometimes things will break in ways that you didn't anticipate. Because you can't get that level of feedback until things reach production, it means that moving fast is inextricably tied with the process of deployment.[38]

McCollum recalls that in Facebook's early days the operations team suggested building a staging environment in which new code could be properly tested before it reached the live production environment and Facebook's then audience of over a billion users. Adam D'Angelo, the company's future CTO, argued against the change, and ultimately convinced Zuckerberg to forgo the additional testing stage, reinforcing the company's now-infamous attitude that prioritizes growth above safety and security.

The primacy of growth, particularly in the context of a global audience, necessitates a number of compromises and, in many cases, precludes the possibility of responsible innovation. As journalist Fred Vogelstein and Wired CEO Nick Thompson explain, Facebook's "move fast" dictum "wasn't just a piece of advice to [Zuckerberg's] developers; it was a philosophy that served to resolve countless delicate trade-offs—many of them involving user privacy—in ways that best favored the platform's growth."[39] The compromises Vogelstein and Thompson describe continue to pile up at Facebook: from the devastating effects of the Cambridge Analytica scandal, to the emails that show Zuckerberg and his colleagues discussing the pros and cons of decisions impacting privacy and user experience, to Facebook's secret partnerships with over 150 companies that granted access to users' data without their consent. Tech journalist Alison Griswold explains how the unmitigated demand for speed, growth, and profit quietly underpin the actual aims of the "move fast and break things" myth.

> The startups that moved fast and broke things have been egged on by return-hungry venture capitalists and their companion motto, "growth at any cost." These investors poured money into some of the Valley's most tarnished companies, including Theranos, Uber, and human-resources startup Zenefits, which devised software to help employees cheat on state compliance tests. Venture capitalists have also spent years looking the other

way on tech's egregious lack of diversity and a culture of sexual harassment that hurt and disempowered women. Today, as funding rounds that exceed $100 million—so-called "mega-rounds"—have become the new norm, startups remain under pressure from investors to raise as much money and grow as quickly as possible.[40]

One startup founder, who had worked in tech for over twenty years, put it this way: "there are many things wrong with the industry; but the one thing it always comes back to is the endless pursuit of capital. It's never enough to satiate the VCs; you have to just grow and grow and grow." The entrepreneur was bootstrapping his newest company in order to distance himself and his team from the "short-term thinking and bad values" he associated with many VC firms.

The consequences of embracing Facebook's "do it now, ask forgiveness later" ideology, unfortunately, aren't always clear until it's too late. One of the most obvious and notable examples is Uber's cataclysmic series of mistakes leading up to CEO Travis Kalanick's removal in 2017. From its infancy in 2009, the company has been a perfect cocktail of truly disruptive and innovative technology, unmitigated growth, and abundant funding, without any of the requisite cultural, legal, or social checks one might expect from a global corporation of its scale and reach. Hempel explains how Uber's second CEO, Dara Khosrowshahi, recognized how the company's misplaced worship of growth had "left a trail of wreckage" in its wake.

> [Uber] disregarded and even undermined laws and regulations; it squandered the loyalty of its drivers, who felt mistreated under its contractor system; and it became notorious for a workplace culture that exemplified the worst tendencies of the Silicon Valley bro. By the time investors moved to demand Kalanick's resignation in June 2017, observers were calling Uber the world's most dysfunctional startup. But where others saw Uber's travails as a symbol of Silicon Valley comeuppance, Khosrowshahi saw something less loaded: a sophisticated tech company that had taken on too much, too quickly, and whose systems groaned under the weight and confusion. Growth, not quality, had been its guiding principle for too long, he said.[41]

The reality of innovating at speed and without proper safety precautions is that, eventually, people will get hurt, as Facebook, Twitter, and Uber's platforms have demonstrated. The bro culture at Uber may have been quelled by a renewed sense of maturity and stability thanks to Khosrowshahi, but the demands for growth and market share still affect the company's ability to think about the implications of its actions. In March 2018, one of Uber's self-driving cars, which was being tested on the streets of Tempe, Arizona, hit and killed pedestrian Elaine Herzberg, a 49-year-old mother of two. The company has also been accused of attempting to silence a growing number of female riders who have been sexually assaulted by Uber's partner drivers.[42] Such cases are a sobering reminder that growth, without caution or concern, can have real, human consequences.

The pace at which Silicon Valley insists organizations and developers must move and scale is intricately linked to its tendency to break the things, people, and systems it claims to be helping. As tech companies align themselves with an ethos that caters to growth and profit over the safety of people, the gravity of the consequences now associated with untested or unfit technology have become more urgent. Award-winning technology journalist Christina Larson has warned that the myth that tech companies must scale and break things in order to succeed, encapsulates "the twin totems of speed and aggression that animate many programmers and venture capitalists in the U.S. tech industry." "It's a lot less appealing," Larson says, "when the things being broken are people."[43] Angus Hervey, a journalist and co-founder of FutureCrunch, explains that as Silicon Valley's technology has been subsumed into a greater number of industries, the industry now bears a responsibility that historically it was not expected to shoulder.

> Traditionally, digital enthusiasts haven't had to worry about stuff like this. Code has always been relatively harmless. Daily interaction with pain, physical harm or death was a lot less likely if you were working with bits and bytes, than if you were working with human bodies (medicine) or heavy machinery (transportation). In order to fulfil the ethical warrant of the profession, all you had to do was make the product work. It was up to other people to figure out the applications or the social mission. That's no longer the case. Software can now propel steel and glass into human flesh, or be turned into propaganda by foreign agents.[44]

A conversation about what it means to be the custodian of public safety in the digital era has simply not been sufficiently or transparently discussed.

Neither those in power, nor those of us who entrusted the tech industry with it, as yet have a clear understanding of what standards of behavior and ethical frameworks in tech should include. What is clear, however, is the immensity of power digital companies wield, and the magnitude of responsibility that accompanies it.

> If information is power in the digital age (and it is), then Google has a fair claim to being the most powerful company in the world. It has collected, digitised, arranged and presented more information than any company in history. It knows more about you than anyone. Does the NHS or HMRC know if you have a dog or not? Google does. With great power, supposedly, comes great responsibility. The powerful should not abuse their position and should perhaps play a role in supporting the societies in which they operate. Do Google and the other titans of the digital age like Apple, Facebook and Amazon pass those tests?[45]

Based on their behaviors to date, many would likely argue that the industry has not proven itself to be sufficiently mature or capable of handling such responsibility. Alex Stamos, Facebook's former CSO, has put forth the argument that the attitude towards responsibility in Silicon Valley has not kept pace with the changing landscape, power, and influence of the industry.

> While the times have changed, the community and the industry have not really changed with them. The truth is that we are no longer the upstarts, we are no longer the hacker kids fighting against corporate conformity.... We don't fight the man anymore, in some ways we are the man. But we haven't really changed our attitude towards what kind of responsibility that puts on us.[46]

What Stamos touches on here is a critical shortcoming of the industry, with far-reaching implications: the tendency to grow without necessarily maturing, and the willingness to assume the most important professions of the digital age without assuming the corresponding moral demands those roles entail.

In addition to the nebulous ethical responsibilities and as-yet-unformulated expectations of the tech industry, there is an important point to be made about the perception of distance and responsibility in today's digital world. In bygone days, when privacy included our physical space and tangible belongings, what constituted harm or misconduct was, for the most part, unequivocal. Today, however, the lines of property, data, possessions, harm, hate speech, and free speech have been blurred by the new, largely intangible world created behind our screens.

> Perhaps what's set Silicon Valley apart—the difference between Elon Musk and John D. Rockefeller, Elizabeth Holmes and Jay Gould—is that it believes, since the "disruption" is orchestrated from behind a computer, it's not the same. That it was somehow cleaner than coal or oil or steel. This is naive. Disruption is painful. People get hurt. And someone has to do that hurting. It's called creative *destruction* for a reason. Good comes from it, but it's not without its costs—to society or to the people who make it their living. The ability to willfully seek out this destruction on a massive scale is, in its own way, a skill. Not all of us have it. It's probably better that most of us do not. But certain people do.[47]

Tech companies are quick to take credit for the improvements their products make (or claim to make), but they are less likely to take responsibility for the damage their disruption leaves in its wake. Until our systems, laws, and moral expectations have caught up to our machines, there remains a dangerous discrepancy between the responsibility with which the industry has been entrusted and the hands-off approach it assumes.

The disruption myth has persisted thanks, in large part, to the expertly spun narratives of tech founders and marketing wizards intent on exaggerating the benefits of their companies, products, and platforms, without acknowledging the many consequences of disruption. As lawmakers, governments, and individuals become more conscious of the negative impacts the industry brings about, however, things show signs of changing. As Alison Griswold has recently observed, "'move fast and break things' has long been the tech way, but it no longer appears to be working."[48] Griswold cites the array of investigations and allegations against prominent tech companies, including Theranos's fraudulent claims around the company's blood testing capabilities; Tesla's SEC investigation following Musk's false claim that he was taking the company private; Uber's string of cultural misdeeds, which resulted in six federal investigations; and Facebook's role in spreading misinformation and undermining democracy on its platform. The assumption that it is acceptable to break things—truth, civility, laws, human life, mental health, democracy—for one's own advancement is a narrative that, thankfully, appears to be breaking down. David Hanson, a programmer and partner at software firm Basecamp, argues "it takes a while for people to catch up when the world changes, but eventually they do, and now they have."

> It used to be that you could unironically claim to be disrupting this or that, and people would look at you with puppy eyes asking to hear more. Now if you claim to be on some disruptive mission, you're far more likely to be met with skepticism and critical inquiry, if not outright eye rolls. That's because the disruption story hasn't had the neat happy ending its main protagonists would like you to believe. Whether it's the gig economy normalizing, nay, *celebrating*, working three jobs to make ends met. Or specifically ride sharing outsourcing all capital costs and risk to drivers. Or apartment buildings turned into defacto hotels by short-term rentals. There are real, systemic downsides.[49]

Disruption for the sake of growth is neither a pardonable nor a permissible ideology. New laws and organizational ethos should reflect the breadth of responsibility that has been conferred upon technology companies, while Silicon Valley must figure out a way to disrupt its own ideology of "move fast and break things" to something comparable to the medical community's ethos to "first, do no harm."

Tech Knows Best

Two of the underlying beliefs that have enabled the above myths to survive and proliferate are the assumption that those leading the tech industry know what's best—for our relationships, for society at large, for the laws that govern them—and that they are trustworthy, upstanding custodians of our wellbeing. Let me say this unequivocally: neither of these beliefs is accurate. Tech author and journalist John Battelle notes the problematic paternalist attitude of platforms like Facebook, which he argues communicate, "[w]e know what's best for you, better than you do in fact, so trust us, we'll roll the code, you consume what we put in front of you."[50] This dynamic has persisted unchallenged thanks, in large part, to Silicon Valley's positive public image. According to Ben Tarnoff, who has reported on the industry for the past decade, as it ascended to public consciousness and market dominance, Silicon Valley companies has been absolved of numerous transgressions, while repeatedly proving themselves undeserving of the positive and deferential treatment they enjoy.

> Silicon Valley benefits from an enormous amount of positive coverage. It's hard to think of another industry that everyone seems to give the benefit of the doubt to. This may have begun to shift a little bit, but when people think of the motivations of Google or Facebook, until relatively recently, they've largely thought of those motivations as being altruistic in nature. Which again is preposterous if we were to think about say, the fossil fuel industry or the financial industry or the restaurant industry—the notion that the executives at those companies were motivated by anything other than profit maximization would strike anyone as absurd. But somehow when we think of the leaders of tech companies, particularly a figure like Elon Musk, who receives an enormous amount of, frankly, quite sycophantic press coverage—they're seen as heroic figures, which is how they see themselves, as figures who have the capacity to liberate mankind. That does the industry a lot of very concrete favors; it's eased and accelerated its success with lobbies, for instance—the top five in tech firms now outspend Wall Street 2:1 on lobbying in D.C. Obviously, that buys a lot of influence, but one of the things that makes that purchase of influence easier is the fact that a significant portion of the general public has bought into this idea that the tech industry really is a force for good in the world. And no other industry enjoys that advantage.[51]

The assumption that the leaders of the tech industry, across the board, have the public's best interests at heart is a common but misguided fallacy, often referred to as technopaternalism. There are certainly lovely human beings who work in tech, but to assume they have a special understanding of what is best for the population at large or are motivated by altruism rather than profits is a dangerous cultural delusion.

In 2018, a survey by HarrisX found that 63 percent of Americans considered technology to be a force for good in society, while 68 percent thought it was having a "positive impact on the world," indicating the myth of the benevolent tech company was alive and well.[52] A 2017 Gallup poll, by comparison, found that, across all industries, only 21 percent of Americans surveyed had a favourable opinion of big businesses in general,[53] suggesting people do not necessarily associate tech companies with traditional corporate America. The unique ability of the tech industry to psychologically uncouple itself from big business is a myth in and of itself, which the following chapter will seek to dispel. Dritan Nesho, CEO of HarrisX, suggests the results of her company's survey illustrate that "the public has a complex relationship with personal technology. Broadly speaking, a majority of Americans perceive technology to be a good force on the world. But dig deeper and you find very conflicted views on a series of important social issues."[54] This ambivalence is reflected in other research, including a poll by Axios and SurveyMonkey, which found that from October 2017 to March 2018, favorability had dropped for Facebook (−28%), Amazon (−13%), Google (−12%), Apple (−10%), Twitter (−7%), and Microsoft (−3%).[55] Nesho puts these numbers down to tech's recent "series of scandals around fake news, platform bias, foreign interference and privacy concerns,"[56] which have begun to dismantle the popular myths of tech companies as a force for social good.

Despite recent trends in public opinion, however, Silicon Valley's worst offenders continue to dominate the market. Simon Jack points to a troubling discrepancy in public perception: that regardless of the transgressions of leading tech companies such as Facebook, Google, Uber, and Twitter—and the accompanying lawsuits, fines, and Congressional, Senate, and Parliamentary hearings that have resulted from their actions—"tech giants enjoy incredible customer loyalty which is perhaps why they genuinely do not believe they are the bad guys in the story of the new industrial revolution."[57] This shared misconception may soon be invalidated, according to author and journalist Scott Rosenberg, as people begin "to ask hard questions about whether tech platforms are weakening democracy, promoting ignorance, and fostering a new wave of authoritarian nationalism."[58]

Anyone would have a hard time answering these questions. But the Silicon Valley founder is uniquely ill prepared. Many founders begin their careers embracing high-minded ideals: freedom of speech, tolerance of difference, equality of opportunity, support for the underdog, respect for the law, and more. They believe, ardently and innocently, that they are doing good in the world, and they see their companies as levers for world-changing improvements.[59]

The problem of assigning responsibility becomes more difficult when those in power believe and defend their own myths. When we have a narrative to which we can attribute our behaviors, our actions often become detached from our original intentions, well-meaning as they may be, and instead become unconsciously justified by our narrative. As tech companies move toward what they perceive to be their goal—bolstered by whatever mantra they keep repeating ("connecting people," "giving everyone a voice," "doing the right thing")—their actions can become oddly self-perpetuating if they fail to reflect on their behavior. If myths serve to inform our understanding of the world and how we must comport ourselves in it, the notion that tech companies are the "good guys" gives them unprecedented license to behave in entirely unbecoming ways.

Dismantling the Myths

We believe stories for a number of reasons. Mostly, however, we believe them because they're easy. Stories are less complicated than the full, messy, unadulterated truth. In the same way it's easier to read a headline than an entire article, our brains are prone to take the path of least resistance between making a judgment about something or connecting two ideas. In our current climate of attention warfare and information overload, we are even more likely to choose myth over fact, as long as it makes some semblance of sense or corresponds to something we already believe or wish to be true. Myths and stories that explain the world are especially powerful, in that they provide us with a rationalization about who or what something is or how it works. As we deconstruct the narratives that have shaped our beliefs about Silicon Valley, we need to ensure they are not replaced with equally inaccurate myths.

Silicon Valley's recent cacophony of misdeeds has revealed, in some cases, deception on a global scale. The discrepancy between Silicon Valley's myths and the realities of its behaviors has created significant cognitive dissonance (to put it lightly) and have exposed a range of challenges that, if left unresolved and unregulated, will have profound implications for the future. The media and the public spent the better part of 2017 and 2018 attempting to reconcile the image portrayed by tech companies with their actions, which have disappointed on both ethical and social grounds. Journalist Maria Bustillos explains the public has been conditioned to believe the archetypal tech leader is "generous, a thoughtful and responsible custodian of our private information, a wise and intelligent leader,"[60] a myth "crafted to evoke warmth, admiration, and good feelings so the people keep coming, keep reading, keep liking, keep paying."[61] PR and communications employees are hired at major tech firms, such as Facebook, with the express purpose of measuring and improving the public's perception of their executives. Others, such as Wennmachers, are tasked with crafting the warm, fuzzy stories we are meant to believe about Silicon Valley's benevolent intentions.

In some cases, what we believe, even if it is patently false, doesn't really matter—in the case of Silicon Valley, it very much does, and we can no longer afford the price we pay for believing its false and misleading narratives. The myths of making the world a better place, of the virtue of moving fast and breaking things, and of the benevolent, socially responsible tech company have survived because we have not sufficiently questioned them. We have collectively allowed and set a precedent that needs to be reversed as soon as possible and replaced with a better, healthier, and more mature narrative based on awareness, fact, and more sophisticated thinking about cultural health. While the myths of Silicon Valley have begun to break down en masse, we must continue to examine and dismantle them in order to truly understand and correct the underlying problems that drive them.

Our next question might be: why? What are the motivations behind the narratives tech feels compelled to tell? What drives an industry like Silicon Valley to behave in the way it has?

Notes

1. Harari, Y. N. (2018, August 5). Yuval Noah Harari Extract: 'Humans have Always Lived in the Age of Post-truth. We're a Post-truth Species.' *The Observer*. Retrieved from https://www.theguardian.com/culture/2018/aug/05/yuval-noah-harari-extract-fake-news-sapiens-homo-deus
2. Ibid.
3. Betuel, E. (2018, August 22). Scientists Reveal the Number of Times You're Actually Conscious Each Minute. Retrieved August 27, 2018, from *Inverse* website: https://www.inverse.com/article/48300-why-is-it-hard-to-focus-research-humans
4. Murfin, R., & Ray, S. M. (Eds.). (2003). Myth. In *The Bedford Glossary of Critical Literary Terms* (2nd ed., p. 284). Boston: Bedford-St. Martin's.
5. Hempel, J. (2018, January 21). The Spin Master Behind Facebook, Airbnb, and Silicon Valley as You Know It. *Wired*. Retrieved from https://www.wired.com/story/margit-wennmachers-is-andreessen-horowitzs-secret-weapon/
6. Bowles, N. (2013, September 22). Marketing Guru Margit Wennmachers' New Venture. Retrieved December 4, 2018, from *SFGate* website: https://www.sfgate.com/news/article/Marketing-guru-Margit-Wennmachers-new-venture-4833221.php
7. Hempel, J. (2018, January 21). The Spin Master Behind Facebook, Airbnb, and Silicon Valley as You Know It. *Wired*. Retrieved from https://www.wired.com/story/margit-wennmachers-is-andreessen-horowitzs-secret-weapon/
8. Ibid.
9. Ibid.
10. Ibid.
11. Ibid.
12. Abi-Heila, G. (2018, March 1). Attention Hacking is the Epidemic of Our Generation.... Retrieved August 27, 2018, from *Hacker Noon* website: https://hackernoon.com/attention-hacking-is-the-epidemic-of-our-generation-e212e111c675
13. Solon, O. (2018, March 24). 'A Grand Illusion': Seven Days that Shattered Facebook's Facade. *The Guardian*. Retrieved from https://www.theguardian.com/technology/2018/mar/24/cambridge-analytica-week-that-shattered-facebook-privacy

14. Giridharadas, A. (2018, August 25). Beware Rich People Who Say They Want to Change the World. *The New York Times*. Retrieved from https://www.nytimes.com/2018/08/24/opinion/sunday/wealth-philanthropy-fake-change.html
15. Giridharadas, A. (2018). *Winners Take All: The Elite Charade of Changing the World* (1st ed., First Printing edition, p. 11). New York: Knopf.
16. Ibid., p. 12.
17. Bronson, K. (2019, March 14). Read T Bone Burnett's Keynote Speech at SXSW. Retrieved May 23, 2019, from *buzzbands.la* website: http://buzzbands.la/2019/03/13/t-bone-burnetts-keynote-speech-at-sxsw-dire-warnings-vs-the-goal-of-art-to-create-conscience/
18. Solon, O. (2017, December 23). Tech's Terrible Year: How the World Turned on Silicon Valley in 2017. *The Observer*. Retrieved from https://www.theguardian.com/technology/2017/dec/22/tech-year-in-review-2017
19. Haque, U. (2018, March 26). Why Capitalism is Obsolete. Retrieved September 17, 2018, from *Eudaimonia and Co* website: https://eand.co/why-capitalism-is-obsolete-d10197b5bca2
20. Tarnoff, B. (2017, September 5). *Interview with Ben Tarnoff* (K. Cook, Interviewer).
21. Ibid.
22. Kulwin, N. (2018, April 13). An Apology for the Internet—From the Architects Who Built It. *Select All*. Retrieved from http://nymag.com/intelligencer/2018/04/an-apology-for-the-internet-from-the-people-who-built-it.html
23. Ibid.
24. Morozov, E. (2014). *To Save Everything, Click Here: The Folly of Technological Solutionism* (p. 5). New York: PublicAffairs.
25. Relander, B. (2015, February 27). #1 Country for Tech Start-Ups: U.S.A. Retrieved December 6, 2018, from *Investopedia* website: https://www.investopedia.com/articles/investing/022815/1-country-tech-startups-usa.asp
26. Lu, Y. (2018, January 19). Silicon Valley's Youth Problem. *The New York Times*. Retrieved from https://www.nytimes.com/2014/03/16/magazine/silicon-valleys-youth-problem.html
27. Ibid.
28. Norman, D. (2018, September 27). *Interview with Don Norman* (K. Cook, Interviewer).
29. Ibid.

30. Wilson, M. (2017, April 20). My Day with Juicero, Silicon Valley's Absurd $400 Juicer. Retrieved August 19, 2018, from *Fast Company* website: https://www.fastcompany.com/90110876/my-day-with-silicon-valleys-absurd-400-juicer
31. Ibid.
32. Smiley, L. (2015, March 25). The Shut-In Economy. Retrieved September 16, 2018, from *Matter* website: https://medium.com/matter/the-shut-in-economy-ec3ec1294816
33. Goodwin, T. (2017, August 3). *Interview with Tom Goodwin* (K. Cook, Interviewer).
34. Herrman, J. (2018, July 15). Have the Tech Giants Grown Too Powerful? That's an Easy One. *The New York Times*. Retrieved from https://www.nytimes.com/2018/07/11/magazine/facebook-google-uber-tech-giants-power.html
35. Harari, Y. N. (2017). *Homo Deus: A Brief History of Tomorrow* (p. 409). London: Vintage.
36. Morozov, E. (2014). *To Save Everything, Click Here: The Folly of Technological Solutionism* (p. 5). New York: PublicAffairs.
37. Hervey, A. (2018, May 25). Move Slowly, and Don't Break Things. Retrieved August 27, 2018, from *Future Crunch* website: https://medium.com/future-crunch/move-slowly-and-dont-break-things-693f00601b19
38. McCollum, A. (2015, March 10). The Unavoidable Truth of Moving Fast and Breaking Things. Retrieved December 7, 2018, from *Tech Crunch* website: http://social.techcrunch.com/2015/03/10/move-fast-and-break-things/
39. Vogelstein, F., & Thompson, N. (2018, February 12). Inside Facebook's Two Years of Hell. *Wired*. Retrieved from https://www.wired.com/story/inside-facebook-mark-zuckerberg-2-years-of-hell/
40. Griswold, A. (2018, September 8). "Move Fast and Break Things" is Broken. Retrieved December 7, 2018, from *Quartz* website: https://qz.com/1380490/move-fast-and-break-things-is-broken/
41. Hempel, J. (2018, April 19). Can this Man Help Uber Recover from the Travis Kalanick Era? *Wired*. Retrieved from https://www.wired.com/story/uber-move-slow-test-things/
42. Levin, S. (2018, March 16). Uber Accused of Silencing Women Who Claim Sexual Assault by Drivers. *The Guardian*. Retrieved from https://www.theguardian.com/technology/2018/mar/15/uber-class-action-lawsuit-sexual-assault-rape-arbitration

43. Larson, C. (2017, November 7). Facebook Can't Cope with the World It's Created. *Foreign Policy*. Retrieved from https://foreignpolicy. com/2017/11/07/facebook-cant-cope-with-the-world-its-created/

44. Hervey, A. (2018, May 25). Move Slowly, and Don't Break Things. Retrieved August 27, 2018, from *Future Crunch* website: https:// medium.com/future-crunch/move-slowly-and-dont-break-things-693f00601b19

45. Jack, S. (2017, November 21). *Google—Powerful and Responsible?* Retrieved from https://www.bbc.com/news/business-42060091

46. Stamos, A. (2017). *Black Hat Keynote: Stepping Up Our Game: Re-focusing the Security Community on Defense and Making Security Work for Everyone*. Retrieved from https://www.youtube.com/watch?v=YJOMTAREFtY

47. Holiday, R. (2018, March 15). It's Time to Get Real about Power in Silicon Valley. Retrieved August 28, 2018, from *Medium* website: https:// medium.com/the-mission/its-time-to-get-real-about-power-in-silicon-valley-b59b4772138d

48. Griswold, A. (2018, September 8). "Move Fast and Break Things" is Broken. Retrieved December 7, 2018, from *Quartz* website: https:// qz.com/1380490/move-fast-and-break-things-is-broken/

49. Hanson, D. (2017, December 19). Silicon Valley Should Welcome the Scrutiny. Retrieved May 27, 2019, from *Signal v. Noise* website: https://m.signalvnoise.com/silicon-valley-should-welcome-the-scrutiny/

50. Battelle, J. (2018, January 24). Is this the Society We Really Want? Retrieved 27 August 2018, from *Newco Shift* website: https://shift. newco.co/2018/01/24/is-this-the-society-we-really-want/

51. Tarnoff, B. (2017, September 5). *Interview with Ben Tarnoff* (K. Cook, Interviewer).

52. HarrisX. (2018). *Inaugural Tech Media Telecom Pulse Survey 2018*. Retrieved from http://harrisx.com/wp-content/uploads/2018/04/ Inaugural-TMT-Pulse-Survey_-20-Apr-Final.pdf

53. Newport, F. (2017). *Business Gets Bigger Even as Americans Prefer Small*. Retrieved from *Gallup* website: https://news.gallup.com/opinion/poll-ing-matters/216674/business-gets-bigger-even-americans-prefer-small. aspx

54. Solon, O. (2018, April 20). Americans Want Tougher Rules for Big Tech Amid Privacy Scandals, Poll Finds. *The Guardian*. Retrieved from http:// www.theguardian.com/technology/2018/apr/20/facebook-tech-companies-us-privacy-poll

55. Hart, K., & Fried, I. (2018, March 26). Exclusive Poll: Facebook Favorability Plunges. Retrieved August 26, 2018, from *Axios* website: https://www.axios.com/exclusive-poll-facebook-favorability-plunges-1522057235-b1fa31db-e646-4413-a273-95d3387da4f2.html

56. Solon, O. (2018, April 20). Americans Want Tougher Rules for Big Tech Amid Privacy Scandals, Poll Finds. *The Guardian*. Retrieved from http://www.theguardian.com/technology/2018/apr/20/facebook-tech-companies-us-privacy-poll

57. Jack, S. (2017, November 21). Google—Powerful and Responsible? *BBC News*. Retrieved from https://www.bbc.com/news/business-42060091

58. Rosenberg, S. (2017, November 8). The End of the Cult of the Founder. *Wired*. Retrieved from https://www.wired.com/story/the-end-of-the-cult-of-the-founder/

59. Ibid.

60. Bustillos, M. (2018, March 8). The Smallness of Mark Zuckerberg. Retrieved August 31, 2018, from *Medium* website: https://medium.com/s/story/the-smallness-of-mark-zuckerberg-4e94a88bba02

61. Ibid.

5

Motivation

Whatever a man depends upon, whatever rules his mind, whatever governs his affections, whatever is the chief object of his delight, is his god.
–Charles Spurgeon

Our motivations are an incredibly complex web of impulses and instincts, influenced both by forces we understand and those we do not. More than any other component of our psychology, our motivations direct our behavior, guide our thinking, and shape the direction of our lives. Psychologist Jeffrey Nevid explains that motivation "refers to factors that activate, direct, and sustain goal-directed behavior... Motives are the 'whys' of behavior—the needs or wants that drive behavior and explain what we do."[1] As the primary drivers of our behavior, our motivations are one of the most powerful components of our psychology.

Certain types of motivations are universal: hunger, sex, and safety from physical harm, for instance, are largely shared, instinctual behaviors based on biological drives. We are born with these and retain them throughout our lives.[2] In addition to our biological needs, we are also driven by psychological, cognitive, and psychosocial needs. These may take the form of

© The Author(s) 2020
K. Cook, *The Psychology of Silicon Valley*,
https://doi.org/10.1007/978-3-030-27364-4_5

affiliation needs (social connection, interpersonal relationships, belonging); *incentives* (the stimuli we associate with rewards and punishments); or the *need for achievement*.[3] These drives, unlike our biological drives, are more variable, more nuanced, and tend to vary from person to person, business to business, culture to culture. Our motivations can also be extrinsic and intrinsic—that is, they may be a reflection of our "desire for external rewards, such as money or the respect of one's peers or family," or a more individual "desire for internal gratification, such as the self-satisfaction or pleasure derived from accomplishing a particular goal or performing a certain task."[4] While there are certainly commonalities to our cognitive and psychosocial motives, we are each impelled by our unique history and environment to pursue different paths, explore different experiences, and chase different dreams. Our motivations, in other words, are responsible for directing our actions towards whatever we deem most worthy of our limited energy, time, and resources.

What, then, determines our motivations? More than any other element of our psychology, motivations are shaped by the values we hold. What we choose, or are taught, to assign value to informs our personal set of motives, which in turn directs our behaviors. Both our values and our motivations, however, are often not fully conscious; the majority of the time we don't stop to think about what motivates us to behave in certain ways, let alone what underpins those motivations. Because behaviors are much easier to observe than motivations or values, Nevid explains we can often extrapolate why we act the way we do from the behaviors we observe. We never actually observe a motive, Nevid states, "rather, we infer that one exists based on the behavior we observe."[5] In order to determine our motivations and values, then, we need to work backwards: observing behavioral patterns in order to uncover both the impulse driving the behavior and the value that shapes the impulse.

The role values play in our lives is perhaps one of the most important and ignored conversations in modern history. What we assign value to not only determines our motivations and behaviors, but also shapes our thoughts and beliefs, determines how we interact with others, and what we pursue and devote our lives to. Individually, our values shape who we become; collectively, our values move our world, for better or worse, in one direction or another. If we collectively prioritize and value equality, for example, we will make strides toward equal pay for all, equal rights, and equal treatment, regardless of gender, ethnicity, sexual orientation, or any other perceived differences. If we decide we value individualism, on the other hand, we will put our own needs first and make decisions in line with what is best for us individually rather than as a society. This might mean we vote to defund programs that would help others, such as affordable healthcare, homelessness initiatives, or affordable education, or against tax breaks for those who need it most.

An awareness of our values is paramount to creating both systems and standards that affect and order our actions. When we are aware of our values individually, we develop a personal set of ethics or moral standards that direct our behavior. Values that are developed at an organizational or societal level allow us to create ethical frameworks that help direct and orient social behavior more broadly.[6] In the event that we are not clear on our collective values—as I would argue is the case now—it is impossible to determine what a set of ethics should entail.

While many have called for ethical standards to be developed around technology, we have failed to discuss what values should underpin these guidelines. In the absence of such a dialogue, the values that have been embraced in the tech industry have been born in the vacuum of Silicon Valley and are not necessarily aligned with collective social values. The behavioral patterns of Silicon Valley illustrate a variety of motives that are at once intrinsically and extrinsically motivated; transparent and hidden; conscious and unconscious. Moreover, there is a profound tension between the original intrinsic and more compassionate motivations of the tech industry, and the more extrinsic and financial motivations that have taken hold in recent years. Distilling the primary motivations and values of the industry allows us to appreciate the most basic and problematic discrepancy in Silicon Valley: the tension of socially liberal values and technocapitalist incentives.

Same, but Different

The economic philosophy of capitalism as envisioned by Adam Smith, the father of modern capitalism, highlighted not only the need for free trade, private ownership, and competition, but also the necessity of ethics and empathy.[7] The version of capitalism we endure today has very little to do with Smith's original vision and everything to do with a relentless devotion to profits and shareholders. As John Mackey and Rajendra Sisodia argue in their book *Conscious Capitalism*, the modern capitalist paradigm is a perverse and skewed version of capitalism that has gone "off the rails" in pursuit of short-term gains.[8] Mackey and Sisodia suggest that capitalism as it stands requires "both a new narrative and a new ethical foundation,"[9] reenergized by the original intentions of an economic system that aims to lift everyone up, rather than just an elite few. Throughout this book, I refer to this second, "off the rails" type of capitalism as hypercapitalism.

So pervasive and profound are the intricacies and effects of technology and hypercapitalism, that the resultant system has assumed its own classification: technocapitalism. Luis Suarez-Villa, author of *Globalization and Technocapitalism: The Political Economy of Corporate Power and Technological Domination* and Professor Emeritus at the University of California, Irvine, defines technocapitalism as "an evolution of market capitalism that is rooted in technological invention and innovation. It can be considered an emerging era, now in its early stage, which is supported by such intangibles as creativity and new knowledge."[10] Like hypercapitalism, "technocapitalism is driven, first and foremost, by commercial objectives,"[11] which are focused on accumulating "capital by concocting means to seize it in ever faster and larger quantities."[12] That is to say, tech, like other for-profit industries, is all about the Benjamins.

Anyone who has studied Marx will appreciate the fluidity of capitalism that Suarez-Villa describes, and its unique ability to evolve by readjusting to fill previously unexplored crannies of potential profit. As we have moved more and more elements of our world online, hypercapitalism has followed, determined to commodify whatever it can in the new digital age, including our information, relationships, and attention. Ben Tarnoff describes Silicon Valley as the place "where American capitalism has gone to renew itself and find new forms of value creation and new methods of capital stimulation" which are predicated on "finding new ways to monetize our everyday lives."[13] Tarnoff's estimation is similar to Suarez-Villa's. And to journalist Kevin Kelly's.[14] And to economist Paul Mason's.[15] And to historian Yuval Harari's.[16] The ways in which technocapitalism monetizes our personal lives, information, and data on a global scale raises a

number of questions, particularly when the world's largest tech corporations are not transparent about their motives, do not act in accordance
with their stated values, and continue to conceal their business practices
and negligent actions.

In this new iteration of hypercapitalism, the most significant differences are a deprioritization of tangible products and a focus on networks, information, and data. In the information economy, Suarez-Villa
explains, the "most valuable resource of the technocapitalist era is
intangible and therefore inherently social."[17] Every day, we are all collectively participants in the great experiment of technological progress,
contributing our knowledge, ideas, creativity, and social interactions to
the next great frontier of money-making. Our connections, attention,
and habits are translated, in the form of vast amounts of data, which are
then used either to sell us things, or target and influence us with particular ideas. In place of compensation for our information and the
degradation of our privacy, users of "free" platforms, like Facebook,
Google, and Twitter, receive zero compensation. Instead, profits go
directly to the companies that collect and lease our data to any number
of third parties willing to pay for it. The result is two-fold. First, an
extraordinary level of power has been conferred to those driving technocapitalism: tech executives, VCs, and other stockholders. Second, an
uncomfortable and unhealthy dynamic has arisen between society and
technology corporations, filled with both contradictions and what
Suarez-Villa calls concerning "pathologies," including unprecedented
levels of intrusion, industrial disruption, job displacement, and economic insecurity.[18]

The fact that Silicon Valley is driven by capitalist imperatives might
not be surprising, but the consequences of prioritizing profit above all
else is a dynamic that problematizes and undermines the industry's original objectives. The tension between greed and goodness in Silicon Valley
has changed the landscape and ambitions of the industry, which now
finds itself obligated to pursue new motivations, such as market share and
revenue, which have affected its behaviors and the way in which its products and services are designed and developed. The tech industry's trans-
gression is not its for-profit and corporate priorities, but a gross
misrepresentation of its motives.

Mo Money, Mo Problems

Silicon Valley has spent years and billions of dollars persuading the public to worship an industry that claims to have its best interests at heart. The myths and the messaging of the tech industry communicate that its companies are motivated by the desire to build communities, spread information, and improve the lives and happiness of their customers. As corporations are beholden to fiscal targets, shareholders, and growth, however, more often than not, lofty social ideals have taken a backseat to the financial motivations that drive the industry. This is not to say that all tech companies put their financial incentives above the public good, merely that, in the majority of cases, companies are encouraged to do so by a financial system that values monetary gains over social benefit and ethical corporate behavior. As a result, over the last decade, the space between the stated motivations and actual motivations of many large tech companies have diverged, resulting in the sense that Silicon Valley is in the business of peddling platitudes and lining its pockets rather than denting the universe and making the world a better place.

Losing sight of our original motivations comes at a profound cost. No matter who we are, a misalignment between our stated values and what actually drives our behavior will result in a diminished sense of authenticity. At an individual level, inauthenticity can be psychological jarring and emotionally uncomfortable; we may feel guilty or ashamed if we know our actions and motives are incongruous, particularly if we cause harm to others. If others uncover that we're full of crap, the reverberations of our actions are wider; we may damage a relationship or lose a friend. If we are public-facing, however—or worse, a company; or worse still, an industry—inauthenticity can have a far more pervasive effect, particularly when it comes to maintaining public trust. As Scott Galloway explains,

> [Silicon Valley's] public-relations efforts paid off handsomely but also set the companies up for a major fall. It's an enormous letdown to discover that the guy who seems like the perfect gentleman is in fact addicted to opioids and a jerk to his mother. It's even worse to learn that he only hung out with you because of your money (clicks).[19]

Having spent the last two years watching scandals and PR disasters pave the road to public meltdowns, Congressional hearings, and apology tours, Silicon Valley's customers are finally getting a more accurate, but far less flattering picture of the tech industry and the motivations that drive it.

While we have collectively operated under the impression that Silicon Valley was in some way an exception to the corporate system in which it operates, the tech industry is driven by the same market forces as any other for-profit industry. Regardless of how they portray themselves, Galloway explains, Google, Facebook, Apple, and Amazon are, from a market perspective, "doing what they're supposed to be doing" as for-profit companies.[20]

> [T]hey're no less or better people than any other organization… As a matter of fact, I would argue that there's a lot of very civic-minded, decent leadership. But this is the issue: when you control 90 percent points of share in a market… and you're primarily compensated and trying… to increase that market share, you can't help but leverage all the power at your disposal. And that is the basis for regulation, and it's the basis for the truism throughout history that power corrupts. They're not bad people; we've just let them get out of control.[21]

Google is not evil. Neither is Facebook, or Twitter, or Uber, or even Theranos. Thinking in terms of good and evil is not only unproductive, it misses the point. What Facebook and friends suffer from is not demonic depravity, but a lack of transparency and awareness about their values and motivations. Add to this an economic system that increasingly values profits over more socially-minded objectives, and it's no wonder the behaviors and decisions of many large tech companies continue to prove so toxic.

The problem with prioritizing profits over people is hopefully glaringly and obviously wrong. Placing greater importance on making money than on taking care of people's needs results in a society with deeply unhealthy values, in which people come second to financial objectives. A society built on such values loses a great deal of its capacity for humanity. Yuval Harari has argued that as this mentality takes hold in Western society and "money brings down the dams of community, religion and state, the world is in danger of becoming one big and rather heartless marketplace."[22]

> Modernity turned the world upside down. It convinced human collectives that equilibrium is far more frightening chaos, and that because avarice fuels growth, it is a force for good. Modernity accordingly inspired people to want more, and dismantled the age-old disciplines that curbed greed. The resulting anxieties were assuaged to a large extent by free-market capitalism [which tells us not to worry and that everything] will be okay. 'Provided the economy grows, the invisible hand of the market will take care of everything else.' Capitalism has thus sanctified a voracious and chaotic system that grows by leaps and bounds, without anyone understanding what is happening and whither we are rushing.[23]

Many prominent economic and political figures have called for a reimagining of the current hypercapitalist system, such that it is more aligned with Mackey and Sisodia's conception of conscious capitalism. The problem with taking profit as a value in and of itself, without attendant moral and social values, is at the heart of current debates about the future of capitalism. Harari goes on to say:

> Capitalism began as a theory about how the economy functions. It was both descriptive and prescriptive—it offered an account of how money worked and promoted the idea that reinvesting profits in production leads to fast economic growth. But capitalism gradually became far more than just an economic doctrine. It now encompasses an ethic—a set of teachings about how people should behave, educate their children and even think. Its principal tenant is that economic growth is the supreme good, or at least a proxy for the supreme good, because Justice, freedom and even happiness all depend on economic growth. Ask a capitalist how to bring justice and political freedom to a place like Zimbabwe or Afghanistan, and you are likely to get a lecture on how economic affluence and a thriving middle-class are essential for stable democratic institutions, and about the need therefore to inculcate Afghan tribesmen in the values of free enterprise, thrift and self-reliance.[24]

As profit, growth, and hypercapitalism have themselves become values, they have forged a new trajectory driven by financial priorities, which have begun to undermine the foundations of modern society. The result is a world that is increasingly dehumanized, where individualism is revered above the collective good, and the chaos and whims of the market are valorized.

In an interview with Sandy Parakilas, a former Facebook employee who uncovered the extent of the data breach that led to the Cambridge Analytica revelations, Lesley Stahl questioned the motivations that led to the company's most infamous scandal.

> *Lesley Stahl*: Did you bring this to the attention of the higher-ups, the executives?
>
> *Sandy Parakilas*: Yeah, a number of folks, including several executives.
>
> *Lesley Stahl*: So were the executives' hair on fire? Did they say, "Oh my God, we have to fix this. We have to do something?"
>
> *Sandy Parakilas*: I didn't really see any traction in terms of making changes to protect people. They didn't prioritize it, I think, is how I would phrase it.
>
> *Lesley Stahl*: So would you say that they didn't prioritize privacy?
>
> *Sandy Parakilas*: Yes. I would say that they prioritize the growth of users, the growth of the data they can collect and their ability to monetize that through advertising. That's what they prioritized because those were the metrics and are the metrics that the stock market cares about.[25]

Parakilas's account illustrates the transition of capitalism as an economic theory to a cultural value. The decision at Facebook to prioritize growth, data collection, advertising, and profits over its customers reframes capitalism; it is no longer the system in which the company operates, but the primary value that informs its motivations and, in turn, its behaviors. In 2016, a day after a Chicago man's death was live streamed on Facebook, one of Zuckerberg's longest-serving deputies, Andrew Bosworth, circulated an internal memo defending what reporters Ryan Mac, Charlie Warzel, and Alex Kantrowitz have described as Facebook's "relentless quest for growth."[26]

Andrew Bosworth
June 18, 2016

The Ugly

We talk about the good and the bad of our work often. I want to talk about
the ugly.
We connect people.
That can be good if they make it positive. Maybe someone finds love.
Maybe it even saves the life of someone on the brink of suicide.
So we connect more people.
That can be bad if they make it negative. Maybe it costs a life by expos-
ing someone to bullies. Maybe someone dies in a terrorist attack coordi-
nated on our tools.
And still we connect people.
The ugly truth is that we believe in connecting people so deeply that
anything that allows us to connect more people more often is *de facto*
good. It is perhaps the only area where the metrics do tell the true story as
far as we are concerned.
That isn't something we are doing for ourselves. Or for our stock price
(ha!). It is literally just what we do. We connect people. Period.
That's why all the work we do in growth is justified. All the questionable
contact importing practices. All the subtle language that helps people stay
searchable by friends. All of the work we do to bring more communication
in. The work we will likely have to do in China some day. All of it.
The natural state of the world is not connected. It is not unified. It is
fragmented by borders, languages, and increasingly by different products.
The best products don't win. The ones everyone use win.
I know a lot of people don't want to hear this. Most of us have the luxury
of working in the warm glow of building products consumers love. But
make no mistake, growth tactics are how we got here.

In a 2019 op-ed for the New York Times, Facebook co-founder Chris
Hughes expressed his concern that Facebook's focus on growth was
undermining its users' safety, information security, and social civility.[27]
Hughes explained that while the company's priorities rested with
Zuckerberg, the focus on growth at any cost had been enabled by an
executive team unwilling to question its CEO's decisions. Facebook is
one example of a Silicon Valley tech company whose lapse in its original

motivations and values left the door open for a new set of values, driven by the incentives of the economy in which they so successfully operate.

Taking capitalism and profits as its primary values is at the heart of both Silicon Valley's most significant problems and its inability to rectify them. We have allowed the tech industry, through a lack of regulation and the proliferation of unhealthy behavioral norms, to become the bastion of an economic order that has abandoned morality in favor of dividends for an elite few. As Galloway observes, "[w]e no longer worship at the altar of character, of kindness, but of innovation and people who create shareholder value,"[28] a social dynamic that has both cultural and political implications. The question of collective values—of what we worship and why—says a great deal not only about our current economic and social crises, but also about where we're headed as a species. As tech behemoths like Facebook, Twitter, and Google lose their moral compass, rather than use this as an occasion to punish, humiliate, or reprimand, we might instead assess the culture that has allowed these values to proliferate and seize the opportunity to reinvent the world as we would like it to be. Part of that process entails pausing to examine not only the behaviors we find problematic, but also the motivations that drive them.

Control

The difficulty of remaining true to our original objectives in the face of success is hugely difficult. The corrupting influence of power is a well-worn truth, captured by British historian Lord Acton's famous statement that "power tends to corrupt, and absolute power corrupts absolutely." The majority of us set out to have a positive effect on the world, act in good faith, and generally have honorable intentions—our intentions, however, are tested once we find ourselves in positions of power. What happens to us psychologically when we accumulate power is fascinating. Over the past two decades, studies have shown how power rewires our brains in a way that Dacher Keltner, a professor of psychology at University of California, Berkeley, explains is comparable to a traumatic brain injury. Research by Keltner and others have found evidence of an inverse relationship between elevated social power and the capacity for empathy and compassion.[29,30] These studies suggest that the degree of power people experience changes how their brains respond to others, most notably in the regions of the brain associated with mirror neurons, which are highly correlated with empathy and compassion.[31] Keltner explains that as our sense of power increases, activity in regions of the orbito-frontal lobe decreases, leading those in positions of power to "stop attending carefully to what other people think,"[32] become "more impulsive, less risk-aware, and, crucially, less adept at seeing things from other people's point of view."[33]

Silicon Valley has experienced tremendous success over the past two decades, accompanied by tremendous power, which has had a multitude of effects on its character as an industry. The impulsivity, risk-seeking behavior, and diminished capacity for empathy and compassion in the industry follow the trajectory that Keltner describes. While those in positions of power in major tech corporations are not bad people, many represent a subset of tech executives whose motivations and values have veered profoundly off-track, from what we can assume were originally prosocial intentions. As the custodians of the world's most powerful platforms, which have the capacity to do tremendous harm or tremendous good, tech giants have not proved themselves to be responsible stewards of the public good. They have lost touch with the original ideals of their organizations—which remain awkwardly embedded in company slogans—on their rise to power. Among psychologists and cultural anthropologists, this dynamic is often referred to as the paradox of power. According to Dacher Kelter, author of *The Power Paradox: How We Gain and Lose Influence*, the "skills most important to obtaining power and leading effectively are the very skills that deteriorate once we have power."[34] Keltner points to multiple studies which demonstrate that "once people assume positions of power, they're likely to act more selfishly, impulsively, and aggressively, and they have a harder time seeing the world from other people's points of view."[35] The shift from the original values that gave birth to the internet—sharing, freedom, open-source platforms, connection, knowledge—to its more recent and less socially responsible motivations—profit, shareholder value, market dominance—represent what we might expect from any person or group in a position of unchecked power.

This shift illustrates how the myths and stories of benevolence that pervade the industry have become tarnished, and in some cases, completely dismantled. "Change the world" and "dent the universe" are now idiomatic relics of the original intentions of Silicon Valley that have become lost along the way to different, more corporate objectives. The industry now sits amidst a paradox of confused self-contradiction, clinging to its disruptor mentality and hippie origins, seemingly unaware that it has become the powerhouse of big business it once sought to disrupt. Holmes Wilson, co-founder of Fight for the Future, a nonprofit aimed at expanding the internet's capacity for good, explains that as Silicon Valley "companies grow past a certain threshold, they become less antagonistic to existing power and more an extension to that power."[36] "What once was a place where 'change the world' was proclaimed in earnest," journalist Nick Statt explains, "is now looking much more like a fervent breeding ground for egoism run amok and the corrupting nature of power, wealth, and success."[37] Ryan Holiday, author of *The Obstacle is the Way* and *Ego is the Enemy*, writes that the values that have proliferated in Silicon Valley perfectly illustrate the effects of unchecked success and power:

> It's easy to be good when the stakes (and the valuations) are low. We can count on it as an immutable law of history: in any space where fame and fortune and power are up for grabs, Machiavelli eventually makes his appearance. Even if you started as the little guy or you were certified as a B Corp or put 'Don't Be Evil' in your public filing documents.[38]

The dichotomy Wilson, Statt, and Holiday describe is palpable. And uncomfortable. The transposition of values that has occurred in tech, in which the industry's prosocial hippie roots have been replaced by pro-market libertarian principles, has mirrored its accrual of power and success and its loss of public trust. It has also reflected its pursuit to preserve its status and influence, at any cost.

Tech Goes to Washington

We can expect those in power to fight to maintain their position and protect their interests, whether those are focused on wealth, influence, or social control. In the case of the tech industry, such efforts can be seen in a number of endeavors, including the influx of money into the U.S. lobbying industry.[39] Technology journalist Olivia Solon has reported that "the five largest tech companies—desperate to avoid the kind of antitrust regulation that disrupted IBM and Microsoft's dominance—are flooding Washington with lobbyists,"[40] with the aim of limiting competition, reducing corporate taxes, avoiding regulation, and allowing for the collection of more data. According to federal records, the tech industry now outspends Wall Street in Washington by a margin of two to one. In 2018, Google alone spent just under $22 million on lobbying—more than any tech company (Facebook, Amazon, Microsoft, and Apple spent $12.6 million, $14.4 million, $9.6 million, and $6.6 million, respectively).[41] Tech has not only made its financial presence known in Washington, but its physical presence as well. In 2013, Alphabet, Google's parent company, "signed a lease on a 55,000-square-foot office, roughly the same size as the White House, less than a mile away from the Capitol Building."[42]

A healthy portion of lobbying budgets from Google, Facebook, and their tech counterparts have been used to oppose consumer privacy initiatives and online advertising regulations. Alvaro Bedoya, the executive director of the Center on Privacy & Technology at Georgetown University, has expressed concern about the implications of the tech industry's escalating lobbying budgets, which are largely deployed to hoard "the data they are collecting on Americans," making it difficult "to pass new and meaningful consumer protection laws."[43] During Mark Zuckerberg's Congressional hearing in April 2018, Bedoya observed the disconnect between Facebook's rhetoric that promised to protect its customers and its active opposition of consumer privacy legislation.

> I'm sitting here watching Mark Zuckerberg say he's sorry and that Facebook will do better on privacy, yet literally as he testifies lobbyists paid by Facebook in Illinois and California are working to stop or gut privacy laws.… If Facebook wants to do better on privacy, it needs to put its money where its mouth is, it needs to stop paying lobbyists to gut critical privacy initiatives in these states.[44]

Thus far, the only new piece of U.S. legislation that has been introduced is the Honest Ads Act (HAA). Sandy Parakilas, a former Facebook platform operations manager, notes that despite being a step in the right direction, the HAA only "addresses election-specific foreign advertising, a small part of the much larger set of problems around election interference."[45] One would assume even tech companies would support such legislation, meant to protect future elections from the influence of foreign agents. As Parakilas points out, however, the Information Technology Industry Council, a lobbying group that represents companies such as Facebook, Google, and Twitter, was originally opposed to the bill. It was only after they came under pressure from lawmakers that Facebook and Twitter executives stated during their congressional hearings that they would support the HAA.[46]

In addition to exercising their power through lobbying and corporate donations, employees at top Silicon Valley companies have also begun to leave tech to work in government, and vice versa, which Olivia Solon and Sabrina Siddiqui describe as the "well-oiled revolving door of Silicon Valley executives to and from senior government positions."[47] Solon and Siddiqui report that "Google alone employs 183 people who previously worked in the federal government under Barack Obama, while 58 Googlers have taken jobs in Washington, according to the Campaign for Accountability."[48] Solon and Siddiqui explain that the industry's influence in American politics began during the Obama administration, as tech giants began to rise in power and influence.

> [Google] executives enjoyed lavish parties and regular contact with the highest-ranking people in the executive branch. Personnel seemingly moved from one entity to the other and back on a regular basis. This kind of integration with one company and the executive branch is extraordinary.... Throughout the Obama administration "googlers" attended White House meetings more than once a week. That includes at least 21 intimate conferences with Obama. In total, there were some 427 White House meetings, so it's not surprising the president eventually endorsed the Federal Communications Commission's new plan to open up the set-top box market, something industry opponents of the plan refer to as the "Google Proposal."[49]

In addition to the tech-government employee exchange phenomenon, Silicon Valley's influence can also be found within U.S. defense bodies, such as the Pentagon's Defense Innovation Board, which counts Alphabet board member and former Google executive chairman, Eric Schmidt, as well as Google's vice president, Milo Medin, as board members.[50]

Silicon Valley also flexes its influence in less politically obvious ways. Beyond its lobbying spending, Solon and Siddiqui outline how the industry "exerts influence on policymakers and citizens through opaque 'soft power' techniques," including funding particular thinktanks, research bodies, and trade associations whose findings or influence furthers the industry's objectives.[51] The ability to direct policy and public opinion through the manipulation or coercion of information is a hugely problematic dynamic that is not unique to Silicon Valley. As Solon and Siddiqui point out, industries such as pharma, banks, and oil have been doing the same for decades. The purchase of influence in U.S. politics is a problem bigger than tech and beyond the scope of this book, but it is a problem all the same, and one in which Silicon Valley is actively involving itself. Whether you agree with Silicon Valley's politics or not—which fall predominantly on the socially liberal, economically libertarian side of the political spectrum—the degree of intimacy and influence between tech and Washington should give us all pause to consider the implications of having companies like Facebook, Amazon, Google, Apple, and Microsoft embedded in the political sphere.

In addition to funding research and thinktanks, the industry also controls the flow and visibility of media globally. Online news and journalism are the primary means by which we access information (for better or worse), the sheer power of which cannot be overstated. Tech executives have also become increasingly involved in the procurement of legacy media publications. Some examples include Salesforce CEO Marc Benioff's purchase of Time magazine; Amazon CEO Jeff Bezos's purchase of The Washington Post; a majority purchase of the Atlantic by Steve Jobs's widow, Laurene Powell Jobs; biotech billionaire Patrick Soon-Shiong's purchase of the Los Angeles Times; and former Facebook exec Chris Hughes's purchase, and subsequent sale, of The New Republic.[52] Though tech-cum-media owners have assured us they do not influence the editorial direction of their publications, this claim must be continually monitored.

In addition to controlling the flow of information online and acquiring traditional media outlets, Silicon Valley execs and companies also have the ability to silence them. Peter Thiel famously shut down Gawker after the news outlet exposed his sexual orientation, funding lawsuits against the company until it was eventually forced to file for bankruptcy. A more disturbing example is the closure of the New America Foundation, a thinktank that studied the growing power of tech giants. In June 2017, while working as a researcher for Open Markets, part of the New America Foundation, scholar Barry Lynn published a press release that supported the EU's historical $2.7 billion fine against Google for anti-trust practices.[53] Although Lynn had served as a researcher on the Open Markets team for 15 years without incident, he was fired within days of publishing the press release.

> [Lynn] believes it's because Google, one of the thinktank's biggest funders, was unhappy with the direction of his research, which was increasingly calling for tech giants including Google, Facebook and Amazon to be regulated as monopolies. Leaked emails suggest the foundation was concerned that Lynn's criticism could jeopardise future funding. In one of them, the organisation's president, Anne-Marie Slaughter, wrote: "We are in the process of trying to expand our relationship with Google on some absolutely key points ... just think about how you are imperiling funding for others." Slaughter denies that Lynn was fired for his criticism of Google. It's a difficult story to swallow, given that Google's parent company, Alphabet, along with its executive chairman Eric Schmidt, have donated $21m to New America since 1999.[54]

The rest of the Open Markets team, comprised of approximately 10 people, were fired along with Lynn, and the group now operates a stand-alone non-profit called Citizens Against Monopoly.

The Happiness Fallacy

As Silicon Valley grows more financially successful, powerful, and influential, its motivations become increasingly synonymous with those of corporate America, whose success rests on its ability to equate economic prosperity with happiness.[55] (Twenty years ago, the founders of Google would not have encouraged you to trust the invisible hand of the market or advertisers; today, however, they're big fans of both.) Hiding behind the popular marketing myths of "making the world a better place" and "putting a dent in the universe," the tech industry has quietly helped advance a very different narrative: the myth of consumerism. Yuval Harari describes the myth of consumerism as the cultural imperative which "tells us that in order to be happy we must consume as many products and services as possible."[56]

> [W]e are inspired to constantly increase our incomes and our standards of living. Even if you are quite satisfied with your current conditions, you should strive for more. Yesterday's luxuries become today's necessities. If once you could live well in a three-bedroom apartment with one car and a single desktop computer, today you need a five-bedroom house with two cars and a host of iPods, tablets and smart phones. It wasn't very hard to convince individuals to want more. Greed comes easily to humans.[57]

Harari explains that

> [T]he view of happiness we have now could not have come about if we didn't have the kind of economic order we have.... the idea of happiness we now have... may have once been a genuinely noble goal, but over time, these values have been co-opted and transformed and used to normalize a deeply unjust and undesirable situation. There really is no way to accurately compare happiness today with happiness 50 or 100 years ago, but this mania for individual satisfaction and this idea that buying and collecting more stuff will make us happy has produced a spectacularly unequal world, and ... left people less fulfilled and more empty inside.[58]

The result of the shift Harari describes has been a form of hypercapitalism that encourages consumption at the expense of collective wellbeing, while maintaining that money and material possessions are synonymous with happiness. This narrative is informed not only by bad values, but also by outright deception. The idea that materialism (more stuff) and lots of money will make us happy has been scientifically disproven.[59] What science tells us promotes true human happiness are strong intimate relationships,[60] self-actualization,[61,62] community,[63] service to others,[64] and living a life that feels authentic.[65]

Professor Carl Cederström, author of *The Happiness Fantasy*, explains that the ideas that underpin the modern story of consumerism were born in the 1970s and 80s, as corporate America learned to co-opt the popular ideals of "liberation, freedom, and authenticity."[66] The marketing tactics that encouraged consumption were predicated on the idea that you needed more because you weren't enough. This helped advance what Cederström describes as "a very individualistic notion of happiness,"[67] alongside a consumer-oriented mindset. The result, according to Cederström, has been a Western culture defined by extreme individualism, competitiveness, and isolation. In such a culture, "people feel constantly anxious, alienated, and where bonds between people are being broken down, and any sense of solidarity is being crushed."[68] As Sean Illing observes in his interview with Cederström,

> Marx got a lot of things wrong, but one of the things he got right was his idea that cultural values are a reflection of the prevailing economic order, and not the other way around.... our idea of happiness has been transformed to make us better consumers and producers.[69]

Cederström and Illing both argue that the hyper-individualist and consumptive priorities of modern hypercapitalist societies have led to a "mania for individual satisfaction," which have resulted in deeply unequal societies and more and more unfulfilled and emotionally bereft consumers.

More stuff, of course, does not make us happy. But it does make the new giants of the economy—Apple, Amazon, Google, Microsoft, and Facebook, currently the top-five valued companies in the world—the wealthiest corporations to ever walk the earth.[70] These corporations, along with hundreds of other, less valuable but equally influential companies, have spent the past decade transitioning the myth of consumerism into a digital context. In the digital era, we are meant to believe that the latest phones, apps, social networks, and other technologies that entertain us or provide more convenience will make us happy. And so we have been encouraged to spend as much of our time and put as much of our lives online as possible, in the name of "bringing us closer together," "broadcasting ourselves," "organizing the world's information," and other patently false myths that have co-opted promises of individual happiness. Scott Galloway, a professor of brand strategy at NYU, cites Apple's understanding of this dynamic, and its unparalleled ability to equate its products with status, sexiness, and exclusivity.

> Apple learned very early on that it could appeal to our need to be desirable—and in turn increase its profit margins—by placing print ads in *Vogue*, having supermodels at product launches, and building physical stores as glass temples to the brand. A Dell computer may be powerful and fast, but it doesn't indicate membership in the innovation class as a MacBook Air does. Likewise, the iPhone is something more than a phone, or even a smartphone. Consumers aren't paying $1,000 for an iPhone X because they're passionate about facial recognition. They're signaling they make a good living, appreciate the arts, and have disposable income. It's a sign to others: If you mate with me, your kids are more likely to survive than if you mate with someone carrying an Android phone. After all, iPhone users on average earn 40 percent more than Android users.[71]

In a 2017 TED talk, Galloway articulates how companies such as Amazon, Facebook, and Google manipulate our emotions in different ways, each with claims to satisfy our most basic human needs. Facebook, for example, feeds on our need for love and connection; Google provides an endless source of answers, which acts almost as an omniscient higher power; Amazon satiates our need to consume, nest, and to fill our homes with ever more stuff. We have been convinced, Galloway argues, through the magic of marketing and a profound manipulation of human psychology, to believe the myths and ignore the true motivations of these companies, which center on financial aims.

The ubiquity and success of hypercapitalism and technocapitalism rests on their ability to convince us that our happiness rests on stuff, money, and the pursuit of individual, rather than collective, satisfaction. This narrative will continue to dominate our society as long as we believe that it is true. As soon as we collectively choose a different narrative, based on true indicators of human happiness and better values, we will begin to see a better world.

Nearly a century ago György Lukács argued that capitalism was still in business because people didn't know their real needs: hence the difference between what he called actual and ascribed consciousness. The sense one gets from reading Harvey is that the gap in consciousness may be narrowing, if only through a growing sense of revulsion at how our societies and economies are organised.[72]

The control and power held by hypercapitalist corporations, such as those that dominate the tech industry, are only powerful as long as we collectively believe in what they're selling. The moment we recognize the core fallacy of hypercapitalism and the values that underpin it, we can begin to re-evaluate the motivations and reprioritize the actions of these corporations such that they align with what actually contributes to our happiness and wellbeing. Thankfully, we appear to be collectively awakening from the stupor of hypercapitalism: a study by Harvard University's Institute of Politics found that 51% of 18- to 29-year-olds in the U.S. no longer support the economic system of capitalism as practiced in its current form.[73]

*   *   *

As Silicon Valley companies and executives refuse to acknowledge the power they have amassed and the responsibility it entails, the effects of their refusal become more profound and problematic. Without an awareness of their motivation, unchecked values like impulsivity, short-term thinking, convenience, profits, and power will proliferate without oversight or the smallest hint of accountability. The original, more altruistic intentions of the tech industry have been lost, but not replaced by anything morally substantial or capable of orienting the industry's values in a socially conscious direction. Instead, the industry has adopted a corporate ethos aligned with hypercapitalistic priorities, leaving a trail of social wreckage in its wake.

The gradual but comprehensive deterioration of Silicon Valley's original motivations has informed the majority of its behavioral problems. What began as an industry genuinely poised to change the world for the better has instead helped usher in an age of individualism, consumption, and inaccurate ideas about human happiness. It has also set into motion a range of human and social impacts unlike anything we have ever known, and which now must be mitigated against as a matter of urgency.

Notes

1. Nevid, J. S. (2013). *Psychology: Concepts and Applications* (p. 288). Belmont, CA: Wadsworth Cengage Learning.
2. There are many schools of thought that attempt to explain how and why we are motivated to behave in certain ways. Instinct theory argues that human behaviors are the result of innate and fixed urges, such as fear, curiosity, and love. Drive theory proposes that our actions aim to keep us in a state of homeostasis; when we lack something, such as food, safety, or sex, to which we are biologically predisposed, our drives will impel us to act in ways such that our needs are met.
3. Nevid, J. S. (2013). *Psychology: Concepts and Applications* (pp. 288–294). Belmont, CA: Wadsworth Cengage Learning.
4. Ibid., p. 294.
5. Ibid., p. 288.
6. Some examples of successful ethical frameworks and bodies that have been created to reflect collective values include: The UN, an international organization charged with promoting international peace, security, and cooperation and ensuring human rights; the Hippocratic Oath, which requires physicians to uphold certain ethical medical practices; the World Health Organization's Global Health Ethics Unit, which examines and advises on ethical issues related to health research, such as bioethics, public health surveillance, and equitable access to health services; and countless religious frameworks, such as the Ten Commandments.
7. Mackey, J., & Sisodia, R. (2014). *Conscious Capitalism* (pp. 16–17). Harvard Business Review Press.
8. Ibid., p. ix
9. Ibid., pp. 15–16.
10. Suarez-Villa, L. (n.d.). Introduction: What is Technocapitalism? Retrieved December 18, 2018, from *technocapitalism.com* website: http://www.technocapitalism.com/Introduction.htm

11. Suarez-Villa, L. (2012). *Technocapitalism: A Critical Perspective on Technological Innovation and Corporatism* (p. 10). Temple University Press.
12. Ibid., p. 19.
13. Tarnoff, B. (2017, September 5). *Interview with Ben Tarnoff* (K. Cook, Interviewer).
14. Kelly, K. (1997, January 9). New Rules for the New Economy. *Wired*. Retrieved from https://www.wired.com/1997/09/newrules/
15. Mason, P. (2016). *Postcapitalism: A Guide to Our Future* (p. 112). St Ives: Penguin.
16. Harari, Y. N. (2017). *Homo Deus: A Brief History of Tomorrow*. London: Vintage.
17. Suarez-Villa, L. (2012). *Technocapitalism: A Critical Perspective on Technological Innovation and Corporatism* (p. 11). Temple University Press.
18. Ibid., p. 16.
19. Galloway, S. (2018, February 8). The Case for Breaking Up Amazon, Apple, Facebook and Google. Retrieved August 31, 2018, from *Esquire* website: https://www.esquire.com/news-politics/a15895746/bust-big-tech-silicon-valley/
20. Galloway, S. (2017). *How Amazon, Apple, Facebook and Google Manipulate Our Emotions*. Retrieved from https://www.ted.com/talks/scott_galloway_how_amazon_apple_facebook_and_google_manipulate_our_emotions
21. Ibid.
22. Harari, Y. N. (2014). *Sapiens: A Brief History of Humankind* (p. 208). London: Vintage.
23. Ibid., p. 255.
24. Ibid., p. 351.
25. Stahl, L. (2018, April 22). Aleksandr Kogan: The Link between Cambridge Analytica and Facebook. Retrieved August 30, 2018, from https://www.cbsnews.com/news/aleksandr-kogan-the-link-between-cambridge-analytica-and-facebook/
26. Mac, R., Warzel, C., & Kantrowitz, A. (2018, March 29). Top Facebook Executive Defended Data Collection in 2016 Memo—And Warned that Facebook Could Get People Killed. *BuzzFeed News*. Retrieved from https://www.buzzfeednews.com/article/ryanmac/growth-at-any-cost-top-facebook-executive-defended-data

27. Hughes, C. (2019, May 14). It's Time to Break Up Facebook. *The New York Times*. Retrieved from https://www.nytimes.com/2019/05/09/opinion/sunday/chris-hughes-facebook-zuckerberg.html
28. Galloway, S. (2017). *How Amazon, Apple, Facebook and Google Manipulate Our Emotions*. Retrieved from https://www.ted.com/talks/scott_galloway_how_amazon_apple_facebook_and_google_manipulate_our_emotions
29. van Kleef, G. A., Oveis, C., van der Löwe, I., LuoKogan, A., Goetz, J., & Keltner, D. (2008). Power, Distress, and Compassion: Turning a Blind Eye to the Suffering of Others. *Psychological Science, 19*(12), 1315–1322. https://doi.org/10.1111/j.1467-9280.2008.02241.x
30. Obhi, S. S., Hogeveen, J., & Inzlicht, M. (2014). Power Changes How the Brain Responds to Others. *Journal of Experimental Psychology: General, 143*(2), 755–762. https://doi.org/10.1037/a0033477
31. Ibid.
32. *How Power Makes People Selfish*. (2015). Retrieved from https://www.youtube.com/watch?v=0vvl46PmCfE
33. Useem, J. (2017, June 18). Power Causes Brain Damage. *The Atlantic*. Retrieved from https://www.theatlantic.com/magazine/archive/2017/07/power-causes-brain-damage/528711/
34. Keltner, D. (2007, December 1). The Power Paradox. *Greater Good*. Retrieved from https://greatergood.berkeley.edu/article/item/power_paradox
35. Ibid.
36. Finley, K. (2017, September 22). Why Big Tech is Clashing with Internet Freedom Advocates. *Wired*. Retrieved from https://www.wired.com/story/why-big-tech-is-clashing-with-internet-freedom-advocates/
37. Statt, N. (2017, June 19). HBO's Silicon Valley is Now a Show about the Destructive Hubris of the Tech Industry. Retrieved August 19, 2018, from *The Verge* website: https://www.theverge.com/2017/6/19/15832878/hbo-silicon-valley-recap-season-4-episode-9-hooli-con
38. Holiday, R. (2018, March 15). It's Time to Get Real about Power in Silicon Valley. Retrieved August 28, 2018, from *Medium* website: https://medium.com/the-mission/its-time-to-get-real-about-power-in-silicon-valley-b59b4772138d
39. Solon, O., & Siddiqui, S. (2017, September 3). Forget Wall Street—Silicon Valley is the New Political Power in Washington. *The Guardian*. Retrieved from https://www.theguardian.com/technology/2017/sep/03/silicon-valley-politics-lobbying-washington

40. Solon, O. (2017, December 23). Tech's Terrible Year: How the World Turned on Silicon Valley in 2017. *The Observer.* Retrieved from https://www.theguardian.com/technology/2017/dec/22/tech-year-in-review-2017

41. Abramson, A. (2018, January 24). Google Spent Millions More Than Its Rivals Lobbying Politicians Last Year. *Time.* Retrieved from http://time.com/5116226/google-lobbying-2017/

42. Solon, O., & Siddiqui, S. (2017, September 3). Forget Wall Street— Silicon Valley is the New Political Power in Washington. *The Guardian.* Retrieved from https://www.theguardian.com/technology/2017/sep/03/silicon-valley-politics-lobbying-washington

43. Hamza, S. (2018, January 23). Google for the First Time Outspent Every Other Company to Influence Washington in 2017. *Washington Post.* Retrieved from https://www.washingtonpost.com/news/the-switch/wp/2018/01/23/google-outspent-every-other-company-on-federal-lobbying-in-2017/

44. Matsakis, L. (2018, April 12). As Zuckerberg Smiles to Congress, Facebook Fights State Privacy Laws. *Wired.* Retrieved from https://www.wired.com/story/despite-zuckerberg-pledge-facebook-fights-state-privacy-laws/

45. Parakilas, S. (2018, January 30). Facebook Wants to Fix Itself. Here's a Better Solution. *Wired.* Retrieved from https://www.wired.com/story/facebook-wants-to-fix-itself-heres-a-better-solution/

46. Ibid.

47. Solon, O., & Siddiqui, S. (2017, September 3). Forget Wall Street— Silicon Valley is the New Political Power in Washington. *The Guardian.* Retrieved from https://www.theguardian.com/technology/2017/sep/03/silicon-valley-politics-lobbying-washington

48. Ibid.

49. Baker, C., & Schwartz, D. (2016, December 19). *PAGA Complaint against Google.* Retrieved from https://www.scribd.com/document/334742749/2016-12-19-PAGA-Complaint-Against-Google

50. Shane, S., & Wakabayashi, D. (2018, July 30). 'The Business of War': Google Employees Protest Work for the Pentagon. *The New York Times.* Retrieved from https://www.nytimes.com/2018/04/04/technology/google-letter-ceo-pentagon-project.html

51. Solon, O., & Siddiqui, S. (2017, September 3). Forget Wall Street— Silicon Valley is the New Political Power in Washington. *The Guardian.* Retrieved from https://www.theguardian.com/technology/2017/sep/03/silicon-valley-politics-lobbying-washington

52. Oremus, W., & Glasser, A. (2018, September 21). What the Washington Post's Margaret Sullivan Makes of the Tech CEOs Taking over the Media—Including her Boss. Retrieved September 25, 2018, from *Slate Magazine* website: https://slate.com/technology/2018/09/what-margaret-sullivan-thinks-about-tech-ceos-buying-media-companies.html

53. Lynn, B. (2017, June 27). Open Markets Applauds the European Commission's Finding Against Google for Abuse of Dominance. Retrieved August 28, 2018, from *New America* website: https://www.newamerica.org/open-markets/press-releases/open-markets-applauds-european-commissions-finding-against-google-abuse-dominance/

54. Solon, O., & Siddiqui, S. (2017, September 3). Forget Wall Street—Silicon Valley is the New Political Power in Washington. *The Guardian*. Retrieved from https://www.theguardian.com/technology/2017/sep/03/silicon-valley-politics-lobbying-washington

55. Easterlin, R. A. (1973). Does Money Buy Happiness? *The Public Interest, 30*. Retrieved from https://search.proquest.com/openview/6ce2d5a919778d8fada2059d39b7ff89/1?pq-origsite=gscholar&cbl=1817076

56. Harari, Y. N. (2014). *Sapiens: A Brief History of Humankind* (p. 129). London: Vintage.

57. Harari, Y. N. (2017). *Homo Deus: A Brief History of Tomorrow* (p. 255). London: Vintage.

58. Cederström, C. (2018, September 4). *A History of Happiness Explains Why Capitalism Makes Us Feel Empty Inside* (S. Illing, Interviewer) [Vox]. Retrieved from https://www.vox.com/science-and-health/2018/9/4/17759590/happiness-fantasy-capitalism-culture-carl-cederstrom

59. Richins, M., & Fournier, S. (1991). Some Theoretical and Popular Notions Concerning Materialism. *Journal of Social Behavior and Personality, 6*, 403–414.

60. Lyubomirsky, S. (2014). *The Myths of Happiness: What Should Make You Happy, But Doesn't, What Shouldn't Make You Happy, But Does*. Penguin.

61. Galati, D., Sotgiu, I., & Iovino, V. (2006). *What Makes Us happy? A Study on the Subjective Representation of Happiness Components* (pp. 60–74). Milano: FrancoAngeli.

62. Cloninger, C. R. (2013). What Makes People Healthy, Happy, and Fulfilled in the Face of Current World Challenges? *Mens Sana Monographs, 11*(1), 16–24. https://doi.org/10.4103/0973-1229.109288

63. Davidson, W. B., & Cotter, P. R. (1991). The Relationship between Sense of Community and Subjective Well-being: A First Look. *Journal of Community Psychology, 19*(3), 246–253. https://doi.org/10.1002/1520-6629(199107)19:3<246::AID-JCOP2290190308>3.0.CO;2-L

64. Borgonovi, F. (2008). Doing Well by Doing Good. The Relationship between Formal Volunteering and Self-reported Health and Happiness. *Social Science & Medicine, 66*(11), 2321–2334. https://doi.org/10.1016/j.socscimed.2008.01.011

65. Mineo, L. (2017, April 11). Over Nearly 80 Years, Harvard Study has been Showing How to Live a Healthy and Happy Life. Retrieved October 23, 2018, from *Harvard Gazette* website: https://news.harvard.edu/gazette/story/2017/04/over-nearly-80-years-harvard-study-has-been-showing-how-to-live-a-healthy-and-happy-life/

66. Cederström, C. (2018, September 4). *A History of Happiness Explains Why Capitalism Makes Us Feel Empty Inside* (S. Illing, Interviewer) [Vox]. Retrieved from https://www.vox.com/science-and-health/2018/9/4/17759590/happiness-fantasy-capitalism-culture-carl-cederstrom

67. Ibid.

68. Ibid.

69. Ibid.

70. Statista. (2018). *The 100 Largest Companies in the World by Market Value in 2018 (in Billion U.S. Dollars)*. Retrieved from https://www.statista.com/statistics/263264/top-companies-in-the-world-by-market-value/

71. Galloway, S. (2018, February 8). The Case for Breaking Up Amazon, Apple, Facebook and Google. Retrieved August 31, 2018, from *Esquire* website: https://www.esquire.com/news-politics/a15895746/bust-big-tech-silicon-valley/

72. Jeffries, S. (2017, November 1). Marx, Capital and the Madness of Economic Reason Review—A Devastating Indictment of How We Live Today. *The Guardian.* Retrieved from https://www.theguardian.com/books/2017/nov/01/marx-capital-and-the-madness-of-economic-reason-review

73. Harvard Kennedy School Institute of Politics. (2016). *Harvard IOP Spring 2016 Poll.* Retrieved from https://iop.harvard.edu/sites/default/files/content/160425_Harvard%20IOP%20Spring%20Report_update.pdf

Part II

Impacts

6

Truth, Information & Democracy

What you are will show in what you do.
–Thomas Edison

The reverberations of Silicon Valley's ascendency can be felt in nearly every corner of our lives. Countless technologies allow us to seamlessly connect with our loved ones around the world, work remotely, access the world's information quickly and easily, and enjoy the immense scientific and medical advancements that technology affords us. In some cases, tech is also working to address what should be humanity's primary concern—making the world more sustainable and environmentally sound— though these companies are still in the minority.

Whether you're a fan of Isaac Newton, Eastern Mysticism, or the Hamilton soundtrack, you'll know that every action has an equal, opposite reaction; forces come in pairs, and rarely is something purely a force for good. Which is why it shouldn't surprise us that for all the benefits technology provides us, there are an equal number of drawbacks and challenges that arise when the world changes at the rate it has without attendant oversight or accountability. The scope of these side effects is

© The Author(s) 2020
K. Cook, *The Psychology of Silicon Valley*,
https://doi.org/10.1007/978-3-030-27364-4_6

vast and, in many cases, hugely complex. This section will illustrate some of the most pervasive problems and challenges that have resulted from technology and the ways in which Silicon Valley's values, behaviors, and psychology have contributed to them.

The products that emerge from Silicon Valley impact us both on a macro, social level, and in more individual and personal ways. This section will examine both, starting with an overview of the industry's more global effects, including democracy, misinformation, economic inequality, and job displacement, and then looking at more individual impacts, such as health and mental health, relationships, and cognition. While these phenomena are not the intended effects of the technology that brought them about, but rather side effects of other motivations, they are, nonetheless, socially destructive, urgent problems that require our immediate attention. Facebook and Twitter did not set out to break democracies and incite hatred; YouTube did not plan to drive extremism; Instagram didn't intend to increase anxiety and depression in young people. Nor did the tech industry as a whole plan to drive inequality and employment instability, demolish individual privacy, create a two-class job market, spread misinformation, upend human connection, or negatively affect our cognition. Each of these is a side effect of other aims and decisions made in the service of certain motivations. The following pages will detail each of these and explore how the psychology of the industry has contributed to the unintended but profound consequences we are now enduring as a result of the technology we have embraced, beginning with an exploration of the crisis of truth, information, and democracy, and the business model that underpins it all.

The Dark Arts

Before we attempt to understand the ways in which technology platforms have undermined social institutions and driven social harm, it's useful to grasp the method by which many of the companies complicit in these problems make the majority of their money. The business model is, in some ways, shockingly simple. In 2018, during Facebook's first congressional hearing, Senator Orrin Hatch asked Mark Zuckerberg how his company sustained a business model in which users didn't pay for the service. Zuckerberg succinctly and honestly replied, "Senator, we run ads." Indeed they do. Advertising accounted for 99 percent of Facebook's 2019 Q1 revenue. The exchange between Hatch and Zuckerberg was mocked for weeks and the hearing largely considered a failure all around; an unblinking Zuck was caricatured as an automaton and Congress as a bunch of out-of-touch fuddy-duddies. The implications of Facebook's business model were never fully fleshed out that day, thanks to everyone's love of the sound of their own voice. It was, however, the most important question and the most lucid answer of the entire hearing.

In 1998, Sergey Brin and Larry Page, then PhD students at Stanford, released a paper about their new project, Google. Google was a search engine prototype designed to organize academic search results. In the paper, the pair acknowledged the increasing commercialization of the internet, and warned against both the "black box" effect of algorithmic search engines and a business model where search could be commoditized and controlled by advertisers.

> Aside from tremendous growth, the Web has also become increasingly commercial over time. In 1993, 1.5% of Web servers were on .com domains. This number grew to over 60% in 1997. At the same time, search engines have migrated from the academic domain to the commercial. Up until now most search engine development has gone on at companies with little publication of technical details. This causes search engine technology to remain largely a black art and to be advertising oriented (see Appendix A in the full version). With Google, we have a strong goal to push more development and understanding into the academic realm.[1]

In October 2000, Google began selling advertising on its platform, embracing the very business model that, less than two years previously, Brin and Page had warned against. As Google's user base grew and the technology driving it advanced, the company invented and pushed targeted advertising, as described by former CEO and Executive Chairman Eric Schmidt:

free platforms such as Facebook, Google, and Twitter do not shout about, however, is why they hoard and protect your data so aggressively—not because selling it would be morally reprehensible, but rather, as New Shift Company explains, because it wouldn't be nearly as profitable. "Facebook does not sell your data. It protects your data like Gollum holding the ring. Selling your data would not be nearly as profitable as leasing access to you, via advertising—over and over again."[9]

What Facebook and Google realized long before the rest of us, and proceeded to build billion dollar businesses off the back of, is the supreme value of data in the information age. There is simply nothing that has lit a fire under capitalism more in the past century than the ability of tech giants to target consumers, using the very data their users agree to give away for free. As Eric Schmidt bragged, Google was the first to capitalize on this realization, which was soon emulated by Twitter and Facebook. Collectively, these companies perfected the art of personalized, targeted advertising.

> Facebook was a social network where legions of users voluntarily offered personally identifying information in exchange for the right to poke each other, like each other, and share their baby pictures with each other. Facebook's founders knew their future lay in connecting that trove of user data to a massive ad platform. In 2008, they hired Sheryl Sandberg, who ran Google's advertising operation, and within a few years, Facebook had built the foundation of what is now the most ruthlessly precise targeting engine on the planet.[10]

Given the now inextricable relationship between advertising and technology, it is perhaps unsurprising that the ethos of the former would bleed into that of the latter. Professor William Irwin, who teaches philosophy at King's College in Pennsylvania, explained to Time magazine reporter Coeli Carr that the advertising industry as a whole "has historically wrestled with questionable ethics and a lack of self-awareness,"[11] the cultural effects of which are now beginning to materialize.

The purpose of advertising, for those of us who didn't major in marketing or watch *Mad Men*, is to change behavior. Historically, marketing campaigns in non-digital spaces focused on changing our behavior in order to make us buy stuff: McDonalds wanted you to buy burgers, Estee Lauder wanted you to buy makeup, and the Marlboro Man wanted to get you hooked on cigarettes. Through the whole of the twentieth century, such advertising campaigns were largely unable to reach their target audience in very meaningful ways. Digital advertising, however, brought sellers closer to their consumers than ever before. Instead of marketing diapers to the general public and hoping expectant couples were on the receiving end of the campaign, diaper companies could now target potential parents based on their past purchases, age, browser history, or any number of demographic factors. In the last few years, a handful of brilliant but morally reprehensible assholes realized targeted advertising could also be used, and indeed was especially effective, at changing public opinion and manipulating emotions—particularly in the political sphere.

> Facebook's business lies in influencing people. That's what the service (sic) it sells to its customers—advertisers, including political advertisers. As such, Facebook has built a fine-tuned algorithmic engine that does just that. This engine isn't merely capable of influencing your view of a brand or your next smart-speaker purchase. It can influence your mood, tuning the content it feeds you in order to make you angry or happy, at will. It may even be able to swing elections.[12]

As its audience was lulled into watching cat videos, posting baby photos, and chatting with long-lost school friends, the bargain between using free services in exchange for personal data seemed relatively innocuous. It is now glaringly apparent that the true cost of free services is far steeper than anyone anticipated. Jaron Lanier, author of *Who Owns the Future?*, describes how the tension between Silicon Valley's advertising business model and its original social ideals led to what has become the most effective social manipulation tool in human history:

> there's only one way to merge [socialism with libertarian ideals], which is what we call the advertising model, where everything's free but you pay for it by selling ads. But then because the technology gets better and better, the computers get bigger and cheaper, there's more and more data—what started out as advertising morphed into continuous behavior modification on a mass basis, with everyone under surveillance by their devices and

receiving calculated stimulus to modify them. So you end up with this mass behavior-modification empire, which is straight out of Philip K. Dick, or from earlier generations, from *1984*. It's this thing that we were warned about. It's this thing that we knew could happen…. And despite all the warnings, and despite all of the cautions, we just walked right into it, and we created mass behavior-modification regimes out of our digital networks. We did it out of this desire to be both cool socialists and cool libertarians at the same time.[13]

Advertising, according to Lanier's assessment, has become the implicit compromise that allows Silicon Valley to simultaneously embrace its socialist roots, entrepreneurial spirit, and libertarian ideals.

As the human and social costs continue to pile up, we might wonder how long it will take to change the "free" advertising-driven business model to something more socially responsible. Barring government regulation or a complete overhaul of the industry's values and psychology, the answer, I'm afraid, is never. As Lanier explains, there is simply no incentive for Facebook, Google, Twitter, or the legions of companies who make money from advertising to change of their own accord. In order to change the practices of the industry, the drivers of its behavior must change.

The Price of Free

The social costs of big tech's current priorities and motivations are plentiful, and examples of its failures in civic responsibility are vast. Umair Haque has argued that "social media's effects on social and civic well-being are worse than they are on emotional well-being: they last longer, do more damage," and require more substantial clean-up and rebuilding efforts,[14] while Tristan Harris argues that society can no longer "afford the advertising business model."

> The price of free is actually too high. It is literally destroying our society, because it incentivizes automated systems that have these inherent flaws. Cambridge Analytica is the easiest way of explaining why that's true. Because that wasn't an abuse by a bad actor—that was the inherent platform. The problem with Facebook is Facebook.[15]

Harris's argument that Facebook's issues are built into the company's DNA raises a problematic truth: that so long as the fundamental structures, financial incentives, and business models of such companies do not change, the issues we're uncovering will continue to pile up. We are only beginning to collectively realize that "free" services like Facebook and Google are never really free, that we simply offer payment in different ways, such as with our time, attention, and the cohesion and civility of our society.

Of all the problems and PR disasters that have transpired in Silicon Valley, one of the most unsettling is the role technology and social media companies have played in the erosion of democracy. The breakdown of civic discourse, the dissemination of false information online, the targeting of individuals with particular information, and the polarizing effect of social media platforms each contribute to the widening gap between what is needed for democracy to function effectively and the disruptive technological factors at play.

While there has always been inaccurate information in circulation, never before has there been so much, and never before has it been weaponized at scale. The modern phenomenon of misinformation and disinformation have proliferated on the internet, where there remains no system by which to determine the accuracy of information online. We may instinctively know that certain sites or sources, such as peer-reviewed journal articles, are based on controlled research and fact, just as we may know that other sites are meant to be satirical. Wading through the other two plus billion websites on the internet, however, it can often be difficult to tell a reputable site from a biased or intentionally fake news site. Even if we are aware of fact checking sources, such as snopes.com or mediabiasfactcheck.com, the majority of us rarely bother to check the quality of every site we visit. The lack of built-in quality assurance on the internet makes the web simultaneously a treasure trove of high-quality information—academic research, scholarly essays, investigative journalism, and books—and a landmine of bad and misleading information.

If the extent of the problem was simply how best to categorize and sort information based on its quality, we wouldn't have a terribly treacherous path ahead. Sure, it would be a pain to fact-check the whole of the internet, but it wouldn't be impossible. The problem facing democracy is complicated by the ways in which the advertising ecosystem of the internet dictates the flows of information online. Algorithms, including those used on Twitter, Google, YouTube, Facebook, and Instagram, are designed to show you whatever will engage you as much as possible. This is because engagement—defined as more clicks, more interactions, and more time spent on apps or websites—is synonymous with greater ad revenue for ad brokers like Facebook and Google; the more engaged you are, the more ads you see, the more money they make. Engagement, according to technology consultant and writer Tobias Rose-Stockwell is "the currency of the attention economy,"[16] which means it is in the financial interests of tech companies that are reliant on advertising to keep us online and engaged in whatever way possible for as long as possible. The impacts of this model are corrupting, to put it lightly. Having ads dictate the flows of information has resulted not only in the spread of misinformation and disinformation, but also in the prioritization of sensationalized content, filter bubbles, and the ability to micro-target individuals with particular information.

Given that the internet boasts to hold the sum total of the world's knowledge, it has become the place we increasingly inhabit to gather (and in some cases mainline) information. Where facts about the world around us used to be mediated by a variety of factors and channels, such as local news (subsidized by the government and/or paid for by mass, untargeted TV commercials), national newspapers (paid for by the reader), and the time it took to report a story (lag time that ensured increased accuracy of information), this is no longer the case. The uncertain quality of the content we see online has spawned the phenomena of misinformation, disinformation, "alternative facts," and "fake news," each of which is either born of or intensified by the advertising ecosystem that drives the internet. At some point between its conception by Tim Berners-Lee as a mechanism to share ideas and information, and its commoditization and commercialization, the internet has become a place where truth is subjective.

Data from Pew Research Center suggests two-thirds of adults in the U.S. get news from social media, and about half rely on Facebook for news (half of these users get their news from Facebook alone, while just one-in-five rely on three or more sites for news).[17] These findings suggest several troubling implications: that the content prioritized by Facebook's algorithm contributes significantly to the average American's news consumption; that many users do not rely on a diverse sample of news from various online sources; and that advertising-driven businesses are feeding a substantial portion of our collective news diet. Combine this with the unchecked quality of most news online, and you get a veritable dumpster-fire of good, bad, and downright ugly information, all mixed up together in one unpoliced internet. The result, according to Rose-Stockwell, has been the normalization of propaganda and the evisceration of traditional journalism.

> Today we have democratized propaganda—anyone can use these strategies to hijack attention and promote a misleading narrative, a hyperbolic story, or an outrageous ideology—as long as it captures attention and makes a profit for advertisers. Journalism—the historical counter to propaganda—has become the biggest casualty in this algorithmic war for our attention. And without it, we are watching the dissolution of a measured common reality.[18]

A 2016 Stanford study found that middle school through university students "could not distinguish between news and sponsored content, source evidence, or evaluate claims on social media."[19] The results suggest that as entertainment, click-bait, and opinions continue to intermingle with and masquerade as evidence-based information, many young people are not adequately equipped to question the source, accuracy, or quality of information they encounter online.

While there are positive effects unique to the rise of digital information, including the ease of research, the accessibility of information, and proliferation of traditionally marginalized voices and issues, there are also significant costs. The spread of sensationalized and false content has led to a less informed populace, more black and white thinking, and the phenomenon of denialism. The creation of filter bubbles has contributed to a more proliferated, angry, and fragmented society. Our hyper-connected world has allowed for the normalization of extremist content, as fringe or fanatical views—which would naturally be drowned out in a traditional community—can more easily come together in digital spaces worldwide. Add to all this the ability to target information to specific individuals for nefarious purposes, and you get a fair bit of confusion and chaos.

Confusion and Chaos

Perhaps the first thing to understand about false information is its sheer ability to spread, virus-like, to the feeds of unsuspecting and unprepared consumers. A 2018 study on the spread of fake news, the largest ever of its kind, demonstrated that lies spread significantly faster than truth.[20] The researchers of the study explain the reason for this lies in "the degree of novelty and the emotional reactions of recipients" to false stories, as well as the tendency for bots, which are programmed to disseminate reactive content, to spread fake stories. Using 11 years of data from Twitter, which included over 4.5 million tweets, along with information from six different independent fact-checking organizations, researchers demonstrated just how profoundly facts fail compared to fictions:

> A false story reaches 1,500 people six times quicker, on average, than a true story does. And while false stories outperform the truth on every subject— including business, terrorism and war, science and technology, and entertainment—fake news about politics regularly does best. Twitter users seem almost to *prefer* sharing falsehoods. Even when the researchers controlled for every difference between the accounts originating rumors—like whether that person had more followers or was verified—falsehoods were still 70 percent more likely to get retweeted than accurate news.[21]

There are no shortage of examples to illustrate the ways in which false, biased, and misrepresented information have spread on social networks like Facebook, Twitter, and YouTube. Just take Twitter's worst offender, Donald Trump, whose lies and misrepresentations of facts spread like digital wildfire thanks to the digital bullhorn that the platform affords him.

The second important thing to understand about false information is that there are different kinds. The person who knowingly concocts a false news article is sharing a different type of information than the person who reads it, assumes it's accurate, and shares it with his or her online community. Johns Hopkins Sheridan Libraries separate the different types of information available online into four categories, depending on their source, purpose, and quality: information, misinformation, disinformation, and propaganda. Information is pretty straightforward: it's what we're mostly after when we go online, even if we don't always find it. Information communicates factual data or knowledge about a subject or event, with reference to the relevant context and evidence. Good information should both be accurate and free from bias; if it is in some way biased, it should make note of it clearly.[22] The remaining types of information—disinformation, misinformation, and propaganda—deviate from this definition in one or more ways.

Johns Hopkins cites propaganda as a commonly misunderstood and misused term, due to its historical association with the Nazi government in Germany.

[M]any people associate propaganda with inflammatory speech or writing that has no basis is fact. In reality, propaganda may easily be based in fact, but facts represented in such a way as to provoke a desired response.[23]

Propaganda, which is still commonly employed in campaign speeches and political statements, is information with some basis in reality, but which is presented in a misleading way to influence attitudes or behavior. Disinformation, by contrast, "refers to disseminating deliberately false information," in which the sharer is aware of and complicit in spreading falsehoods. Johns Hopkins calls disinformation the "lowest of the low," and explains that it is most typically circulated by "individuals or institutions [in order] to say or write whatever suits a particular purpose, even when it requires deliberate fabrication."[24] (The authors describe the Internet as "an excellent vehicle for disinformation.") A third type of inaccurate information is misinformation, which is similar to disinformation in that it is false, but differs in that the individual or group sharing it is unaware of its inaccuracy. Information may begin as disinformation—that is, information that is knowingly false—and then be circulated as misinformation by people who see it, assume its veracity, and share it with others in good faith. The authors cite misinformation as the most difficult subtype of bad information to identify, suggesting it may also be the most dangerous, due to its obscurity and the fact that it is typically delivered with good intentions.

Examples of the swift and steady spread of misinformation, disinformation, and propaganda online are too numerous to list; so, too, are instances of individual harm, hate speech, and democratic regression that accompany them. Some of the most well-known and horrible examples of the effects of misinformation on democracy, social unrest, and human rights violations include:

1. The spread of false information via Facebook in Myanmar, in which Buddhist extremists spread hate speech and false information about the country's Rohingyan population, which resulted in riots, executions, rape, the burning of hundreds of Rohingyan villages, and the ethnic cleansing of the country's Muslim minority.[25,26] As of September 2018, 725,000 Muslim Rohingya had fled Bangladesh and 10,000 were confirmed dead (widely considered a conservative estimate). A report by an independent Human Rights Council concluded in a UN report that Facebook had been central to the campaign against the Rohingya and had proved itself to be "a useful instrument for those seeking to spread hate."[27] Ashin Wiratho, one of the leaders of the anti-Rohingya movement, likewise credits Facebook with its "success": "If the internet had not come to [Myanmar], not many people would know my opinion and messages … The internet and Facebook are very useful and important to spread my messages."[28]

2. In Sri Lanka, disinformation circulated on Facebook by Sinhalese nationalists was used to incite violence and hatred toward the country's Muslim population. Posts included messages such as, "Kill all Muslims, don't even save an infant" and instructions to "reap without leaving an iota behind."[29] Those who reported such posts, using Facebook's on-site reporting tool, were often told that they did not violate the platform's standards.[30] One man behind the violence, Amith Weerasinghe, shared videos, hateful messages, and warnings with thousands of followers on Facebook, which were reported to the platforms by researchers in Colombo, but never taken down. "Over the next three days, mobs descended on several towns, burning mosques, Muslim-owned shops and homes. One of those towns was

Digana. And one of those homes, among the storefronts of its winding central street, belonged to the Basith family. Abdul Basith, a 27-year-old aspiring journalist, was trapped inside. 'They have broken all the doors in our house, large stones are falling inside,' Mr. Basith said in a call to his uncle as the attack began. 'The house is burning.' The next morning, the police found his body. In response, the government temporarily blocked most social media. Only then did Facebook representatives get in touch with Sri Lankan officials, they say. Mr. Weerasinghe's page was closed the same day."[31]

3. In Indonesia, false messages were spread via Facebook and Whatsapp (a subsidiary of Facebook) that gangs were stealing and killing children and selling their organs. Villagers in nine rural Indonesian communities, upon seeing outsiders enter their towns, lynched those they presumed were coming to murder their children.[32]

4. India, the country with the largest Facebook user base in the world (220 million), experienced a string of lynchings similar to those in Indonesia,[33,34] as well as a misinformation campaign by fringe political parties and religious extremists intended to sow discord and false information to the 49 million voters in India's Karnataka region. Both phenomena were carried out primarily via Whatsapp, where false information was forwarded en masse, with no means to trace or stop the spread of untrue messages.[35] Two men who lost their lives in the wake of one such misinformation campaign were Abijeet Nath and Nilotpal Das, who were driving back through India's Assam province from a waterfall they had visited. When the two men stopped in a village to ask for directions, they were pulled from their vehicle and beaten to death by a mob, who assumed they were coming after the area's children.[36] False information circulated by right-wing Hindu groups were similarly responsible for inciting violence toward Muslim populations. One example included "a grisly video that was described as an attack on a Hindu woman by a Muslim mob but was in fact a lynching in Guatemala. One audio recording on the service from an unknown sender urged all Muslims in the state to vote for the Congress party 'for the safety of our women and children.'.... Like the rest of India, Karnataka is a Hindu majority state. A staple of electoral politics here is pitting Muslims against Hindus, and various Hindu castes against each other."[37]

5. In Brazil, an outbreak of yellow fever was thought to be the result of misinformation spread on Whatsapp regarding anti-vaccine propaganda.[38]

6. In the Philippines, Rodrigo Duterte, along with other candidates, was trained by several Facebook employees during the country's 2016 presidential campaign, which instructed candidates how to set up accounts, drive engagement, and attract followers. Using this knowledge, Duterte's office mobilized itself around an anti-drug and criminal justice campaign, many of which were seeped with "aggressive messages, insults, and threats of violence," as well as disinformation, such as the false claim that the Pope Francis endorsed Duterte.[39] Using fear and falsehoods to drive his message, Duterte was elected in 2016. "He told Filipinos the nation was being ruined by drug abuse and related crime and promised to bring to the capital the merciless strategy he had employed in Davao. Soon, Duterte's death squads prowled the streets at night in search of drug dealers and other criminals. Images of blood-smeared bodies slumped over on sidewalks, women cradling dead husbands, and corpses in satin-lined caskets went viral. As the bodies piled up—more than 7,000 people have been killed as part of Duterte's war on drugs—the social media war escalated."[40] Still, the relationship between Facebook and Duterte appears strong; in November 2017, the social network agreed to a partnership with Duterte's government, in which the company agreed to fund the development of underwater fiber cables in the Philippine's Luzon Strait and "provide a set amount of bandwidth to the government."[41]

The proliferation of propaganda, misinformation, and disinformation on the web is at the heart of the internet's collision with democracy, civic order, and the degradation of human rights. Driving this troubled dynamic is the prioritization of engagement and push for growth into foreign markets, driven by the profit-oriented motivations of the industry.

To their credit, Facebook, Twitter, and YouTube have made some efforts to address the spread of false information. In India, Facebook now limits Whatsapp groups to five people (previously capped at 256 members/group), in an attempt to mitigate the spread of misinformation and rumors on its popular messaging app. The company has also conducted safety workshops in the Philippines for journalists, non-profit employees, and students focused on digital literacy and safety. YouTube released its plans to help ebb the flow of misinformation by investing $25 million in an effort to promote more legitimate and trusted news sources on its platform, which is part of a larger $300 million plan to address misinformation within its parent company, Google.[42] The issue remains, however, that such efforts are at odds with the core business model of such companies. As Olivia Solon aptly points out, "how can [Silicon Valley] condemn the practice on which its business model depends?"[43]

In addition to reconciling the tension between the profits generated by misinformation and the safety of their users, another question many tech companies must grapple with is their position on disinformation and those who spread it. Currently, unless something violates a platform's specific policies, which tend to focus on hate speech and inappropriate content, there is no unified position on how to treat false information online. Even now that the disastrous effects of misinformation and disinformation campaigns have been exposed, platforms like Facebook, YouTube, and Twitter have failed to categorically denounce and expunge such information from their sites, seemingly unsure how to balance free speech with their users' safety.

But why does it matter? Surely everyone has a right to scream and shout their opinion into the void of social media, even if the opinion they espouse or the article they post is false or misinformed. As Mark Zuckerberg has argued, there is merit in leaving such information on Facebook's platform, even when that information is patently false and perpetuates hatred, conspiracy theories, and anti-Semitism.

> [T]here's a set of people who deny that the Holocaust happened. I find that deeply offensive. But at the end of the day, I don't believe that our platform should take that down because I think there are things that different people get wrong. I don't think that they're *intentionally* getting it wrong... What we will do is we'll say, "Okay, you have your page, and if you're not trying to organize harm against someone, or attacking someone, then you can put up that content on your page, even if people might disagree with it or find it offensive."[44]

The suggestion that Holocaust denial should even be included in the realm of "information" is a startling assertion, with deeply troubling implications. Facebook's goal, according to Zuckerberg, is not to be the judge of truth and accuracy, but "to prevent hoaxes from going viral and being widely distributed. The approach that we've taken to false news is not to say, you can't say something wrong on the internet. I think that that would be too extreme."[45] Facebook demotes identified hoaxes but does not necessarily remove them unless moderators believe content will "result in real harm, real physical harm, or if you're attacking individuals, then that content shouldn't be on the platform."[46]

The parameters Zuckerberg and his company cite constitute an extremely literal understanding of harm, free from nuance and more socially contextualized understandings. The most general understanding of harm is typically that which could reasonably cause either physical, mental, or emotional damage. What constitutes mental and emotional damage however, can be rather subjective sticking points. Moral philosopher Bernard Gert defined harm as that which causes pain, death, disability, or the loss of freedom or pleasure, while political and legal philosopher Joel Feinberg determined harm also included what he called "welfare interests," which took into consideration harm that affected one's

> intellectual acuity, emotional stability, the absence of groundless anxieties and resentments, the capacity to engage normally in social intercourse and to enjoy and maintain friendships, at least minimal income and financial security, a tolerable social and physical environment, and a certain amount of freedom from interference and coercion.[47]

The subversion of democracy via orchestrated disinformation campaigns can undoubtedly, then, be counted as harmful? The eradication of trust, also, is surely dangerous to ordered social institutions? The challenge of making democracy work amidst the backdrop of the digital age is a hugely complex task. In *The People vs. Tech*, Jamie Bartlett argues that the primary difficulty in reconciling democracy and technology comes back to the principles that govern each institution and the fact that the rules that guide Western democracies are fundamentally at odds with those that govern cyberspace.[48]

Out of Sight, Out of Mind

Related to the problem of misinformation and disinformation is the phenomenon of denialism, which has really come into its own thanks to the propagation of fake and misleading information. Denialism can be defined as the "refusal to admit the truth of a concept or proposition that is supported by the majority of scientific or historical evidence."[49] As Keith Kahn-Harris explains, while denialists were once confined to the fringes of public discourse, they now occupy a much more visible and central position as a result of the internet's global reach and connectivity.

> As information becomes freer to access online, as "research" has been opened to anyone with a web browser, as previously marginal voices climb on to the online soapbox, so the opportunities for countering accepted truths multiply. No one can be entirely ostracised, marginalised and dismissed as a crank anymore. The sheer profusion of voices, the plurality of opinions, the cacophony of the controversy, are enough to make anyone doubt what they should believe.[50]

Khan-Harris goes on to explain the conflict between science and wishful thinking that underlies many denialist positions.

> Denialism is not stupidity, or ignorance, or mendacity, or psychological pathology. Nor is it the same as lying. Of course, denialists can be stupid, ignorant liars, but so can any of us. But denialists are people in a desperate predicament ... a very modern predicament. Denialism is a post-enlightenment phenomenon, a reaction to the "inconvenience" of many of the findings of modern scholarship. The discovery of evolution, for example, is inconvenient to those committed to a literalist biblical account of creation. Denialism is also a reaction to the inconvenience of the moral consensus that emerged in the post-enlightenment world.[51]

The proliferation of extreme, inaccurate views, taken to its extreme, informs what Khan-Harris calls post-denialism, in which the world is fashioned to take any form the narrator desires.

[I]ts methods liberate a deeper kind of desire: to remake truth itself, to remake the world, to unleash the power to reorder reality itself and stamp one's mark on the planet. What matters in post-denialism is not the establishment of an alternative scholarly credibility, so much as giving yourself blanket permission to see the world however you like…. Whereas denialism explains—at great length—post-denialism asserts. Whereas denialism is painstakingly thought-through, post-denialism is instinctive. Whereas denialism is disciplined, post-denialism is anarchic. The internet has been an important factor in this weakening of denialist self-discipline. The intemperance of the online world is pushing denialism so far that it is beginning to fall apart. The new generation of denialists aren't creating new, alternative orthodoxies so much as obliterating the very idea of orthodoxy itself. The collective, institutional work of building a substantial bulwark against scholarly consensus gives way to a kind of free-for-all.[52]

Denialism represents not only the erosion of information, but also the collective breakdown of order, truth, and the psychological orientation these provide. Two modern and devastating examples of denialism include climate change and the anti-vaccination movement. While certain minority groups have historically expressed scepticism at the idea of global warming, modern scientific evidence and research points unequivocally to the dire and urgent problem of climate change and its effects on our ecosystems, weather, and the inhabitability of the planet. It is a terribly inconvenient truth, to quote Al Gore's 2006 documentary on the same topic, that human industrial activities have caused such severe damage to the planet. No one enjoys thinking about the fact that we are responsible for raising global carbon dioxide, methane, and nitrous oxide levels to the point that they have collectively impacted earth's rapidly rising temperature or threatened millions of plant and animal species.[53,54] It's not fun to think about, but it's true, and it remains our most pressing global problem. None of this, however, can stop tweets from Donald Trump claiming climate change was invented by the Chinese in order to weaken the U.S. manufacturing industry.[55] The assertion, like many Trump makes on Twitter, is accompanied by neither facts nor research; it is merely a succinct, grossly inaccurate claim, sent out on a whim and compressed to 280 characters or less. And Trump is not alone. Denialists, conspiracy theorists, and those who wish to sow discord on any topic can now do so from anywhere, for any reason, to any end, with the push of a button.

Denialist movements have also been used to discredit and misinform global populations about vaccinations. The World Health Organization linked a 2018–2019 surge in measles cases across Europe and the U.S. to widespread erroneous information propagated online, regarding claims that the vaccine was ineffective or even harmful. The false information has contributed to a significant decrease in the uptake of the life-saving MMR vaccine, which has contributed to a staggering 60,000 cases of infection in 2018 (twelve times the number of cases reported in 2016) and dozens of deaths in Europe alone.[56]

> False information about MMR continues to be spread online, particularly on social media, giving a platform to the anti-vaccination movement to push erroneous claims. Some of the posts have hundreds of thousands of 'likes' and include false claims that healthcare professionals have been lying to the public or that immunisation injections amount to nothing more than 'poison being pumped into people's bloodstreams'.[57]

Helen Stokes-Lampard, a professor of medicine and Chair of the Royal College of General Practitioners in the U.K., who has studied the disease's recent progression and its ties to denialist propaganda, also cites the role of false information online in bolstering the re-emergence of what is a lethal but entirely preventable disease.[58] Stokes-Lampard explains that the underlying issue remains a "lack of regulation and enforcement around this material online," which has allowed anti-vax "groups to build momentum without the opportunity for any form of meaningful evidence-based rebuttal."[59]

The epidemic of faulty information and the unwillingness to police it ties back to the tech industry's focus on individualism, its motivation for profit, and its advertising-driven business model. Bold, ridiculous claims naturally attract our attention and trigger our emotions (rage, concern, fervent agreement); the natural result is that these are shared more, which in turn results in more engagement and more profit. While the leaders of YouTube, Twitter, and Facebook probably don't consciously want to contribute to the biggest outbreak of preventable measles deaths in history, the option to aggressively police false information is at odds with both their business models and belief in individual (if erroneous) expression.

Filter Bubbles

Related to the resurgence of denialism is the phenomenon of filter bubbles. The basic concept underlying filter bubbles is that we tend to gravitate towards ideas that confirm what we already believe, which eventually blocks out information that is not in line with our existing opinions. Given the breadth of information available to us, we might assume that the spoils of knowledge would make us more, rather than less informed; after all, the central attraction of the internet lies in its promise of information. With all that knowledge at our fingertips, surely we would become more informed, more knowledgeable, wiser versions of ourselves? Not so, according to historian Timothy Snyder, who explains that

> [I]n assuming that the Internet would make us more rather than less rational, we have missed the obvious danger: that we can now allow our browsers to lead us into a world where everything we would like to believe is true.[60]

The fact that we can find any and all information online means that there is likely to be support for every position, regardless of accuracy. Though the web was built in the name of academic research exchange, the quality of the information that populates the modern internet is, quite obviously, of different calibers. As a result, we are constantly presented with conflicting information, of different qualities, in unfathomable quantities, all the time. The task of sorting through this mass of information is too much for most of us to bear, and the path of least cognitive resistance is often to gravitate towards what already feels comfortable and familiar, rather than challenge ourselves to explore or consider a new position.

The reason we are more likely to see news and information that corresponds to our existing worldview has everything to do with the algorithms and the business models of tech companies who rely on advertising revenue. The algorithms that run the sites we use to peruse information, such as Facebook and YouTube, gather our data in an effort to predict what they think we are most interested in or want to see, in order to drive engagement, show us "relevant" content, and ultimately generate more time spent on the platform. The result is that we start to see only what we want, rather than a range of accurate, balanced information. The more refined our algorithms become, the less likely we are to come across things outside our comfort zone, which might challenge our beliefs. And voila! There you have a filter bubble.

The implication here is actually quite scary. Staying inside our bubbles may hinder our ability to think differently, consider another's perspective, or intelligently defend our own. The more refined the algorithms dictating our newsfeeds become, the more embedded we become in our virtual echo chambers, largely unaware of points of view that differ from our own. Living solely in the company of our own opinions may feel good, but it's not doing us any favors as rational human beings. Research suggests that the more content we have to sort through, the worse we become at differentiating between high- and low-quality information. A 2017 study found that while confirmation bias had originally evolved to help us quickly dispel useless and false information, in the context of the internet, and particularly with social media, "such a bias easily leads to ineffective discrimination."[61] Gene Demby of National Public Radio explains that instead of bridging opinions and encouraging conversation as social media platforms claim to do, these sites in fact make us less aware of different opinions and more insulated in our own.[62]

The other troubling consequence of self-selecting our information is the phenomenon of algorithmic extremism. John Naughton's interview with Zeynep Tufekci outlines the means by which YouTube's algorithm impels us down rabbit holes of increasingly extreme content:

> Tufekci tried watching videos on non-political topics such as vegetarianism (which led to videos about veganism), and jogging (which led to items about running ultramarathons). "It seems," she reflected, "as if you are never 'hardcore' enough for YouTube's recommendation algorithm. It promotes, recommends and disseminates videos in a manner that appears to constantly up the stakes. Given its billion or so users, YouTube may be one of the most powerful radicalising instruments of the 21st century."[63]

The mechanism of YouTube's algorithm works in two ways: first, it takes a topic we have already expressed interest in and gives us even more information on that topic, knowing we're already intrigued. Second, it pushes us towards greater and greater extremes of our chosen topic. Interested in tea? Why not learn how to produce and distribute organic homemade kombucha? Want to know more about the Israeli-Palestinian conflict? Here, have some conspiracy theory videos about Al Jazeera being a secret tool of the Israeli government. Before we know it, we may begin incorporating new, more extreme information into our worldview that, while vaguely related to our original query, is a far cry from where we started. When it comes to the discrepancy between YouTube's financial incentives and its moral obligations to curb extremism, as Chandra Steele points out, it is obvious which is winning: "YouTube has no interest in curbing this, because it quite literally pays: The more extreme the content, the more watchers are hooked, and the more revenue is generated."[64]

Us and Them

If we quietly absorbed and did not act on the information we came across online—be it extreme, biased, or just misinformed—the practical problems of extremist content would perhaps be relatively benign. Unfortunately, the innate desire to share our findings ("you *have* to see this video," "OMG, you should read this," "have you seen this study?") usually outweighs our ability to keep quiet. As social beings, we constantly seek connection with others; particularly in heightened states of emotion—be it outrage, shock, or inspiration—we are especially likely to reach out to other people. In our digital worlds, this translates into a drive to post, comment, engage, and share the radical content we find with others online (a realization social media ad brokers have exploited in full).

Sharing can go one of two ways: If our digital comrades agree with us, we become further entrenched in our position or existing thinking; if people disagree with our ideas, however, we may find ourselves defensive, angry, or indignant, and tempted to distance ourselves from such dissenters. In the real world, we would (hopefully) be unlikely to abuse, belittle, or chastise people with views different from our own. Online, however, behind the safety of our screens, it can be a slippery slope from reasoned debate to outrage and moral fury. While the desire to arrange ourselves into factions based on similarities is a natural human tendency, Thomas Friedman explains that this propensity is drastically exacerbated on the web.

> [W]hile it's true that polarization is primarily driven by our human behavior, social media shapes this behavior and magnifies its impact. Say you want to say something that is not based on fact, pick a fight, or ignore someone that you don't like. These are all natural human impulses, but because of technology, acting on these impulses is only one click away.[65]

The dynamic Friedman describes can be seen in the increased callousness and lack of civility we see online: Twitter wars, bitter Facebook arguments, and endless hateful comments sections, which often descend into ridicule, name-calling, and even threats of violence. The volatility of these examples is heightened by the reduced social costs of such exchanges. As Molly Crockett, a neuroscientist and Assistant Professor of Psychology at Yale explains, "digital media may promote the expression of moral outrage by magnifying its triggers, reducing its personal costs and amplifying its personal benefits"[66]; in other words, the highs we get from expressing ourselves online are amplified, while any potential social costs are diminished.[67]

> Offline, moralistic punishment carries a risk of retaliation. But online social networks limit this risk. They enable people to sort themselves into echo chambers with sympathetic audiences. The chance of backlash is low when you're only broadcasting moral disapproval to likeminded others. Moreover, they allow people to hide in a crowd. Shaming a stranger on a deserted street is far riskier than joining a Twitter mob of thousands. Another cost of outrage expression is empathic distress: punishing and shaming involves inflicting harm on other human beings, which for most of us is naturally unpleasant. Online settings reduce empathic distress by representing other people as two dimensional (sic) icons whose suffering is not readily visible. It's a lot easier to shame an avatar than someone whose face you can see.[68]

We may feel smug and satisfied having belittled our idiot aunt who keeps posting flat earth videos, however, the pain or anger our response elicits in her (or others) and the divisiveness to our relationship is less immediately apparent.

The polarization that results from this dynamic is rooted in our tribalistic instincts, which results in both the separation from and dehumanization of others who do not share our views. Crockett writes that

> there is a serious risk that moral outrage in the digital age will deepen social divides. A recent study suggests a desire to punish others makes them seem less human. Thus, if digital media exacerbates moral outrage, in doing so it may increase social polarization by further dehumanizing the targets of outrage. Polarization in the US is accelerating at an alarming pace, with widespread and growing declines in trust and social capital. If digital media accelerates this process further still, we ignore it at our peril.[69]

In Crockett's estimation, the ring-fencing and protectionism that social platforms encourage is not only negative but dangerous. In an interview with Chris Cox, Facebook's former Chief Product Officer, Nicholas Thompson, editor in chief of Wired magazine, called filter bubbles and the spread of misinformation "the biggest problem with Facebook." Thompson asked Cox whether the radicalization and polarization of Facebook's users was tied to its business model, which Cox quickly denied. This position, of course, is overwhelmingly refuted by research, which continues to find that social media networks like Facebook and Twitter encourage rather than quell digital manifestations of tribalism, which researchers now classify as a systemic global risk.

> This body of work suggests that, paradoxically, our behavioural mechanisms to cope with information overload may make online information markets less meritocratic and diverse, increasing the spread of misinformation and making us vulnerable to manipulation. Anecdotal evidence of hoaxes, conspiracy theories and fake news in online social media is so abundant that massive digital misinformation has been ranked among the top global risks for our society, and fake news has become a major topic of debate in the United States and Europe.[70]

The more platforms corral the information we see, the less likely we are to engage thoughtfully, rationally, and kindly with others on a range of important issues, such as politics, climate change, and economic inequality. Instead, we are more likely to split into factions, unencumbered by many of the social norms that previously held society together.

What social media companies failed to take account of, with their mission to connect the world, is that the human brain is wired to collaborate locally (within-group cooperation) and instinctively dislike or act with hostility towards strangers (between-group competition).[71] Rather than furthering its mission to "build communities," Facebook's ambition to bring two billion people into one gigantic virtual common room, without thought or forward-planning, has actually driven intense polarization, distrust, and prejudice. Moving fast and breaking things in the name of growth has been accomplished to startling effect; unfortunately, what has been broken are communities, trust, and informed discussion, along with the evolution of a new brand of tribalism, which spreads more easily and is more difficult to immobilize.

Our tendency towards polarization is born from our tendency to categorize. Our brains have evolved to observe something, label it, and store that information away, to be retrieved later. This saves us the trouble of assessing each situation, person, and object from scratch each time we encounter something or someone new, which helps us navigate and, in some cases, survive our environment. Most of the time, this cognitive functionality is helpful. If you see someone brandishing a gun and screaming, it's nice your brain instinctively tells you to run away. There are, however, very real downsides to our tendency to think in categorical terms, particularly those that divide people into categories of "us" and "them." In his book *Factfulness*, Hans Rosling describes how each of us unconsciously and "automatically categorizes and generalizes all the time" and the harm this can engender.

> It is not a question of being prejudiced or enlightened. Categories are absolutely necessary for us to function. They give structure to our thoughts.... The necessary and useful instinct to generalize... can also distort our worldview. It can make us mistakenly group together things, or people, or

countries that are actually different. It can make us assume everything or everyone in one category is similar. And, maybe most unfortunate of all, it can make us jump to conclusions about a whole category based on a few, or even just one, unusual example.[72]

The act of psychological categorization is problematized by online dynamics, according to Peter Bazalgette, which tends to heighten our biases and debase our capacity for empathy. In our online worlds, tribal behavior and "unbridled prejudices" can quickly amplify, as they are "given free rein in [the] empathy-free, digital dystopia" of the web.[73] Former human rights lawyer Amanda Taub and journalist Max Fischer similarly suggest that Facebook's biggest flaw and "most consequential impact may be in amplifying the universal tendency toward tribalism."

> Posts dividing the world into "us" and "them" rise naturally, tapping into users' desire to belong. Its gamelike interface rewards engagement, delivering a dopamine boost when users accrue likes and responses, training users to indulge behaviors that win affirmation. And because its algorithm unintentionally privileges negativity, the greatest rush comes by attacking outsiders: The other sports team. The other political party. The ethnic minority. … by supercharging content that taps into tribal identity, [Facebook] can upset fragile communal balances.[74]

In addition to the hit of dopamine Taub and Fischer describe, Amy Chua, an expert on tribalism and its social impacts, explains that in-group instincts that demonize others also raise our oxytocin levels, meaning we are influenced by not one but two of the most powerful neurological motivators in our body's arsenal. The combination, Chua says, "physiologically 'anesthetizes' the empathy one might otherwise feel" towards others,[75] pushing us to unconsciously act differently and more cruelly than we normally would towards others.

Add to the problems of misinformation, disinformation, propaganda, denialism, and tribalism, the rise of troll farms, automated and semi-automated accounts ("bots"), and the ability of any group to target any message to anyone in the world, and you have a recipe for a veritable political catastrophe, the effects of which we began to see in 2016.

2016: U.S. Presidential Election & Brexit

In addition to the divisive misinformation campaigns around the world in countries that rely heavily on Facebook for news and communication, two more internet bombs of extremism and misinformation dropped in 2016: the U.S. presidential election and Britain's decision to leave the European Union. Within the Facebook/Instagram, Google/YouTube, and Twitter ecosystems, the ability to advertise products and messages to target audiences took a dark turn in the years leading up to both 2016 elections. Foreign and domestic agents utilized the micro-targeting technology available on each platform in order to influence and disrupt the political systems of the U.S. and U.K., encouraging "Leave" votes in the U.K. and the election of Donald Trump across the pond. Central to the success of both campaigns was Cambridge Analytica, a data analytics company responsible for hoarding and hijacking information extracted from Facebook's unsuspecting user base.

Way back in 2008, two Cambridge University researchers, Michal Kosinski and David Stillman, discovered that online behaviors and psychometric data were incredibly useful in predicting users' personality, traits, and demographics, such as race, sexual orientation, political affiliation, intelligence, substance use, and even if they were the children of divorced parents.[76]

A few years later, in 2011, the real fun started. Another Cambridge researcher named Aleksandr Kogan collaborated with Facebook on a study published in the journal *Personality and Individual Differences* on friendships.[77] The data for the study was supplied to Kogan by Facebook, which included information on 57 billion Facebook friendships. The same year, Facebook began offering a feature on its platform called "friends permissions," which allowed third-party developers to collect masses of personal information about users and their friends (without their friends' permission). During this time, while approximately 9 million apps were integrated with Facebook, a vast quantity of user data was extracted and harvested by various companies using the feature. Kogan has since estimated that tens of thousands of developers extracted data in the same way he did, and that Facebook was very much aware of this, saying the company considered it "a feature, not a bug."[78]

In 2013, Cambridge Analytica was founded by Christopher Wylie and Alexander Nix as a subsidiary of SCL Group, which described itself as a strategic communications company focusing on "global election management." Using sophisticated data mining and analysis techniques, SCL focused primarily on advising governments and military organizations on behavioral change programs. Later that year, Nix and Wylie demoed Cambridge Analytica's capabilities to billionaire Robert Mercer, a Trump supporter, who put up an initial $15 million in funding; Steve Bannon, who would later become Trump's chief strategist, invested an estimated $1 to 5 million in the company.

The following year, Kogan and his colleague, Joseph Chancellor, founded a company called Global Science Research (GSR) and signed a contract with Cambridge Analytica to create an app that would harvest users' psychometric Facebook data. Kogan and Chancellor extracted data from 270,000 Facebook users and their friends—including their status updates, likes, and private messages—which amounted to a data set of more than 87 million people. Cambridge Analytica then used Kogan and Chancellor's data to create over 30 million user profiles, identify target voter groups, and design specific targeted messaging to influence voters' opinions and behaviors.

In June 2016, the Trump campaign hired Cambridge Analytica for $6 million and began to use Facebook as both its primary fundraising and propaganda vehicle.

> The campaign uploaded its voter files—the names, addresses, voting history, and any other information it had on potential voters—to Facebook. Then, using a tool called Lookalike Audiences, Facebook identified the broad characteristics of, say, people who had signed up for Trump newsletters or bought Trump hats. That allowed the campaign to send ads to people with similar traits. Trump would post simple messages like "This election is being rigged by the media pushing false and unsubstantiated charges, and outright lies, in order to elect Crooked Hillary!" that got hundreds of thousands of likes, comments, and shares. The money rolled in. Clinton's wonkier messages, meanwhile, resonated less on the platform. Inside Facebook, almost everyone on the executive team wanted Clinton to win; but they knew that Trump was using the platform better. If he was the candidate for Facebook, she was the candidate for LinkedIn.[79]

According to Bloomberg reporters Joshua Green and Sasha Issenberg, in addition to spreading false and inflammatory information, Cambridge Analytica data was used to encourage voter suppression: "the Trump campaign used so-called dark posts—nonpublic posts targeted at a specific audience—to discourage African Americans from voting in battleground states."[80] As Tufekci points out, however, Trump's campaign "wasn't deviantly weaponizing an innocent tool. It was simply using Facebook exactly as it was designed to be used."

> The campaign did it cheaply, with Facebook staffers assisting right there in the office, as the tech company does for most large advertisers and political campaigns. Who cares where the speech comes from or what it does, as long as people see the ads? The rest is not Facebook's department.[81]

After Trump's victory in November 2016, Zuckerberg described the idea that his platform may have been used to influence the results of the Presidential election as "a pretty crazy idea." Sixteen months later, Zuckerberg was finally convinced. Facebook suspended SCL and Cambridge Analytica, as well as Wylie and Kogan, from the platform. Chancellor, by contrast, has been gainfully employed by Facebook since 2015. This was followed by a series of events: the suspension of CEO Nix from Cambridge Analytica, Cambridge Analytica's bankruptcy, the suspension of 200 apps from Facebook's platform, the plunging of Facebook's stock by 24 percent, and the company's admission that activities on its service indicated "coordinated inauthentic behavior" from the Russian, Kremlin-linked group, the Internet Research Agency. Cambridge Analytica's parent company, SCL, on the other hand, continues to capitalize on the data obtained from Facebook. In early 2017, armed with the psychometric information of 230 million U.S. citizens, SCL "had won contracts with the US State Department and was pitching to the Pentagon."[82]

Around the same time, British citizens were dealing with their own election nightmare. In a session before the Digital, Culture, Media and Sport Committee, Wylie explained to MPs how the EU referendum vote "was won through fraud" via the Vote Leave campaign "improperly channelling money through a tech firm with links to Cambridge Analytica."[83]

Wylie said it was striking that Vote Leave and three other pro-Brexit groups—BeLeave, which targeted students; Veterans for Britain, and Northern Ireland's Democratic Unionist party—all used the services of the little-known firm Aggregate IQ (AIQ) to help target voters online. He told MPs that AIQ was effectively the Canadian arm of Cambridge Analytica/SCL, deriving the majority of its income by acting as a sub-contractor.[84]

The shuffling of funds between the Vote Leave and BeLeave campaigns, which was spent on AIQ's services, is currently under investigation by the UK Electoral Commission. The EU referendum won by a small margin (2%) of the vote, a result that Wylie believes would have been very different had it not been for AIQ's involvement, combined with the possible violation of campaign spending limits.

Wylie, who was just 24-years-old when he helped Nix form Cambridge Analytica, now describes the company as a "full service propaganda machine."[85] He told Carole Cadwalladr, the Guardian reporter who broke the scandal, he believed the methods employed by Cambridge Analytica and the campaigns that had hired them were "worse than bullying. Because people don't necessarily know it's being done to them."

At least bullying respects the agency of people because they know. … if you do not respect the agency of people, anything that you're doing after that point is not conducive to a democracy. And fundamentally, information warfare is not conducive to democracy.[86]

The importance of sound, accurate information is essential to the institution of democracy. United States District Judge Amy Berman Jackson, who sentenced Trump campaign manager Paul Manafort in 2019 for multiple charges, including tax fraud and conspiracy, stated at the sentencing, if "people don't have the facts, democracy can't work." In an article for *Boston Review*, Clara Hendrickson specifically calls Facebook and Instagram's priorities antithetical to democracy, noting that its policies have "proved to fragment, polarize, and threaten liberal democracy."[87]

According to the University of Gothenburg's 2018 annual Democracy Report, democracy began declining in 2006 and 2007 across a number of regions, including Latin America, the Caribbean, Eastern Europe, Central America, the Middle East, North Africa, Western Europe and North America.[88] These years are, coincidentally, considered to be seminal in tech; 2006 was the year Twitter was launched, Facebook was released to the public, and Google acquired YouTube. In June of the following year, the iPhone made its debut. The only two regions whose democracies the report found to be improving rather than regressing were sub-Saharan Africa and Asia, which, according to the report analysis, are the only two regions whose internet penetration rates fall below the world average (in other words, these two regions don't use the internet as much as those whose democracies are in decline).[89]

In addition to domestic manipulation of U.S. and U.K. elections, foreign influence on social media has also played an important role, particularly Russian interference. In one of its 2018 Congressional hearings, Facebook admitted that 170 Instagram accounts and 120 Facebook pages "were found to have spread propaganda from Russia's Internet Research Agency."[90] If 120 doesn't sound too bad, consider data journalist and research director at Columbia University's Tow Center for Digital Journalism Jonathan Albright's findings: posts from only six of the Russian accounts suspended by Facebook had been shared a whopping 340 million times.[91] Investigations into Trump's victory, Brexit, and Russian interference are currently well under way at the time of this writing and, once complete, will likely illustrate one of the most comprehensive, devastating, and unthinkable attacks on democracy in modern history.

Russia, Facebook, Trump, Mercer, Bannon, Brexit. Every one of these threads runs through Cambridge Analytica. Even in the past few weeks, it seems as if the understanding of Facebook's role has broadened and deepened. The Mueller indictments were part of that, but Paul-Olivier Dehaye—a data expert and academic based in Switzerland, who published some of the first research into Cambridge Analytica's processes—says it's become increasingly apparent that Facebook is "abusive by design". If there is evidence of collusion between the Trump campaign and Russia, it will be in the platform's data flows.[92]

The mechanism by which "Facebook was hijacked, repurposed to become a theatre of war," and "how it became a launchpad for what seems to be an extraordinary attack on the U.S.'s democratic process,"[93] is both scary and complex. The motivation that allowed it to persist, however, is much more straightforward: revenue generated by advertising.

Notes

1. Brin, S., & Page, L. (1998). The Anatomy of a Large-Scale Hypertextual Web Search Engine. *Computer Networks and ISDN Systems, 30*(1), 107–117. https://doi.org/10.1016/S0169-7552(98)00110-X
2. Schmidt, E. (2016, June 9). *Interview with Eric Schmidt* (C. Rose, Interviewer). Retrieved from https://charlierose.com/videos/28222
3. Cohen, N. (2017, October 13). Silicon Valley is Not Your Friend. *The New York Times*. Retrieved from https://www.nytimes.com/interactive/2017/10/13/opinion/sunday/Silicon-Valley-Is-Not-Your-Friend.html
4. Rosenberg, E. (2015, February 5). How Google Makes Money. Retrieved August 27, 2018, from *Investopedia* website: https://www.investopedia.com/articles/investing/020515/business-google.asp
5. Google: Ad Revenue 2001–2018. (n.d.). Retrieved May 27, 2019, from *Statista* website: https://www.statista.com/statistics/266249/advertising-revenue-of-google/
6. Tufekci, Z. (2018, January 16). It's the (Democracy-Poisoning) Golden Age of Free Speech. *Wired*. Retrieved from https://www.wired.com/story/free-speech-issue-tech-turmoil-new-censorship/
7. Tarnoff, B. (2017, August 23). Silicon Valley Siphons Our Data like Oil. But the Deepest Drilling has Just Begun. *The Guardian*. Retrieved from https://www.theguardian.com/world/2017/aug/23/silicon-valley-big-data-extraction-amazon-whole-foods-facebook
8. Zuckerberg, M. (2018, July 18). *Zuckerberg: The Recode Interview* (K. Swisher, Interviewer). Retrieved from https://www.recode.net/2018/7/18/17575156/mark-zuckerberg-interview-facebook-recode-kara-swisher
9. Facebook's Gollum Will Never Give Up Its Data Ring. (2018, May 5). Retrieved September 9, 2018, from *Newco Shift* website: https://shift.newco.co/2018/05/05/facebooks-gollum-will-never-give-up-its-data-ring/

10. Battelle, J. (2017, September 15). Lost Context: How Did We End Up Here? Retrieved September 2, 2018, from *Newco Shift* website: https://shift.newco.co/2017/09/15/lost-context-how-did-we-end-up-here/
11. Carr, C. (2010, August 8). The Meaning of Mad Men: Philosophers Take on TV. *Time*. Retrieved from https://content.time.com/time/arts/article/0,8599,2009261,00.html
12. Chollet, F. (2018, March 28). What Worries Me about AI. Retrieved September 7, 2018, from *François Chollet* website: https://medium.com/@francois.chollet/what-worries-me-about-ai-ed9df072b704
13. Lanier, J. (2018, April 17). *We Won, and We Turned into Assholes* (N. Kulwin, Interviewer) [*New York Magazine*]. Retrieved from http://nymag.com/selectall/2018/04/jaron-lanier-interview-on-what-went-wrong-with-the-internet.html
14. Haque, U. (2017, September 15). Is Social Media a Failure? Retrieved August 27, 2018, from *Eudaimonia and Co* website: https://eand.co/is-social-media-a-failure-f4f970695d17
15. Kulwin, N. (2018, April 13). An Apology for the Internet—From the Architects Who Built It. *Select All*. Retrieved from http://nymag.com/intelligencer/2018/04/an-apology-for-the-internet-from-the-people-who-built-it.html
16. Rose-Stockwell, T. (2017). This is How Your Fear and Outrage are Being Sold for Profit. *Medium*. Retrieved February 18, 2019, from https://medium.com/@tobiasrose/the-enemy-in-our-feeds-e86511488de
17. Shearer, E., & Gottfried, J. (2017). *News Use across Social Media Platforms 2017*. Retrieved from Pew Research Center website: https://www.journalism.org/2017/09/07/news-use-across-social-media-platforms-2017/
18. Rose-Stockwell, T. (2017). This is How Your Fear and Outrage are Being Sold for Profit. *Medium*. Retrieved February 18, 2019, from https://medium.com/@tobiasrose/the-enemy-in-our-feeds-e86511488de
19. Wineburg, S., McGrew, S. Breakstone, J., & Ortega, T. (2016). Evaluating Information: The Cornerstone of Civic Online Reasoning. *Stanford Digital Repository*. Retrieved September 2, 2018, from https://purl.stanford.edu/fv751yt5934
20. Vosoughi, S., Roy, D., & Aral, S. (2018). The Spread of True and False News Online. *Science, 359*(6380), 1146–1151. https://doi.org/10.1126/science.aap9559
21. Meyer, R. (2018, March 8). The Grim Conclusions of the Largest-Ever Study of Fake News. *The Atlantic*. Retrieved from https://www.theatlantic.com/technology/archive/2018/03/largest-study-ever-fake-news-mit-twitter/555104/

22. Johns Hopkins Sheridan Libraries. (2018, June 25). Evaluating Information: Propaganda vs. Misinformation. Retrieved August 22, 2018, from http://guides.library.jhu.edu/evaluate/propaganda-vs-misinformation
23. Ibid.
24. Ibid.
25. Taub, A., & Fisher, M. (2018, April 21). Where Countries are Tinderboxes and Facebook is a Match. *The New York Times*. Retrieved from https://www.nytimes.com/2018/04/21/world/asia/facebook-sri-lanka-riots.html
26. Facebook Chief Fires Back at Apple Boss. (2018, April 2). *BBC News*. Retrieved from https://www.bbc.com/news/technology-43619410
27. Human Rights Council. (2018). *Report of the Independent International Fact-finding Mission on Myanmar* (No. A/HRC/39/64; pp. 1–21). Retrieved from https://www.ohchr.org/EN/HRBodies/HRC/RegularSessions/Session39/_layouts/15/WopiFrame.aspx?sourcedoc=/EN/HRBodies/HRC/RegularSessions/Session39/Documents/A_HRC_39_64.docx&action=default&DefaultItemOpen=1
28. Larson, C. (2017, November 7). Facebook Can't Cope with the World It's Created. *Foreign Policy*. Retrieved from https://foreignpolicy.com/2017/11/07/facebook-cant-cope-with-the-world-its-created/
29. Taub, A., & Fisher, M. (2018, April 21). Where Countries are Tinderboxes and Facebook is a Match. *The New York Times*. Retrieved from https://www.nytimes.com/2018/04/21/world/asia/facebook-sri-lanka-riots.html
30. Ibid.
31. Ibid.
32. Ibid.
33. Harris, J. (2018, May 6). In Sri Lanka, Facebook's Dominance has Cost Lives. *The Guardian*. Retrieved from https://www.theguardian.com/commentisfree/2018/may/06/sri-lanka-facebook-lives-tech-giant-poor-countries
34. Hern, A. (2018, July 20). WhatsApp to Restrict Message Forwarding after India Mob Lynchings. *The Guardian*. Retrieved from https://www.theguardian.com/technology/2018/jul/20/whatsapp-to-limit-message-forwarding-after-india-mob-lynchings
35. Goel, V. (2018, May 16). In India, Facebook's WhatsApp Plays Central Role in Elections. *The New York Times*. Retrieved from https://www.nytimes.com/2018/05/14/technology/whatsapp-india-elections.html

36. Waterson, J. (2018, June 17). Fears Mount Over WhatsApp's Role in Spreading Fake News. *The Guardian*. Retrieved from https://www.theguardian.com/technology/2018/jun/17/fears-mount-over-whatsapp-role-in-spreading-fake-news

37. Goel, V. (2018, May 16). In India, Facebook's WhatsApp Plays Central Role in Elections. *The New York Times*. Retrieved from https://www.nytimes.com/2018/05/14/technology/whatsapp-india-elections.html

38. Waterson, J. (2018, June 17). Fears Mount over WhatsApp's Role in Spreading Fake News. *The Guardian*. Retrieved from https://www.theguardian.com/technology/2018/jun/17/fears-mount-over-whatsapp-role-in-spreading-fake-news

39. Etter, L. (2017, December 7). Rodrigo Duterte Turned Facebook into a Weapon, with a Little Help from Facebook. *Bloomberg.Com*. Retrieved from https://www.bloomberg.com/news/features/2017-12-07/how-rodrigo-duterte-turned-facebook-into-a-weapon-with-a-little-help-from-facebook

40. Ibid.

41. Ibid.

42. YouTube to Invest $25 Million to Boost "Trusted" News Sources (2018, July 10). *ABS-CBN News*. Retrieved from https://news.abs-cbn.com/business/07/10/18/youtube-to-invest-25-million-to-boost-trusted-news-sources

43. Solon, O. (2018, March 24). 'A Grand Illusion': Seven Days that Shattered Facebook's Facade. *The Guardian*. Retrieved from https://www.theguardian.com/technology/2018/mar/24/cambridge-analytica-week-that-shattered-facebook-privacy

44. Zuckerberg, M. (2018, July 18). *Zuckerberg: The Recode Interview* (K. Swisher, Interviewer). Retrieved from https://www.recode.net/2018/7/18/17575156/mark-zuckerberg-interview-facebook-recode-kara-swisher

45. Ibid.

46. Ibid.

47. Feinberg, J., *The Moral Limits of the Criminal Law, Volume 1: Harm to Others* (New York: Oxford University Press, 1984), p. 37.

48. Bartlett, J. (2018). *The People vs Tech: How the Internet is Killing Democracy (and How We Save It)*. New York: Penguin.

49. Definition of denialist. (n.d.). In *Oxford Dictionaries*. Retrieved from https://en.oxforddictionaries.com/definition/denialist

50. Kahn-Harris, K. (2018, August 3). Denialism: What Drives People to Reject the Truth. *The Guardian*. Retrieved from https://www.theguardian.com/news/2018/aug/03/denialism-what-drives-people-to-reject-the-truth

51. Ibid.

52. Ibid.

53. NASA. (2018). *Climate Change Causes: A Blanket Around the Earth* [Vital Signs of the Planet]. Retrieved from https://climate.nasa.gov/causes

54. Díaz, S., Settele, J., & Brondízio, E. (2019). *IPBES Global Assessment Summary for Policymakers*. Retrieved from IPBES website: https://www.ipbes.net/news/ipbes-global-assessment-summary-policymakers-pdf

55. Kahn-Harris, K. (2018, August 3). Denialism: What Drives People to Reject the Truth. *The Guardian*. Retrieved from https://www.theguardian.com/news/2018/aug/03/denialism-what-drives-people-to-reject-the-truth

56. Measles and Rubella Surveillance Data. (2018, August 13). Retrieved August 22, 2018, from World Health Organization website: http://www.who.int/immunization/monitoring_surveillance/burden/vpd/surveillance_type/active/measles_monthlydata/en/

57. Stokes-Lampard, H. (2018, August 21). Anti-vaxxers are Still Spreading False Claims as People Die of Measles. *The Guardian*. Retrieved from https://www.theguardian.com/commentisfree/2018/aug/21/anti-vaxxers-measles-mmr-vaccine-gp-online

58. Ibid.

59. Ibid.

60. Snyder, T. (2018, May 21). Fascism is Back. Blame the Internet. *Washington Post*. Retrieved from https://www.washingtonpost.com/news/posteverything/wp/2018/05/21/fascism-is-back-blame-the-internet/

61. Qiu, X., Oliveira, D. F. M., Shirazi, A. S., Flammini, A., & Menczer, F. (2017). Limited Individual Attention and Online Virality of Low-quality Information. *Nature Human Behaviour, 1*(7), 0132. https://doi.org/10.1038/s41562-017-0132

62. Demby, G. (2016, July 9). *How Social Media Impacts the Conversation on Racial Violence* (L. Neary, Interviewer) [NPR]. Retrieved from https://www.npr.org/2016/07/09/485356145/how-social-media-impacts-the-conversation-on-racial-violence

63. Naughton, J. (2018, March 18). Extremism Pays. That's Why Silicon Valley Isn't Shutting It Down. *The Guardian*. Retrieved from https://www.theguardian.com/commentisfree/2018/mar/18/extremism-pays-why-silicon-valley-not-shutting-it-down-youtube

64. Steele, C. (2018, November 28). Extremism Pays for YouTube, but at What Cost? Retrieved January 16, 2019, from *PC Magazine* website: https://www.pcmag.com/news/365140/extremism-pays-for-youtube-but-at-what-cost

65. Friedman, T. L. (2016). *Thank You for Being Late: An Optimist's Guide to Thriving in the Age of Accelerations* (p. 274). New York: Farrar, Straus and Giroux.

66. Crockett, M. J. (2017). Moral Outrage in the Digital Age. *Nature Human Behaviour, 1*(11), 769–771. https://doi.org/10.1038/s41562-017-0213-3

67. Crockett also notes that expressing our moral outrage online may make us less likely to act in the real world in a meaningful and socially engaged way, such as by donating or volunteering our time, as digital platforms "the way we experience outrage, and limiting how much we can actually change social realities."

68. Crockett, M. J. (2017). Moral Outrage in the Digital Age. *Nature Human Behaviour, 1*(11), 769–771. https://doi.org/10.1038/s41562-017-0213-3

69. Ibid.

70. Qiu, X., Oliveira, D. F. M., Shirazi, A. S., Flammini, A., & Menczer, F. (2017). Limited Individual Attention and Online Virality of Low-quality Information. *Nature Human Behaviour, 1*(7), 0132. https://doi.org/10.1038/s41562-017-0132

71. Bazalgette, P. (2017). *The Empathy Instinct: How to Create a More Civil Society* (p. 221). London: John Murray.

72. Rosling, H., Rosling, O., & Rosling Rönnlund, A. (2018). *Factfulness: Ten Reasons We're Wrong about the World—And Why Things are Better Than You Think* (p. 146). London: Sceptre.

73. Bazalgette, P. (2017). *The Empathy Instinct: How to Create a More Civil Society* (p. 117). London: John Murray.

74. Taub, A., & Fisher, M. (2018, April 21). Where Countries are Tinderboxes and Facebook is a Match. *The New York Times*. Retrieved from https://www.nytimes.com/2018/04/21/world/asia/facebook-sri-lanka-riots.html

75. Chua, A. (2018, June 14). Tribal World. *Foreign Affairs*. Retrieved July/ August 2018, from https://www.foreignaffairs.com/articles/world/2018-06-14/tribal-world

76. The researchers would go on to publish two papers on the subject: "Private traits and attributes are predictable from digital records of human behavior" in 2013, and "Psychological targeting as an effective approach to digital mass persuasion" in 2017. They would also eventually be approached by Christopher Wylie to discuss using their data.

77. Yearwood, M. H., Cuddy, A., Lamba, N., Youyou, W., van der Lowe, I., Piff, P. K., ... Spectre, A. (2015). On Wealth and the Diversity of Friendships: High Social Class People Around the World have Fewer International Friends. *Personality and Individual Differences, 87*, 224–229. https://doi.org/10.1016/j.paid.2015.07.040

78. Stahl, L. (2018, April 22). *Aleksandr Kogan: The Link between Cambridge Analytica and Facebook*. Retrieved from https://www.cbsnews.com/news/aleksandr-kogan-the-link-between-cambridge-analytica-and-facebook/

79. Vogelstein, F., & Thompson, N. (2018, February 12). Inside Facebook's Two Years of Hell. *Wired*. Retrieved from https://www.wired.com/story/inside-facebook-mark-zuckerberg-2-years-of-hell/

80. Tufekci, Z. (2018, January 16). It's the (Democracy-Poisoning) Golden Age of Free Speech. *Wired*. Retrieved from https://www.wired.com/story/free-speech-issue-tech-turmoil-new-censorship/

81. Ibid.

82. Cadwalladr, C. (2018, March 18). 'I Made Steve Bannon's Psychological Warfare Tool': Meet the Data War Whistleblower. *The Guardian*. Retrieved from https://www.theguardian.com/news/2018/mar/17/data-war-whistleblower-christopher-wylie-faceook-nix-bannon-trump

83. Hern, A., & Sabbagh, D. (2018, March 27). EU Referendum Won Through Fraud, Whistleblower Tells MPs. *The Guardian*. Retrieved from https://www.theguardian.com/uk-news/2018/mar/27/brexit-groups-had-common-plan-to-avoid-election-spending-laws-says-wylie

84. Ibid.

85. Memoli, M., & Schecter, A. (2018, April 25). Bannon Turned Cambridge into "Propaganda Machine," Whistleblower Says. Retrieved January 17, 2019, from *NBC News* website: https://www.nbcnews.com/politics/donald-trump/bannon-turned-cambridge-propaganda-machine-whistleblower-says-n869126

86. Cadwalladr, C. (2018, March 18). 'I Made Steve Bannon's Psychological Warfare Tool': Meet the Data War Whistleblower. *The Guardian*. Retrieved from https://www.theguardian.com/news/2018/mar/17/data-war-whistleblower-christopher-wylie-faceook-nix-bannon-trump

87. Hendrickson, C. (2018, April 12). Democracy vs. the Algorithm. Retrieved September 3, 2018, from *Boston Review* website: http://bostonreview.net/science-nature/clara-hendrickson-democracy-vs-algorithm

88. University of Gothenburg Varieties of Democracy Institute. (2018). *V-Dem Annual Democracy Report 2018* (pp. 1–96). Retrieved from https://www.v-dem.net/media/filer_public/3f/19/3f19efc9-e25f-4356-b159-b5c0ec894115/v-dem_democracy_report_2018.pdf

89. World Internet Users Statistics and 2019 World Population Stats. (2019, March 31). Retrieved May 26, 2019, from *Internet World Stats* website: https://www.internetworldstats.com/stats.htm

90. Volpicelli, G. (2018, April 28). Can Instagram Keep Its Nose Clean? *The Observer*. Retrieved from https://www.theguardian.com/technology/2018/apr/28/instagram-at-the-crossroads-profits-facebook-data-scandal-politics-influencers-mental-health

91. Vogelstein, F., & Thompson, N. (2018, February 12). Inside Facebook's Two Years of Hell. *Wired*. Retrieved from https://www.wired.com/story/inside-facebook-mark-zuckerberg-2-years-of-hell/

92. Cadwalladr, C. (2018, March 18). 'I Made Steve Bannon's Psychological Warfare Tool': Meet the Data War Whistleblower. *The Guardian*. Retrieved from https://www.theguardian.com/news/2018/mar/17/data-war-whistleblower-christopher-wylie-faceook-nix-bannon-trump

93. Ibid.

7

Economic Inequality & Employment

An imbalance between rich and poor is the oldest and most fatal ailment of all republics.
–Plutarch

From shifting job categories, the disruption and decimation of industries, and an impending global skills mismatch, to the concentration of extreme wealth, income inequality, and avoidance of corporate taxes, Silicon Valley's role in furthering economic inequality is hugely important, insufficiently understood, and under-actioned. The role technology plays in changing the conditions and types of employment, as well as reshaping global economics, is not the most publicized problem the industry has weathered, but it will be the next—and it will be the worst. Like other harmful social outcomes in which it is complicit, the tech industry's mentality, priorities, and behaviors have intensified the effects of both economic inequality and job displacement.

The changing nature of employment due to automation has been a recent source of fear, uncertainty, and discord. Some experts argue that the growing role of automated technologies will upend traditional

© The Author(s) 2020
K. Cook, *The Psychology of Silicon Valley*,
https://doi.org/10.1007/978-3-030-27364-4_7

employment for a substantial number of people, as machines become increasingly adept at both cognitive and physical tasks. A 2013 study by Oxford researchers Michael Osborne and Carl Frey analyzed 702 distinct occupations and found 47% were at risk of being automated over the next twenty years,[1] which sent both news outlets and the public into an existential employment tailspin. (An article in The Economist subsequently referred to the impending situation as "a jobs apocalypse."[2]) The study is perhaps the most cited (and anxiety-producing) research on the future of employment, but it is also commonly misinterpreted. Frey and Osborne do not say explicitly that nearly half of existing jobs will necessarily be obsolete, only that they will significantly change due to automation. The paper also does not comment on job creation, only job destruction, and thus does not make any predictions about the future of employment or the types of jobs that will be created as technology advances.

Other studies have emerged that mimic Frey and Osborne's research—some with less severe projections, others that paint an even more dire scenario. In 2016, McKinsey predicted that 45% of workers would be susceptible to automation in the next two decades, while the World Bank estimated the number would be closer to 57%. Projections in countries such as Ethiopia (88%), China (77%), and India (69%) are even higher.[3] In the U.K., thinktank IPPR estimates that 44% of roles—equaling the jobs of 13.7 million people—could potentially be automated.[4] Researchers Melanie Arntz, Terry Gregory, and Ulrich Zierahn, however, have much more conservative estimates, putting the number of jobs at risk of full automation at only 9%.[5] The fact of the matter, of course, is that neither the World Bank nor Arntz et al knows with certainty what the future of automation holds, or the exact number of jobs and people that will be affected. What everyone does agree on is that there will be significant changes as certain types of jobs disappear and others are born, that businesses will rely increasingly on automation where possible, that this will put some people out of work, and that the types—and number—of new jobs available are as yet unknown.

The possibility of mass automation in the long-term is an eventuality that should be discussed and prepared for, beginning immediately. The more pressing problem, however, is the transition to a more automated society that will occur over the next several decades, particularly in countries such as the US, that do not have strong social safety nets. Ben Tarnoff asserts that it is not automation itself that is a problem, but the economic and social insecurity of those who will be affected by it.

> It's reasonable to expect at some point in the next 50 years, technology will proceed to the point that a large number, potentially even most occupations, can be partially or fully automated. If that scenario arrives under our present political and economic arrangement, the consequences would be catastrophic.[6]

The current hypercapitalist economic system in the U.S., in other words, combined with a set of highly individualistic values, would exacerbate the sting of economic inequality in the face of technological unemployment. According to Mathew Lawrence, a senior research fellow at IPPR, "[m]anaged badly, the benefits of automation could be narrowly concentrated, benefiting those who own capital and highly skilled workers. Inequality would spiral."[7]

> Mass automation wouldn't necessarily be a negative development, but if it occurs in a capitalist system designed to funnel the spoils of economic and productivity growth to those who are already sitting on billions of dollars, there's no question that most people would not see the benefits and would likely take to smashing the machines responsible for their immiseration, as so many other workers have done before them. And it would be hard to blame them for it.[8]

The only way to mitigate the inevitable consequences of automation is to begin amending governmental policies to include more comprehensive social programs designed to help people whose roles are disrupted or usurped by technological advancements. Thankfully, to design such a system, we need only look to countries where AI and robotic innovations are anticipated enthusiastically.

In societies where strong social safety nets are in place, such as Sweden, research has found that over 80% of workers express positive views about robots, automation, and artificial intelligence in the workplace.[9] In the U.S., however, these numbers are reversed: 72% of Americans express concern about the effects of increased automation in the workplace,[10] 73% worry that AI will displace more jobs than it creates,[11] and 76% believe economic inequality will worsen as a result.[12] MIT Technology Review Space Reporter Erin Winick explains that the fear that underlies many Americans' views about automation is largely the result of differences in governmental services and job security.

> Swedish citizens tend to trust that their government and the companies they work for will take care of them, and they see automation as a way to improve business efficiency. Since Swedish employees actually do benefit from increased profits by getting higher wages, a win for companies is a win for workers. ... the American tendency to worry about robots' replacing human workers is driven by the severe consequences of losing a job in the U.S. ... Sweden's free health care, education, and job transition programs dampen the risk of such undertakings—which may be why people in the country are mostly happy to pay income tax rates of up to nearly 60 percent. The U.S., by contrast, provides almost none of these services. The difference is especially stark in the area of employment assistance: the U.S. spends only about 0.1 percent of GDP on programs designed to help people deal with changes in the workplace.[13]

If increased automation is coming—and it is, perhaps faster than we can currently appreciate—countries such as Sweden and their Nordic neighbors will be vastly better prepared than the U.S., due in large part to their social policies.

A follow-up question, should we decide to help workers navigate the coming wave of change, is, who exactly do we help? Who will require reskilling in their current professions and who will require training for entirely new jobs? Many researchers and futurists have argued that automation will hit those with low and mid-level skills hardest in the coming years,[14] citing multiple studies which have found that, already, "a range of low-skill and medium-skill occupations exposed to automation have suffered employment declines and sluggish or even negative wage growth."[15] A 2017 analysis by PriceWaterhouseCoopers projected the industries most affected by automation will be administrative services, retail, construction, manufacturing, defense, transportation, and the financial sector.[16] Yet there is also growing evidence that highly-skilled workers, such as physicians, lawyers, teachers, professors, and accountants will soon feel the effects of automation.[17] As Arwa Mahdawi explains,

Today's technological revolution is an entirely different beast from the industrial revolution. The pace of change is exponentially faster and far wider in scope. As Stanford University academic Jerry Kaplan writes in *Humans Need Not Apply*: today, automation is "blind to the color of your collar." It doesn't matter whether you're a factory worker, a financial advisor or a professional flute-player: automation is coming for you.[18]

The idea that white-collar jobs are equally at risk to the effects of automation is also supported by employment experts Richard and Daniel Susskind, whose book, *The Future of the Professions*, outlines the impending wave of automation and its effects on white collar jobs. As robots and AI encroach on every role from surgery,[19] to military jobs,[20] to the 70 million drivers employed worldwide,[21] we will collectively feel the changes of automation across nearly every industry in the very near future.

There is also the issue of geographic impacts on job loss and economic inequality. IPPR reports that 48% of jobs in the north-east of England are at high risk of being automated, compared to just 39% in London, which the report suggests "could lead to wider geographical inequalities."[22] The same is true in the U.S., according to a 2019 report from the Metropolitan Policy Program at the Brookings Institute, which found that non-metro, "Heartland" states would be significantly more affected than urban centers,[23] a finding echoed by a 2018 Philadelphia Fed report.[24] Stephane Kasriel, CEO of Upwork, has emphasized the "need to acknowledge the uneven geographic impact of automation and take steps, as businesses and collectively as a society, to increase opportunity in geographic areas that are affected adversely."[25] Kasriel cites the research of Daron Acemoglu and Pascual Restrepo,[26] whose work has demonstrated the uneven impacts of automation across different localities:

What [Acemoglu and Restrepo] found is a strong regional impact: for every new robot introduced in a particular metro region, an estimated 6.2 jobs were lost in the same geographic area. But when examining the country as a whole, they found that the impact was about half or equivalent to three workers losing their jobs for each additional robot. One possible explanation is that the automation of industrial jobs in the Midwest and US south is partially offset by new types of jobs in coastal cities. But that's no comfort if you're living in one of the states with a net decline in jobs.[27]

As the prowess of automated machines and AI continues to improve, we can expect to see the impacts of job losses in industries such as manufacturing, which are historically concentrated in more rural cities and states, worsen considerably.

Many experts cite the historical truism that new technology has always replaced human labor, particularly in times of great technological advancement, but new jobs invariably follow to replace those that are lost. The difference in the current technological revolution is not only the outstanding pace of change (writers at the Economist argue that "never before have so many jobs been threatened at once"[28]), but also the quality of forthcoming jobs, and the question of who is equipped to perform them. Even in the event that there is a net job creation, the skills required to fill those jobs will likely not match the skillsets of those whose jobs are displaced. The most pressing problems in the short- to medium-term, then, are (1) the skills gap that will exist between existing jobs that will become automated and new jobs that will be created, and (2) the ability of organizations and governments to help prepare, educate, and transition workers to new roles. The Automation Readiness Index, which studies the preparedness of countries for the coming wave of automation, has found that few policies and programs are in place worldwide to address such changes.

Business leaders are not displaying much fear. Such anxieties as they have about these technologies are more about being caught out by market disruption. Thus many are speeding ahead to integrate AI or advanced robotics into their operations. That pace will accelerate in the next few years, and the actual impacts on economies and workforces will begin then to become clearer. To avoid a vacuum, countries will need to put policies and plans in place to help individuals (and to some extent businesses) take maximum advantage of the opportunities that these technologies offer. Policies will also be needed to mitigate the negative impacts resulting from the displacement of some categories of workers from their familiar roles. In both cases it is a matter of policies and strategies that help workforces make the transition to a more automated economy.[29]

Regardless of the types of jobs affected by automation, a new social need will arise for programs that support, train, and reskill workers who are displaced by technology, alongside more comprehensive social safety nets. In a New York Times op-ed, Louis Hyman suggests it is not technology that will displace humans from their jobs, but the values at play in the corporations driving technological change.

> The history of labor shows that technology does not usually drive social change. On the contrary, social change is typically driven by *decisions* we make about how to organize our world. Only later does technology swoop in, accelerating and consolidating those changes. This insight is crucial for anyone concerned about the insecurity and other shortcomings of the gig economy. For it reminds us that far from being an unavoidable consequence of technological progress, the nature of work always remains a matter of social choice. It is not a result of an algorithm; it is a collection of decisions by corporations and policymakers.[30]

At the heart of the employment problem is again the subject of values, particularly those that are informed by profit rather than social value.

The Gig Economy & Workers' Rights

The adaptability of the workforce in the face of such swift and unprecedented change is complicated by the type of work that has become available. According to Daniel Alpert, a senior fellow in macroeconomics at Cornell Law School, there has been a resounding degradation in the quality of jobs over the last 25 years, noting that we have "become far more dependent, especially since the recession, on low-wage, low-hour jobs... [which] don't pay very much at all."[31] The employment options that for many decades fueled the middle-class are going missing. Such jobs, which were based primarily on "routine manual and routine cognitive tasks,"[32] have been increasingly automated as the world shifts from a "material-based economy" to a "knowledge-based economy."[33] The decimation of such roles leaves workers in a precarious situation: more and more people have been forced to take on not only lower-skilled jobs but, in many cases, multiple jobs, in order to replace the income they have lost as their previously better paid, middle class jobs have disappeared. As MIT professor Erik Brynjolfsson explains, "the great paradox of our era" is that

[p]roductivity is at record levels, innovation has never been faster, and yet at the same time, we have a falling median income and we have fewer jobs. People are falling behind because technology is advancing so fast and our skills and organizations aren't keeping up.[34]

As robotics are combined with advancements in deep learning and AI, Brynjolfsson and others expect the effects of the burgeoning two-class job market to become even more pronounced.

The effects of an increasingly bifurcated employment landscape can be seen in the growing number of freelancers, gig economy workers, and those working multiple jobs. As job stability, working opportunities, and pay have all decreased, many have had to scramble to cobble together work by any means necessary. While unemployment in the U.S. remains at the lowest level in decades, the type and amount of work people are undertaking has changed dramatically—and not for the better. As Scott Galloway describes, "[i]t's never been easier to get a job, but it's never been harder to get a well-paying job." The result, he argues, is "an economy that is bifurcating into what could loosely be described as 350 million serfs serving 3 million lords," an intensely divided "labor market, where people with advanced skills earn higher wages but where workers without those skills see technology drive down demand for their services, depressing their pay."[35] The reason, again, comes back to corporate priorities.

Effectively we've decided again that what's good for the consumer and good for the shareholder is good for society writ large. There are three entities here: there's consumers, there's shareholders, and there's workers. We have purposefully opted to treat the consumers like royalty, to treat shareholders like kings and queens, and the serfs are the workers…. We have literally reshaped the economy to serve a small number of very talented and very lucky people.[36]

You don't have to look very far to see Galloway's fears being realized. If you have taken Uber or Lyft, had packages delivered from Amazon, or used Seamless, DoorDash, or any number of food delivery apps, you have already witnessed first-hand the divided labor market Galloway describes.

The rise of the gig economy, or what the U.S. Bureau of Labor Statistics refers to as those working in "alternative working arrangements," accounted for over 10% of the U.S. workforce in 2017.[37] This includes "Uber drivers, freelance graphic designers, and people who find work through temp agencies"; it does not, however, include those who work full-time and have a second gig job, nor does it include those who have diversified sources of income from multiple sources of employment.[38] A more accurate picture of gig work is reflected in a report from the Federal Reserve, which found that almost one-third of adults participated in some form of gig work,[39] or a study by Upwork, which reported that in 2017, 36% of the U.S. workforce was freelancing.[40] In addition to the more obvious examples of gig work, such as drivers, on-demand cleaning services, and an army of freelancers, contractors at large tech companies within Silicon Valley face many of the same issues. In 2018, over half of Google's workforce was comprised of contractors, who did not receive the same benefits as regular employees, such as stocks, job stability, insurance, paid leave, and healthcare.[41]

The central promise of the gig economy rests on the notion of autonomy and the idea that people can choose to work when and where they want. The flexibility promised by gig jobs—particularly service-related positions in the app-driven on-demand economy—is often overshadowed by the unpredictability of work available, the flooding of the market, and the lack of worker protections. The most well-known example is Uber's creation of "driver-partners," who act as contractors for the company, carrying out the brilliant day-to-day service that customers pay for, but who do not in any way share in its vast $75 billion of equity.[42,43]

Of all those Uber has managed to anger—regulators, cabbies, riders—it has done worst by its own drivers. Treated as contractors, not employees, drivers have complained that they can't make enough money under Uber's pricing system. They have protested the service's constantly changing rules. They've been frustrated when no one at Uber has helped to resolve problems quickly. At best, Kalanick seemed to ignore them, and at worst he intimated they'd be eventually replaced by autonomous vehicles. By the start of 2017, the company recognized it had a problem. Only a quarter of the people who'd signed up to drive for Uber were still doing so a year later, according to news reports.[44]

In May 2018, Uber and Lyft drivers staged massive protests and strikes in response to low wages and lack of pricing transparency for drivers. The protests were held across a number of Uber's biggest markets, including San Francisco, London, and New York, and occurred just days before Uber went public. (Uber, it should be noted, has yet to make a profit in its 10-year history.)

The pressures workers experience in the gig economy bring up important questions around workers' rights in the digital age. Should workers in the delivery companies utilized by Amazon, for example, be eligible for sick pay, holiday pay, and the national minimum wage? The GMB union, which represents the drivers used by Amazon in the U.K., believe so, and have taken legal action to dispute Amazon's classification of these workers as "self-employed."[45]

> The day to day reality for many of our members who deliver packages for Amazon is unrealistic targets, slogging their guts out only to have deductions made from their pay when those targets aren't met and being told they're self-employed without the freedom that affords. Companies like Amazon and their delivery companies can't have it both ways—they can't decide they want all of the benefits of having an employee, but refuse to give those employees the pay and rights they're entitled to (sic). Guaranteed hours, holiday pay, sick pay, pension contributions are not privileges companies can dish out when they fancy. They are the legal right of all UK workers, and that's what we're asking the courts to rule on.[46]

Uber faced a similar lawsuit, which argued drivers should be classified as employees. The drivers won, but Uber has appealed the ruling.

Yet another troubling finding related to the employment dynamics of several Silicon Valley companies is the working conditions endured by employees, particularly those whose products and services rely on large numbers of manufacturing and warehouse staff. Amazon's fulfillment centers are amongst the most prolific offenders, with charges ranging from "intolerable working conditions," to penalizations for sick days, and wages so low that employees have been seen camping outside.[47] Conditions inside Amazon's facilities have been documented by journalists and undercover reporters, including James Bloodworth, who worked in an Amazon warehouse as part of his research for *Hired: Six Months Undercover in Low-Wage Britain.* Bloodworth found not only were Amazon employees regularly injured on the job, but also that fulfillment demands necessitated they work impossibly long hours and not take scheduled breaks. In order to meet Amazon's productivity requirements, some employees urinated in bottles, rather than take bathroom breaks and risk penalization for missing their targets, Bloodworth reported.[48] Former Amazon employee Vickie Shannon Allen recounts her experience working for the company in a series of videos posted to YouTube, in which she chronicles the back injury she suffered due to faulty equipment and subsequent abuses by Amazon, which included sending her home without workers compensation and eventually dropping her medical coverage. In the months that followed, Allen lost her home, was forced to live out of her car, and would go days without eating.[49]

Stories similar to Allen's are plentiful, as are legal filings against the company related to workers compensation and unsafe working conditions. In 2018, Amazon's U.S. warehouses "were listed on the National Council for Occupational Safety and Health's 'dirty dozen' list of most dangerous places to work."[50] Reporter Michael Sainato explains the reason for the escalating hazardous working conditions, injuries, and harm come back to "Amazon's emphasis on fulfilling a high demand of orders [which] has resulted in unsafe working conditions for its warehouse employees."[51] A similar dynamic has ensued at Tesla, where long hours, high stress, infrequent breaks, and production targets have led many workers to leave and/or take legal action against the company for injuries and unsafe working conditions. In 2018, the company came under investigation by the Division of Occupational Safety and Health to determine whether it had incorrectly reported safety issues and injuries, after charges were leveled that Tesla had mislabeled employee injuries as personal medical cases rather than work-related injuries.[52]

Such examples illustrate that the financial, social, and human consequences of alternative work go far beyond the obvious, important problem of making ends meet. Injuries, deteriorating mental health, and decreased worker protections are each central to the rise of the bifurcated job market and its reliance on part-time, contracted, and low-wage workers.

The Haves and the Have Nots

As of early 2019, Amazon's CEO Jeff Bezos ranked as the world's richest person, with an estimated net worth of $112 billion. Bill Gates ranked second with $90 billion; Mark Zuckerberg fifth with $71 billion. Of the top 26 places on the list, 11 were tech executives or VCs.[53] Those same 26 people, according to Oxfam's annual inequality report, now control the same amount of wealth as 3.8 billion people.[54] (The previous year, that number was 42.) Let that sink in for a second, because it's really important we all agree how bizarre and tragically unequal these numbers are. Twenty-six. Compared to 3,800,000,000. A group the size of a kindergarten classroom currently controls the same amount of wealth as half the planet's population. Regardless of what you think about how these 26 people spend, save, or distribute their money, the fact that such a small group has been allowed to accumulate such extreme wealth is hugely problematic. Perhaps nothing further needs to be said to illustrate the tragedy of wealth concentration amongst executives and the rest of the world's population, or the increasing role tech corporations and their executives play in controlling that wealth. (Just try to stop me, though; I find myself fueled by both a deep revulsion and a lot of coffee.)

If you were to read up on global prosperity—if you do, I cannot recommend Hans Rosling's book *Factfulness* highly enough—you would discover that, all in all, the world is vastly improving. Our achievements over the past several decades alone include: improved education for women and children, markedly fewer human rights violations, increased life expectancy, fewer wars, health improvements across a number of fronts, greater access to water and electricity, and the uptake of life-saving vaccinations. We have also reduced the proportion of people living in extreme poverty by almost half. Indeed, with the exception of impending environmental catastrophe, we're doing quite well on the majority of challenges we face as a species, particularly economic growth.

Explain these happy findings to someone living in rural West Virginia, however, where both labor force participation and job growth are among the lowest in the U.S. and living standards have dramatically decreased over the past two decades, and you'll probably be met with righteous skepticism. This is because the U.S. is, according to the 2016 Poverty and Inequality Report, "the most unequal rich country on earth, a conclusion that holds equally for absolute or relative measurement."[55] For good reason, over two-thirds of U.S. and European citizens are worried about current levels of economic inequality.[56] Despite economic growth, increased democracy, and better health outcomes globally, in a number of Western countries, including the U.S. and U.K., both wealth and income inequality have become far more pronounced. The misrepresentation in these countries that the economy is healthy because the markets are performing well can only be touted for so long. A booming stock market doesn't matter to the masses of people who can't afford to buy stock, let alone groceries or healthcare.

The concentration of wealth identified in Oxfam's inequality report illustrates the problem of increased capital held by a small elite, and the economic struggles faced by the majority of the population. In 2017, a UN report on poverty and human rights found that more than 40 million Americans were living in poverty (which equates to 12.7% of the U.S. population), half of whom were considered to be living in deep poverty, meaning their income was "below one-half of the poverty threshold."[57] A 2019 report by the National Low Income Housing Coalition (NLIHC) illustrates why this might be the case for so many Americans. NLIHC found that in order to afford a modest 2-bedroom apartment in every one of the 50 states across the U.S. required an income of at least twice the federal minimum wage.[58] In states like Hawaii, California, and Massachusetts, the cost of a basic apartment required an income approximately five times the federal minimum wage, meaning someone in Hawaii making $7.25 an hour would need to work 3.6 full-time minimum wage jobs to afford an apartment in the state.[59] In the U.K., poverty statistics are even worse. The Joseph Rowntree Foundation puts the poverty rate in London at 27% and the U.K. national average at 21%. The report also showed the number of people living in poverty in the U.K. had more than doubled between 2005 and 2016, from 2.2 million to 4.5 million people. As in the U.S., the majority of these people (3.8 million in the U.K.) are actively employed, meaning that 1 in 8 workers in the U.K. live in poverty, often while working more than one job.[60]

Poverty is a notoriously hard measure to calculate, given the differences in costs of living across the world. One of the most useful methods to determine poverty thresholds is the Supplemental Poverty Measure, which defines poverty as "the lack of economic resources for consumption of basic needs."[61] This takes into account the cost of living in different states, which includes housing, taxes, food, clothing, utilities, and government assistance programs, all of which may be appreciably higher or lower than the national average.[62] Interestingly, the state with the highest supplemental poverty level in the U.S.—by a longshot—is California, with an estimated 23.8% of its residents living at or below the poverty line.[63] California, which has the fifth largest economy in the world and the largest in the U.S., ranks 46th in the nation for opportunity, 43rd for fiscal stability, and dead last for the quality of life, according to McKinsey's and U.S. News's Best States Project, which ranks states across eight categories using 77 metrics.[64]

The extreme wealth and extreme poverty in California illustrate the problem of concentrating money in a small number of hands (or bitcoin accounts, or mattresses, or wherever they put it these days), as well as the fact that trickle-down economics does not work. The pain of wealth concentration, according to Anand Giridharadas, is an issue that bridges political divisions and is felt equally among both conservative and liberal voters.

> Millions of Americans, on the left and the right, feel one thing in common: that the game is rigged against people like them. Perhaps this is why we hear constant condemnation of 'the system,' for it is the system that people expect to turn fortuitous developments into societal progress. Instead, the system—in America and around the world—has been organized to siphon the gains from innovation upward, such that the fortunes of the world's billionaires now grow at more than double the pace of everyone else's.[65]

Another compelling warning against the vast and swelling economic inequality in the U.S. comes neither from an economist nor a social activist, but from billionaire Nick Hanauer, the first non-family investor in Amazon. In an open letter to his fellow billionaires in POLITICO Magazine, Hanauer explains the dangers of allowing extreme amounts of wealth to become concentrated in a small subset of the population.

> [L]et's speak frankly to each other. I'm not the smartest guy you've ever met, or the hardest-working. I was a mediocre student. I'm not technical at all—I can't write a word of code. What sets me apart, I think, is a tolerance for risk and an intuition about what will happen in the future. Seeing where things are headed is the essence of entrepreneurship. And what do I see in our future now? I see pitchforks. At the same time that people like you and me are thriving beyond the dreams of any plutocrats in history, the rest of the country—the 99.99 percent—is lagging far behind. The divide between the haves and have-nots is getting worse really, really fast. In 1980, the top 1 percent controlled about 8 percent of U.S. national income. The bottom 50 shared about 18 percent. Today the top 1 percent share about 20 percent; the bottom 50 percent, just 12 percent. But the problem isn't that we have inequality. Some inequality is intrinsic to any high-functioning capitalist economy. The problem is that inequality is at historically high levels and getting worse every day. Our country is rapidly becoming less a capitalist society and more a feudal society. Unless our policies change dramatically, the middle class will disappear.

Hanauer points to an essential truth that corporations everywhere will soon discover the hard way: that economic inequality in the U.S. is gutting the middle class and, by extension, its customer base. Citing Henry Ford's decision to pay his workers lavishly above their market value, Hanauer observes that if you demolish the middle class, there will be no one left to buy home assistants and smart refrigerators. Instead, he advocates for "middle-out" economics, which he describes as a "long-overdue rebuttal to the trickle-down economics worldview that has become economic orthodoxy across party lines—and has so screwed the American middle class and our economy generally."

Middle-out economics rejects the old misconception that an economy is a perfectly efficient, mechanistic system and embraces the much more accurate idea of an economy as a complex ecosystem made up of real people who are dependent on one another. Which is why the fundamental law of capitalism must be: If workers have more money, businesses have more customers. Which makes middle-class consumers, not rich businesspeople like us, the true job creators. Which means a thriving middle class is the source of American prosperity, not a consequence of it. The middle class creates us rich people, not the other way around.

Finally, Hanauer ends with an extrapolation of the existing economic paradigm:

> If we don't do something to fix the glaring inequities in this economy, the pitchforks are going to come for us. No society can sustain this kind of rising inequality. In fact, there is no example in human history where wealth accumulated like this and the pitchforks didn't eventually come out. You show me a highly unequal society, and I will show you a police state. Or an uprising. There are no counterexamples. None. It's not if, it's when.[66]

Hanauer recognizes a series of truths that other billionaires, such as Chris Hughes, one of Facebook's co-founders, are starting to realize: not only do people suffer in an economically unequal society, but there is also very real danger inherent in unchecked economic inequality. In 2019, Hanauer and Hughes, along with 16 other billionaires, wrote an open letter to U.S. 2020 presidential candidates in support of a wealth tax on America's 75,000 wealthiest families. The group argued that higher taxes on the ultra wealthy would both constitute the ethical course of action and could also "help address the climate crisis, improve the economy, improve health outcomes, fairly create opportunity, and strengthen our democratic freedoms."[67]

Though pitchforks may not be the weapons of choice, the likelihood of uprisings in the face of grossly uneven wealth distribution is historically substantiated. In Branko Milanovic's book *Global Inequality*, the economist and professor explains that inequality is cyclical, as are the revolts against it that almost always result. Milanovic uses the example of the industrial revolution, in which wealth vastly increased for some and was depressed for others, creating a "divergence of paths [that] widened global inequality."[68] According to Milanovic, the more unequal a society becomes, the greater chance there is for social unrest, riots, revolution, and war. This has been the case in numerous historical uprisings, including the French Revolution, American Revolution, and even as far back as ancient Greece, where Aristotle famously observed "poverty is the parent of revolution and crime."[69] The research of historian Walter Scheider, author of *The Great Leveler: Violence and the History of Inequality from the Stone Age to the Twenty-First Century*, also indicates that, historically, extreme economic inequality is almost always followed by war, uprisings, or social violence.[70]

Let's take Amazon as an example. On one hand, customers get their products at lightning speed, investors and stockholders happily watch the company's shares skyrocket, and Jeff Bezos gets to sit around one of his six mansions with $112 billion in his bank account. On the other hand, the working conditions at a number of its facilities have been exposed to be subpar, to say the least, and in some cases downright dangerous. One employee called Amazon's warehouse an "isolating colony of hell," another said warehouse staff were "treated like robots."[71] Employees sleep on the ground outside of fulfilment centers, skip bathroom breaks, and pee in jars to meet their targets; some sustain life-changing injuries in the process. Many others threaten or commit suicide. Between 2013 and 2018, journalists Max Zahn and Sharif Paget report that employees called 911 "189 times for suicide attempts, suicidal thoughts, and other mental-health episodes."[72] Half of the company's employees make less than $28,446 a year and, according to reports, one-third of Amazon employees in Arizona are on food stamps. By all accounts, Amazon does not take care of its factory employees. In November 2018, following significant public scrutiny, Amazon raised its minimum wage to $15/hour. The same month, presumably in order to balance its books, the company ended its Variable Compensation Plan, which offered employees attendance and productivity bonuses in the form of stock incentives. At Whole Foods, which Amazon owns, employee hours were cut significantly following the wage increase.[73] As Annie Lowrey reports, Amazon has also fought to keep its workers from unionizing.

Since its founding nearly three decades ago, Amazon has again and again sought to prevent the unionization of its workforce, a development that would likely bolster wages and improve working conditions. Amazon has reportedly shut down operations where workers were seeking to organize, fired employees advocating for unionization, hired law firms to counter organizing drives at warehouses around the country, and given managers instructions on how to union-bust.[74]

Whether employees are eventually able to unionize or not, how long would you expect them to continue accepting the circumstances in which they find themselves, working for the world's richest man, under some of the poorest conditions?

Lowrey goes on to say that Bezos is hardly to blame for the wealth he has accumulated and should not be criticized for his choice not to donate to philanthropic causes. (Bezos, famously, "unlike Gates or Zuckerberg, has given away only a tiny fraction of his fortune", Lowrey explains.) What Lowrey argues is to blame, is in fact a series of policy failures at the very highest levels of government.

> [W]ealth concentration is bad for the economy and the country itself, and the government has failed to counter it. Rising inequality fuels political polarization and partisan gridlock. It slows economic growth, and implies a lack of competition that fuels economic sclerosis. It makes the government less responsive to the demands of normal people, potentially putting our very democracy at risk. Bezos's extraordinary fortune shows that the game is rigged.[75]

Experts agree that the policies that have birthed such profound inequality must be rectified if we are to avoid potential civic unrest. New York City Mayor Bill De Blasio has argued repeatedly that the hypercapitalist economic system in the U.S. is rigged to benefit the rich and contended that too much money has been "in the wrong hands" for too long.

> Look what's happening... all over the country: millions upon millions of people literally can barely make ends meet. Working people—who are working one job, two jobs—working harder than ever, working longer hours than ever, the pace of our lives gets tougher and tougher and people

get less and less back. Why? Because the 1% really has rigged the system, including [Trump's] recent tax law, that gave a huge windfall to the corporations and the wealthy. This is systematic… this has been an agenda, from Reagan's administration right on through to Trump's: to take money from working people and give it to the 1%. So when I say there's plenty of money in this country, it's just in the wrong hands, it means to say, we need policies that give back to working people, like guaranteeing healthcare for all. It's clear to me why it's wrong, because government policies gave the 1% every conceivable leg up. This was not by accident, this was an agenda, it was systematic.[76]

The U.S. Democratic party's 2020 Presidential race has been largely structured by the narrative of economic inequality; candidates like Elizabeth Warren, Bernie Sanders, and Pete Buttigieg, have campaigned on the message that the corporate-political game is rigged in favor of the rich, with Warren drawing attention to the central role tech companies have played in furthering economic inequality.

The problem of mounting economic inequality is larger than Silicon Valley. The system that has allowed such deep concentrations of money to become lodged in the pockets of so few—mostly white, mostly male— executives is not the tech industry's fault. As the world increasingly shifts to a knowledge- and information-based economy we must readily acknowledge that this is where the majority of wealth and income will continue to be diverted. The economic advantages and vast wealth of both the industry's executives and its corporations have become more pronounced every year. In 2006, only one tech corporation, Microsoft, ranked among the world's most valuable six companies; by 2016, five of the top six spots were claimed by tech companies (Apple, Alphabet, Microsoft, Amazon, and Facebook). Information is the most valuable resource in the world; it is the future of the economy; and it is increasingly held by a very small number of obscenely wealthy executives and stockholders.

A solid first step would be to take off the rose-colored glasses that have led us to believe tech companies are different than other multinational corporations. As Scott Galloway contends, we have found ourselves "in the midst of a dramatic market failure, one in which the government has been lulled by the public's fascination with big tech."[77] A second measure is to ensure billionaires (and millionaires and corporations, for that matter) are appropriately taxed and regulated. Lowrey points out that because Bezos "takes paltry salary, in relative terms... his gains are subject to capital-gains taxes, which top out at just 20 percent; like Warren Buffett, it is possible he pays effective tax rates lower than his secretary does." According to a report from the Institute on Taxation and Economic Policy (ITEP), despite making hundreds of millions and, in Amazon's case billions of dollars in profits, several tech companies not only didn't pay any federal corporate taxes, but actually got tax rebates. Amazon netted over $10.8 billion in profits in 2018, paid no federal corporate income tax, and received a rebate of $129 million. IBM similarly earned $500 million in income in the U.S., paid no federal tax, and received a tax rebate of $342 million, making their effective rate a staggering −68%. Netflix also had a negative tax rate: they made $856 million in profits and received $22 million in tax rebates.[78] In addition to tax breaks for the world's wealthiest companies and the billionaires who run them, tech companies like Facebook, Apple, and Google have been criticized for avoiding corporate taxes, which they accomplish largely by shifting profits to lower-tax regions, such as Ireland (Amazon moves its profits as well, but records its European sales in Luxembourg).[79] As Galloway notes, Google paid more in fines in the E.U. in 2018 than it did in taxes.

* * *

Inequality is not only associated with acute financial stress at an individual level, it is also correlated with political polarization,[80] violence, homicide, decreased health and mental health outcomes.[81] Researchers have repeatedly demonstrated how capitalist values, when taken to an extreme, directly contribute to a decline in social wellbeing, a decrease in social capital, and an increase in psychopathology throughout society.[82,83] These findings hold true not only for those on the losing end of the economy, but everyone in an economically inequitable society, even its richest citizens. Inequality.org explains that high levels of inequality "negatively affect the health of even the affluent," as inequality decreases social cohesion, which "leads to more stress, fear, and insecurity for everyone."[84] The social environment of modern industrialized hypercapitalist countries, according to researcher and family medicine practitioner Brandon Hidaka, has become significantly depleted in countries such as the U.S., which are increasingly competitive, threatening, and socially isolating.[85] Unequal, competitive societies tend to abandon interest in the collective good, while in more equal societies, such as Sweden and Japan, members of the community are more likely to help one another, contribute to common social goals, such as volunteering, and support initiatives that benefit the population as a whole.[86] In their book, *The Inner Level*, epidemiologists Kate Pickett and Richard Wilkinson show that highly unequal societies suffer far worse outcomes in nearly every measurable category, including happiness. They conclude that happiness comes down not to how much money a country has, but how its wealth is distributed.

Everyone deserves to have a job and, as Elizabeth Warren is fond of saying, "one job should be enough." Everyone deserves to make a fair income, access basic human rights, like education and health care, have agency over their decisions, and contribute to the conversation about where the world is going. The richest countries in the world should not be the most unequal. A more equitable distribution of wealth and opportunity is the only answer to what is fast becoming the most important existential question in America and abroad: why do the rich keep getting richer while economic inequality worsens? Likewise, if we are to fix the social impacts born of our technological products, Silicon Valley must reconsider the individualist, libertarian ideals that motivate it.

Notes

1. Frey, C. B., & Osborne, M. A. (2017). The Future of Employment: How Susceptible are Jobs to Computerisation? *Technological Forecasting and Social Change, 114*, 254–280. https://doi.org/10.1016/j.techfore.2016.08.019
2. Cukier, K. N. (2018, April 18). Technology and Its Discontents. *The Economist*. Retrieved from https://www.economist.com/open-future/2018/04/16/technology-and-its-discontents

3. Abdu, A. Z. (2016, November 22). Robotics and Artificial Intelligence: Mankind's Latest Evolution. *Newsweek Middle East*. Retrieved from http://newsweekme.com/robotics-artificial-intelligence-mankinds-latest-evolution/

4. Partington, R. (2017, December 28). UK's Poorest to Fare Worst in Age of Automation, Thinktank Warns. *The Guardian*. Retrieved from https://www.theguardian.com/technology/2017/dec/28/uks-poorest-to-fare-worst-in-age-of-automation-thinktank-warns

5. Acemoğlu, D., & Restrepo, P. (2017, April 10). Robots and Jobs: Evidence from the US. Retrieved September 19, 2018, from *VoxEU.org* website: https://voxeu.org/article/robots-and-jobs-evidence-us

6. Tarnoff, B. (2017, September 5). *Interview with Ben Tarnoff* (K. Cook, Interviewer).

7. Partington, R. (2017, December 28). UK's Poorest to Fare Worst in Age of Automation, Thinktank Warns. *The Guardian*. Retrieved from https://www.theguardian.com/technology/2017/dec/28/uks-poorest-to-fare-worst-in-age-of-automation-thinktank-warns

8. Marx, P. (2018, May 10). The Growing Backlash to Elite-Focused Automation. Retrieved September 16, 2018, from *Paris Marx* website: https://medium.com/@parismarx/the-growing-backlash-to-elite-focused-automation-2bb88406386b

9. European Commission. (2017). *Attitudes Towards the Impact of Digitisation and Automation on Daily Life*. Retrieved from https://ec.europa.eu/digital-single-market/en/news/attitudes-towards-impact-digitisation-and-automation-daily-life

10. Smith, A., & Anderson, M. (2017). *Automation in Everyday Life*. Retrieved from Pew Research Center website: http://www.pewinternet.org/2017/10/04/automation-in-everyday-life/

11. Gallup & Northeastern University. (2018). *Optimism and Anxiety: Views on the Impact of Artificial Intelligence and Higher Education's Response*. Retrieved from https://news.gallup.com/reports/226475/gallup-northeastern-university-artificial-intelligence-report-2018.aspx

12. Smith, A., & Anderson, M. (2017). *Automation in Everyday Life*. Retrieved from Pew Research Center website: http://www.pewinternet.org/2017/10/04/automation-in-everyday-life/

13. Winick, E. (2017, December 27). While U.S. Workers Fear Automation, Swedish Employees Welcome It. Retrieved January 23, 2019, from *MIT Technology Review* website: https://www.technologyreview.com/the-download/609857/while-us-workers-fear-automation-swedish-employees-welcome-it/

14. Kasriel, S. (2017, August 14). 6 Ways to Make Sure AI Creates Jobs for All and Not the Few. Retrieved September 19, 2018, from World Economic Forum website: https://www.weforum.org/agenda/2017/08/ways-to-ensure-ai-robots-create-jobs-for-all/

15. Acemoğlu, D., & Restrepo, P. (2017, April 10). Robots and Jobs: Evidence from the US. Retrieved September 19, 2018, from *VoxEU.org* website: https://voxeu.org/article/robots-and-jobs-evidence-us

16. Kollewe, J. (2018, July 16). Artificial Intelligence will be Net UK Jobs Creator, Finds Report. *The Guardian*. Retrieved from https://www.theguardian.com/technology/2018/jul/17/artificial-intelligence-will-be-net-uk-jobs-creator-finds-report

17. Harari, Y. N. (2017). *Homo Deus: A Brief History of Tomorrow* (pp. 363–369). London: Vintage.

18. Mahdawi, A. (2017, June 26). What Jobs will Still be Around in 20 Years? Read This to Prepare Your Future. *The Guardian*. Retrieved from https://www.theguardian.com/us-news/2017/jun/26/jobs-future-automation-robots-skills-creative-health

19. Adams, T. (2018, July 29). The Robot will See You Now: Could Computers Take Over Medicine Entirely? *The Observer*. Retrieved from https://www.theguardian.com/technology/2018/jul/29/the-robot-will-see-you-now-could-computers-take-over-medicine-entirely

20. Abdu, A. Z. (2016, November 22). Robotics and Artificial Intelligence: Mankind's Latest Evolution. *Newsweek Middle East*. Retrieved from http://newsweekme.com/robotics-artificial-intelligence-mankinds-latest-evolution/

21. Ibid.

22. Partington, R. (2017, December 28). UK's Poorest to Fare Worst in Age of Automation, Thinktank Warns. *The Guardian*. Retrieved from https://www.theguardian.com/technology/2017/dec/28/uks-poorest-to-fare-worst-in-age-of-automation-thinktank-warns

23. Muro, M., Maxim, R., & Whiton, J. (2019). *Automation and Artificial Intelligence: How Machines are Affecting People and Places* (pp. 1–108). Retrieved from Brookings Institute website: https://www.brookings.edu/wp-content/uploads/2019/01/2019.01_BrookingsMetro_Automation-AI_Report_Muro-Maxim-Whiton-FINAL-version.pdf

24. Ding, L., Leigh, E. W., & Harker, P. (2018). *Automation and Regional Employment in the Third Federal Reserve District*. Retrieved from Federal Reserve Bank of Philadelphia website: https://www.philadelphiafed.org/-/media/community-development/publications/special-reports/automation-and-regional-employment.pdf?la=en

25. Kasriel, S. (2017, August 14). 6 Ways to Make Sure AI Creates Jobs for All and Not the Few. Retrieved September 19, 2018, from World Economic Forum website: https://www.weforum.org/agenda/2017/08/ways-to-ensure-ai-robots-create-jobs-for-all/

26. Acemoglu, D., & Restrepo, P. (2017). *Robots and Jobs: Evidence from US Labor Markets* (Working Paper No. 23285). https://doi.org/10.3386/w23285

27. Kasriel, S. (2017, August 14). 6 Ways to Make Sure AI Creates Jobs for All and Not the Few. Retrieved September 19, 2018, from World Economic Forum website: https://www.weforum.org/agenda/2017/08/ways-to-ensure-ai-robots-create-jobs-for-all/

28. Cukier, K. N. (2018, April 18). Technology and Its Discontents. *The Economist*. Retrieved from https://www.economist.com/open-future/2018/04/16/technology-and-its-discontents

29. The Economic Intelligence Unit. (2018). *The Automation Readiness Index 2018: Executive Summary* [Executive Summary]. Retrieved from http://automationreadiness.eiu.com/

30. Hyman, L. (2018, August 20). It's Not Technology That's Disrupting Our Jobs. *The New York Times*. Retrieved from https://www.nytimes.com/2018/08/18/opinion/technology/technology-gig-economy.html

31. Rushe, D. (2018, March 9). US Economy Adds 313,000 Jobs in Strong Monthly Display but Wage Growth Slows. *The Guardian*. Retrieved from https://www.theguardian.com/business/2018/mar/09/us-economy-february-jobs-wage-growth

32. Autor, D. H., Levy, F., & Murnane, R. J. (2003). The Skill Content of Recent Technological Change: An Empirical Exploration. *The Quarterly Journal of Economics, 118*(4), 1279–1333. https://doi.org/10.1162/003355303322552801

33. Harari, Y. N. (2017). *Homo Deus: A Brief History of Tomorrow* (p. 17). London: Vintage.

34. Malik, O. (2016, November 28). Silicon Valley has an Empathy Vacuum. *The New Yorker*. Retrieved from https://www.newyorker.com/business/currency/silicon-valley-has-an-empathy-vacuum

35. Irwin, N. (2018, June 18). If the Robots Come for Our Jobs, What Should the Government Do? *The New York Times*. Retrieved from https://www.nytimes.com/2018/06/12/upshot/if-the-robots-come-for-our-jobs-what-should-the-government-do.html

36. Galloway, S. (2018, July 24). *Amazon Raking in Billions, Some Employees Relying on Food Stamps* (S. Ruhle, Interviewer). Retrieved from https://www.msnbc.com/stephanie-ruhle/watch/amazon-raking-in-billions-some-employees-relying-on-food-stamps-1284302915600

37. *Contingent and Alternative Employment Arrangements Summary.* (n.d.). Retrieved from https://www.bls.gov/news.release/conemp.nr0.htm

38. Boro, M. (2018, July 11). The Gig Economy is Bigger than US Government Data Makes It Look. Retrieved August 19, 2018, from *Quartz at Work* website: https://qz.com/work/1324292/gig-economy-data-why-the-us-department-of-labor-numbers-are-misleading/

39. U.S. Federal Reserve. (2018). *Report on the Economic Well-being of U.S. Households in 2017.* Retrieved from https://www.federalreserve.gov/consumerscommunities/shed.htm

40. Upwork. (2017). *Freelancing in America: 2017 Survey.* Retrieved from https://www.upwork.com/i/freelancing-in-america/2017/

41. Bergen, M., & Eidelson, J. (2018, July 25). Inside Google's Shadow Workforce. *Bloomberg.Com.* Retrieved from https://www.bloomberg.com/news/articles/2018-07-25/inside-google-s-shadow-workforce

42. Galloway, S. (2018, February 8). The Case for Breaking up Amazon, Apple, Facebook and Google. Retrieved August 31, 2018, from *Esquire* website: https://www.esquire.com/news-politics/a15895746/bust-big-tech-silicon-valley/

43. Reddy, A. (2019, May 10). How Uber's $75.5 Billion Valuation Stacks Up. *MSN.* Retrieved from https://www.msn.com/en-us/money/top-stocks/how-ubers-dollar755-billion-valuation-stacks-up/ar-AABbpcl

44. Hempel, J. (2018, April 19). Can this Man Help Uber Recover from the Travis Kalanick Era? *Wired.* Retrieved from https://www.wired.com/story/uber-move-slow-test-things/

45. Butler, S., & Smithers, R. (2018, June 3). Amazon Delivery Firms Face Legal Action over Workers' Rights. *The Guardian.* Retrieved from https://www.theguardian.com/technology/2018/jun/04/amazon-delivery-firms-face-legal-action-over-workers-rights

46. Ibid.

47. Osborne, H. (2016, December 12). Amazon Accused of "Intolerable Conditions" at Scottish Warehouse. *The Guardian.* Retrieved from https://www.theguardian.com/technology/2016/dec/11/amazon-accused-of-intolerable-conditions-at-scottish-warehouse

48. Liao, S. (2018, April 16). Amazon Warehouse Workers Skip Bathroom Breaks to Keep Their Jobs, Says Report. *The Verge*. Retrieved from https://www.theverge.com/2018/4/16/17243026/amazon-warehouse-jobs-worker-conditions-bathroom-breaks

49. Burke, C. (2018, August 2). Vickie Shannon Allen, Homeless Amazon Employee: 5 Fast Facts. Retrieved August 30, 2018, from *Heavy.com* website: https://heavy.com/news/2018/08/vickie-shannon-allen-homeless-amazon-employee/

50. Sainato, M. (2018, July 30). Accidents at Amazon: Workers Left to Suffer after Warehouse Injuries. *The Guardian*. Retrieved from https://www.theguardian.com/technology/2018/jul/30/accidents-at-amazon-workers-left-to-suffer-after-warehouse-injuries

51. Ibid.

52. Evans, W., & Jeong Perry, A. (2018, April 16). Tesla Says Its Factory is Safer. But It Left Injuries Off the Books. *Reveal*. Retrieved from https://www.revealnews.org/article/tesla-says-its-factory-is-safer-but-it-left-injuries-off-the-books/

53. The World's Billionaires. (2019, March 5). Retrieved January 23, 2019, from *Forbes* website: https://www.forbes.com/billionaires/list/

54. Oxfam International. (2019). *Public Good or Private Wealth?* (pp. 1–106). Retrieved from https://www.oxfam.org/en/research/public-good-or-private-wealth

55. Grusky, D. B., Mattingly, M. J., & Varner, C. E. (2016). *The Poverty and Inequality Report 2016*. Retrieved from Stanford Center on Poverty and Inequality website: https://inequality.stanford.edu/sites/default/files/Pathways-SOTU-2016.pdf

56. As inequality grows, so does the political influence of the rich. (2018, July 21). *The Economist*. Retrieved from https://www.economist.com/finance-and-economics/2018/07/21/as-inequality-grows-so-does-the-political-influence-of-the-rich

57. Alston, P. (2017). *Statement on Visit to the USA, by Professor Philip Alston, United Nations Special Rapporteur on Extreme Poverty and Human Rights*. Retrieved from United Nations Human Rights Office of the High Commissioner website: https://www.ohchr.org/EN/NewsEvents/Pages/DisplayNews.aspx?NewsID=22533&LangID=E

58. National Low Income Housing Coalition. (2019). *Out Of Reach*. Retrieved from https://reports.nlihc.org/sites/default/files/oor/OOR_2019.pdf

59. Paddison, L. (2019, June 18). Grim New Report Shows Rent is Unaffordable in Every State. Retrieved 24 June 2019, from *HuffPost* website: https://www.huffpost.com/entry/rent-afford-state-salary-housing_n_5cb6e4aee4b098b9a2dc8297

60. Tinson, A., Ayrton, C., Barker, K., Barry Born, T., Aldridge, H., & Kenway, P. (2016). *Monitoring Poverty and Social Exclusion 2016.* Retrieved from Joseph Rowntree Foundation website: https://www.jrf. org.uk/report/monitoring-poverty-and-social-exclusion-2016

61. Jacob, A. (n.d.). The Supplemental Poverty Measure: A Better Measure for Poverty in America? *UC Davis Center for Poverty Research, 1*(6). Retrieved from https://poverty.ucdavis.edu/policy-brief/supplemental-poverty-measure-better-measure-poverty-america

62. Short, K. (2015). *The Research Supplemental Poverty Measure* (No. hdl:SSDS/11309). Retrieved from U.S. Census Bureau website: http://dataverse.ucdavis.edu/dvn/dv/CPR/faces/study/StudyPage.xhtml?globalId=hdl:SSDS/11309

63. Berlinger, J. (2012, November 15). New Census Data on Poverty Rates Yields Some Pretty Shocking Results. *Business Insider.* Retrieved from https://www.businessinsider.com/new-census-data-on-poverty-rates-yields-some-pretty-shocking-results-2012-11

64. U.S. News & McKinsey. (2017). *Where Does California Place in the U.S. News Best States Rankings?* Retrieved from https://www.usnews.com/news/best-states/california

65. Giridharadas, A. (2018). *Winners Take All: The Elite Charade of Changing the World* (1st ed., 1st Printing ed., pp. 4–5). New York: Knopf.

66. Hanauer, N. (2014, August). The Pitchforks are Coming… For Us Plutocrats. *POLITICO Magazine.* Retrieved from https://www.politico.com/magazine/story/2014/06/the-pitchforks-are-coming-for-us-pluto-crats-108014.html

67. Bowditch, L. J., Bowditch, R. S., Disney, A., Eldridge, S., English, S. R., Gund, A., … Soros, G. (2019, June 24). *An Open Letter to the 2020 Presidential Candidates: It's Time to Tax Us More.* Retrieved from https://medium.com/@letterforawealthtax/an-open-letter-to-the-2020-presidential-candidates-its-time-to-tax-us-more-6eb3a548b2fe

68. Milanovic, B. (2016). *Global Inequality* (p. 119). Cambridge, MA: Harvard University Press.

69. Archer, D. (2013, September 4). Could America's Wealth Gap Lead to a Revolt? Retrieved September 10, 2018, from *Forbes* website: https://www.forbes.com/sites/dalearcher/2013/09/04/could-americas-wealth-gap-lead-to-a-revolt/

70. Scheidel, W. (2017). *The Great Leveler*. Princeton, NJ: Princeton University Press.
71. Paget, S., & Zahn, M. (2019, March 11). 'Colony of Hell': 911 Calls From Inside Amazon Warehouses. *The Daily Beast*. Retrieved from https://www.thedailybeast.com/amazon-the-shocking-911-calls-from-inside-its-warehouses
72. Ibid.
73. Sainato, M. (2019, March 6). Whole Foods Cuts Workers' Hours after Amazon Introduces Minimum Wage. *The Guardian*. Retrieved from https://www.theguardian.com/us-news/2019/mar/06/whole-foods-amazon-cuts-minimum-wage-workers-hours-changes
74. Lowrey, A. (2018, August 1). Jeff Bezos's $150 Billion Fortune is a Policy Failure. Retrieved August 17, 2018, from *The Atlantic* website: https://www.theatlantic.com/business/archive/2018/08/the-problem-with-bezos-billions/566552/
75. Ibid.
76. De Blasio, B. (2019, January 12). *De Blasio on his Plan to Redistribute Wealth* (J. Tapper, Interviewer) [CNN]. Retrieved from https://www.cnn.com/videos/politics/2019/01/13/sotu-de-blasio-wealth.cnn
77. Galloway, S. (2018, February 8). The Case for Breaking up Amazon, Apple, Facebook and Google. Retrieved August 31, 2018, from *Esquire* website: https://www.esquire.com/news-politics/a15895746/bust-big-tech-silicon-valley/
78. Gardner, M., Wamhoff, S., Martellotta, M., & Roque, L. (2019). *Corporate Tax Avoidance Remains Rampant under New Tax Law*. Retrieved from Institute on Taxation and Economic Policy (ITEP) website: https://itep.org/wp-content/uploads/04119-Corporate-Tax-Avoidance-Remains-Rampant-Under-New-Tax-Law_ITEP.pdf
79. Titcomb, J. (2017, November 22). Tech Giants Face Tax Avoidance Crackdown. *The Telegraph*. Retrieved from https://www.telegraph.co.uk/technology/2017/11/22/budget-2017-tech-giants-face-tax-avoidance-crackdown/
80. Stewart, M. (2018, June). The 9.9 Percent is the New American Aristocracy. *The Atlantic*. Retrieved from https://www.theatlantic.com/magazine/archive/2018/06/the-birth-of-a-new-american-aristocracy/559130/
81. Inequality and Health. (n.d.). Retrieved September 17, 2018, from *Inequality.org* website: https://inequality.org/facts/inequality-and-health/

82. Kasser, T., Cohn, S., Kanner, A. D., and Ryan, R. M. (2007). Some Costs of American Corporate Capitalism: A Psychological Exploration of Value and Goal Conflicts. *Psychological Inquiry, 18*, 1–22. https://doi.org/10.1080/10478400701386579

83. Putnam, R. D. (1995). Tuning In, Tuning Out: The Strange Disappearance of Social Capital in America. *PS: Political Science & Politics, 28*, 664–683. https://doi.org/10.2307/420517

84. Inequality and Health. (n.d.). Retrieved September 17, 2018, from *Inequality.org* website: https://inequality.org/facts/inequality-and-health/

85. Hidaka, B. H. (2012). Depression as a Disease of Modernity: Explanations for Increasing Prevalence. *Journal of Affective Disorders, 140*, 205–214. https://doi.org/10.1016/j.jad.2011.12.036

86. Wilkinson, R., & Pickett, K. (2018, June 10). Inequality Breeds Stress and Anxiety. No Wonder so Many Britons are Suffering. *The Guardian.* Retrieved from https://www.theguardian.com/commentisfree/2018/jun/10/inequality-stress-anxiety-britons

8

Mental Health, Relationships & Cognition

Enslave the liberty of but one human being and the liberties of the world are put in peril.
—William Lloyd Garrison

Beyond its wider cultural and social impacts, we are also affected in more individual and personal ways by the technology in our lives. Because the purpose of this book is not to inventory the positive effects of technology, it will have to suffice to recognize that there are significant favorable impacts born of digital technologies. Apps for improving health, platforms for informed discussion, video communication technology, 3D-printed affordable homes (and 3D printed organs, for that matter), research repositories, drones for medical services delivery. There are countless wonderful uses and applications of technology and the companies and people who build them should be celebrated.

We can recognize technology as an incredible force for good, while, at the same time working to mitigate the ways in which it causes harm. While democracy, misinformation, economic inequality, and job displacement encapsulate some of the most important social concerns in

© The Author(s) 2020
K. Cook, *The Psychology of Silicon Valley*,
https://doi.org/10.1007/978-3-030-27364-4_8

relation to technology, the impacts on our health, mental health, cognition, and relationships are among the most pressing challenges we face at a more personal level.

First, Do No Harm

While the mental health effects of tech have, quite rightly, captured the attention of journalists and researchers alike, the physical effects of technology have been relatively less prominent in public discourse. The physical impacts of technology may take considerably longer to materialize, but evidence increasingly points to the need for both awareness and caution.

In 2018, researchers from the University of Toledo found that the blue light emitted from devices such as phones, laptops, and tablets triggers the creation of toxic molecules in the eye's retina. Over time, the light, which has a different, shorter wavelength and more energy than other types of light, can cause permanent damage, such as macular degeneration, which leads to blindness.[1] Other studies have focused on the phenomenon of sleep deprivation as a result of technology. The addictive effects of phones in particular, have led both to less sleep and lower quality sleep.[2,3,4] (The health benefits of sleep and the health impacts of insufficient sleep are wide-ranging and well-documented throughout scholarly research.[5])

A more contentious area of research is the relationship between digital technology and cancer. A large-scale study by the U.S. National Toxicology Program (NTP) exposed rats and mice to a radiofrequency (RF) energy similar to that emitted by mobile phones for two years (a period equivalent to 70 years in humans). The study found "clear evidence" for an increased risk of heart tumors and a "possible risk" of increased brain and adrenal gland tumors in the male rats exposed to RF radiation. Interestingly, the female rats showed no increased risk of developing cancer and all the mice of both genders were fine.[6,7] Research on human subjects has, for obvious reasons, been far more limited. While some studies follow large cohorts and track their phone use and rates of cancer, the majority have looked retrospectively at patients with brain tumors and relied on self-reported phone use to determine correlations between technology and cancer. Throughout these studies, findings have been mixed and the rates and risks of cancer and other impacts remain unclear. A closer look at the history of research around phone radiation and cancer paints a disturbing picture as to why this might be.

In 1993, the Cellular Telecommunications and Internet Association (CTIA) hired epidemiologist George Carlo to investigate the physical risks of cellular phone radiation. At the time, there were neither restrictions nor government safety testing on phones, but a growing number of cases were beginning to be brought against companies alleging the potential harm of mobile devices, particularly an increased risk of cancer. For six years, Carlo acted as chairman of a research initiative called the Wireless Technology Research project (WTR), which carried out over 50 studies and reviewed dozens more. In October 1999, Carlo wrote to CEOs at 32 major tech and telecom companies, including Apple and AT&T, to explain WTR's findings, which included an increased risk of benign tumors, lethal tumors, and genetic damage. In a letter to AT&T CEO Michael Armstrong, Carlo expressed concerns about what he believed to be "an emerging and serious problem concerning wireless phones." In addition to the research findings themselves, Carlo also expressed concern about the disingenuous approach of technology firms in truthfully communicating these risks with their customers.

Alarmingly, indications are that some segments of the industry have ignored the scientific findings suggesting potential health effects, have repeatedly and falsely claimed that wireless phones are safe for all consumers including children, and have created an illusion of responsible follow up by calling for and supporting more research. The most important measures of consumer protection are missing: complete and honest factual information to allow informed judgment by consumers about assumption of risk; the direct tracking and monitoring of what happens to consumers who use wireless phones; and, the monitoring of changes in the technology that could impact health.... As an industry, you will have to deal with the fallout from all of your choices, good and bad, in the long term. But short term, I would like your help in effectuating an important public health intervention today. The question of wireless phone safety is unclear. Therefore, from a public health perspective, it is critical for consumers to have the information they need to make an informed judgment about how much of this unknown risk they wish to assume in their use of wireless phones. Informing consumers openly and honestly about what is known and not-known about health risks is not liability laden—it is evidence that your industry is being responsible, and doing all it can to assure safe use of its products. The current popular backlash we are witnessing in the United States today against the tobacco industry is derived in large part from perceived dishonesty on the part of that industry in not being forthright about health effects. I urge you to help your industry not repeat that mistake.[8]

The following day, Tom Wheeler, president of the CTIA, began to discredit Carlo's research findings, releasing his own letter to the same tech CEOs, contradicting WTR's findings, and trashing Carlo in the press. The Wireless Technology Research project ceased operations and George Carlo was pushed out of the organization.

Since Carlo released the results of his research over twenty years ago, tens of thousands of studies have been published on the topic of mobile phones and cancer, which variously support or fail to find evidence for an increased risk of cancer from phone radiation. As Mark Dowie and Mark Hertsgaard report, however, the industry's practice of funding research that fails to correlate mobile phones with negative health outcomes is symptomatic of the industry's self-interest.

A closer look reveals the industry's sleight of hand. When Henry Lai, a professor of bioengineering at the University of Washington, analysed 326 safety-related studies completed between 1990 and 2006, he discovered that 44% of them found no biological effect from mobile phone radiation and 56% did; scientists apparently were split. But when Lai recategorised the studies according to their funding sources, a different picture emerged: 67% of the independently funded studies found a biological effect, while a mere 28% of the industry-funded studies did. Lai's findings were replicated by a 2007 analysis in *Environmental Health Perspectives*, which concluded that industry-funded studies were two and a half times less likely than independent studies to find health effects.[9]

Dowie and Hertsgaard point to the practical effect this tactic serves: by suggesting evidence is inconclusive, further research is called for, which

postpones the influx of regulations that companies would face if a majority of independent research findings concluded mobile phones increased
the risk of certain cancers.

> Central to keeping the scientific argument going is making it appear that
> not all scientists agree. Towards that end, and again like the tobacco and
> fossil-fuel industries, the wireless industry has "war-gamed" science, as a
> Motorola internal memo in 1994 phrased it.[10] War-gaming science involves
> playing offence as well as defence—funding studies friendly to the industry
> while attacking studies that raise questions; placing industry-friendly
> experts on advisory bodies such as the World Health Organisation and
> seeking to discredit scientists whose views differ from the industry's.[11]

Dowie and Hertsgaard compare the tech industry's funding of sympa-
thetic research to the tobacco and fossil-fuel industries, which have
famously funded studies that cast doubt on the risks of smoking and climate change, respectively.[12]

It has taken decades and millions of cases of death and disease to begin
to undo the damage done by research funded by special interests. In the
same way oil, gas, tobacco, pharma, and sugar industries have positioned
themselves in Washington, contradicted independent research, and
funded studies that further their interests, tech has followed suit, becoming the most prolific lobbying force in the U.S. and funding research that
promotes its interests. In the absence of definitive evidence in either
direction, most expert bodies such as the World Health Organization
currently classify mobile phones as "possibly carcinogenic."[13] As 5G connectivity becomes the norm and digital assistants and smart home devices
become more common, radiation from these devices will grow exponentially, while industry-funded studies continue to cast doubt on their
potentially negative health effects.

Mental Health

Perhaps owing to my background, combined with the sheer amount of
research available on the subject of mental health and technology, I
wrongly assumed this would be the easiest section of this book to write.

Instead, it has proved the hardest. The psychological effects of mobile phones and social media were what drew me to this work nearly ten years ago, and yet, it has become no easier and no less upsetting to see how technology affects our mental health and wellbeing. The eruption of digital technologies into every corner of our lives has upended the social norms that science tells us are good for our health: deep connections, thoughtful communication, strong relationships, and a sense of community. There is strong evidence that internet-based technology, and social media sites in particular, diminish the things that improve our wellbeing while promoting the things that don't.

Over twenty years ago, researchers at Carnegie Mellon conducted a study that suggested spending time online made you lonely, depressed, and antisocial.[14] Since then, thousands of researchers have replicated their results. While there are typically subtle changes to the specific research question or environment, study after study tells us that social media is negatively correlated with wellbeing[15,16,17] and life satisfaction,[18] and is associated with increased levels of negative emotions,[19] loneliness,[20] and depression.[21] These outcomes are not the result of a single mechanism or social tool, but a convergence of significant social changes, propelled by the internet and underpinned by a number of business priorities that exist in conflict with human wellbeing. Increased depression and anxiety, for example, can be, in part, attributed to a change in the type and quality of human connection, an increase in comparison of one's life to others, and the addictive and frenetic quality of social media.

Central to the problem of technology's negative impact on our mental health is its false promise of sociability. Platforms such as Snapchat, Twitter, Facebook, Instagram, and Reddit, which have been globally marketed as a form of social connection and community, are, for many, inherently isolating. Ethan Cross and his colleagues, who have carried out numerous studies on the mental health effects of social networks, concluded that, "[o]n the surface, Facebook provides an invaluable resource for fulfilling the basic human need for social connection. Rather than enhancing well-being, however, these findings suggest that Facebook may undermine it."[22] Social platforms like Facebook would argue that they create opportunities for "meaningful connections," but research has repeatedly demonstrated that this is simply not the way humans work. A

2005 study found that the internet, when used for the purpose of sociability and intimacy, was in fact inversely correlated to quality of life.[23]

The reason for this is, in some ways, pretty straightforward. The more time we spend on our phones and devices, the less time we have available to spend with others in person. The method of contact in our social relationships actually matters a lot, especially when it comes to depression. The authors of one study concluded that in-person interactions should be encouraged as much as possible, as the "[p]robability of having depressive symptoms steadily increased as frequency of in-person [interaction]... decreased."[24] A study in the journal *American Psychologist* found that internet use was correlated with less family communication, smaller social circles, more depressive symptoms, and greater feelings of loneliness,[25] suggesting increased screen time may lead to a decrease in the types of interactions that promote wellbeing. A follow-up study by the same researchers refined these results and found that, four years later, many of the negative social effects had dissipated for some of their cohort but remained high for others. In general, the researchers found, "using the Internet predicted better outcomes for extraverts and those with more social support but worse outcomes for introverts and those with less support."[26]

The importance of in-person connection and communication is true not only of our deeper, more intimate relationships, but our brief social interactions as well. Gillian Sandstrom and Elizabeth Dunn have spent years studying the power of acquaintances and "weak social ties," which include people we may interact with once or repeatedly, for a short period of time, such as our barista, a professor, or a colleague down the hall. Those who increased their number of such interactions reported an elevation of their mood and decreased loneliness, "suggesting that even [in-person] social interactions with the more peripheral members of our social networks contribute to our well-being."[27] Other people, it turns out, are good for our health. While relationships can certainly be forged online (such as on dating apps or in chat rooms), real human connection and intimacy are the domains of offline interactions. Communal dinners, social meet-ups, team sports, classrooms, parties, intimate meals, brunches with friends, nights on the sofa, and shared activities and adventures are all infinitely better for us than scrolling through a newsfeed or communicating in the comments section.

The false equation of social media with true connection is compounded by the nature of interactions online. The divisiveness and anger omnipresent on social media are accompanied, in many cases, by threats of violence and bullying. The toxicity of such interactions is, quite obviously, extremely dangerous for our mental health, particularly for children, who may lack the resilience or tools to manage such harassment. Researcher Jean Twenge has suggested that increased engagement in social media use "may account for the increases in depression and suicide"[28] in young people, as studies show that teenagers who spend two or more hours a day online have a significantly increased risk of suicide.[29] Data from both U.S. children's hospitals, which saw the number of suicide-related admissions double,[30] and the National Center for Health Statistics (NCHS), which reported a 24% increase in suicides across the U.S.,[31] support Twenge's hypothesis and findings. Interestingly, the NCHS reported that the pace of the increase was greatest after 2006/07, the same two years Twitter, Facebook, YouTube, and the iPhone were made available to the public (or in YouTube's case, went mainstream). While these correlations may not tell the entire story and should not be mistaken for causation, experts express concern that, taken together, the effects of the internet and social media on our wellbeing are more dangerous than tech companies would like us to believe. Dr. Safiya Umoja Noble, an Associate Professor at UCLA and author of *Algorithms of Oppression: How Search Engines Reinforce Racism*, has argued that lawmakers should take note of the "mounting evidence, that unregulated digital platforms cause serious harm" across a number of mental health categories.[32]

In addition to the depressive effects of social media, the rise and inundation of technology plays a role in our individual and collective anxiety. Breaking news, updates, emails, notifications, and the incessant buzz of messages across a variety of platforms have become increasingly difficult to escape, as has the perceived need to document and catalogue our lives online. Dr. Edward Shorter, a professor at the University of Ontario who lectures on the History of Medicine, argues that social media has "created a universal climate of apprehension,"[33] an argument confirmed by Gallup's 2019 Global Emotions Report, which found U.S. citizens to be among the most stressed out in the world. In *The Age of Anxiety*, Sarah

Dunant and Roy Porter explain that the root of our collective anxious-ness stems from an uncertainty about the future, magnified by an unprec-edented number of accelerating social changes.

> For many people in the western world the unprecedented expansion of everything from technology through communication to shopping has brought with it not only increased demands of choice (in itself some-thing of an anxiety) but also an expanding potential for feeling out of control.[34]

Dr. Harsh Trivedi, president and CEO of Sheppard Pratt Health System, contends that while technology may not be the only cause of this con-tinuous source of stress, it is certainly responsible for exacerbating it. The "constant noise from the internet and social media," combined with the stream of notifications and alerts we receive all day, Trivedi explains, heightens our alert system, amps up our "anxiety and angst,"[35] and leaves us feeling busy and apprehensive round the clock.

Twenge has a wholly different theory than Shorter and Trivedi about the increase in anxiety, specifically when it comes to young adults. A 2010 study by Twenge and her colleagues found that a shift from intrin-sic to more extrinsic goals has mirrored the increase of anxiety and depres-sion among young adults.[36] Where previously intrinsic pursuits, such as strong relationships, community, and competence were more central to young people's life goals, Twenge's team found a pronounced shift to extrinsic goals, such as appearance, social status, and wealth in the young adults they studied. Peter Gray, a psychology professor at Boston College explains that Twenge's findings represent "a general shift toward a culture of materialism, transmitted through television and other media," in which "young people are exposed... to advertisements and other mes-sages implying that happiness depends on good looks, popularity, and material goods."[37] Where intrinsic goals "have to do with one's own development as a person—such as becoming competent in endeavors of one's choosing and developing a meaningful philosophy of life,"[38] extrin-sic goals, by contrast, require an audience. And, as luck would have it, we each have an ever-present audience, at all hours, conveniently located in our pocket.

The shift from internal achievements to external attainment mirrors the escalation of our online lives, which has precipitated the rise of personal brands, self-aggrandizing content, and digital personas. Elements of who we are have shifted online to a series of digital representations of ourselves (Instagram account, Twitter handle, LinkedIn profile) that capture only a sliver of our true selves—typically only the most positive and favorable snippets of who we are (or rather, who we want others to believe we are). The psychological consequences of this phenomenon on our identity is a concern for many academics, such as Baroness Susan Greenfield, an Oxford researcher and member of the House of Lords, who studies the neuroscience of consciousness and the impacts of technology on the brain.

> People feel they have to sell themselves, have lots of friends, and offer their constant thoughts all the time, as if they have to have some kind of cyber presence or they won't exist. And that is deeply troubling, because if you see your identity simply as a brand, as someone who has 500 friends, who has eaten chocolate cake, or downloaded this or that, or gives a particularly savage reaction to something to get attention—who are you?[39]

The focus on status and materialism is intimately linked to what we have, what we do, or how we look, Greenfield explains, and thus is dependent on the judgment of others.[40] Allowing our identity to be increasingly defined by external factors, rather than relying on our internal sense of self, creates greater dependence on our audience and the digital markers of social affirmation and approval we get from them.

The anxiety Twenge and Greenfield describe is linked to this mercurial process, wherein our sense of who we are is variously confirmed, invalidated, or ignored by others. The result is a constant comparison between our lives and the lives of others, which may leave us feeling dissatisfied, jealous, elated, depressed, anxious, or validated, depending on the day, the engagement we receive, and our perception of our extrinsic worth.[41] When we see ourselves in comparison to our contemporaries, we experience "status anxiety," a term coined by Alain de Botton, which in turn causes "an assault on [our] feeling of self-worth."[42] Wilkinson and Pickett, who study the psychosocial effects of economic inequality, explain that status anxiety "increases what psychologists have called the 'social evaluative threat', where social contact becomes increasingly stressful."[43] The results can range from "low self-esteem and a collapse of self-confidence,"[44] to depression, narcissism, and addiction,[45] as more favorable feedback is continually sought. German researchers have dubbed this cycle of sharing and comparing our lives online the "the self-promotion-envy spiral,"[46] where likes, comments, views, and engagement come to define our sense of self-worth. Knowing social media is the world's most effective vehicle for social comparison, that it heightens and amplifies status anxiety, and negatively affects our wellbeing across a variety of measures, why do we keep coming back for more?

The Science of Addiction

Have you ever wondered why digital notifications are red? Or why a dot dot dot appears while your mom is crafting her latest emoji-heavy text message? (Just kidding, mom, you know I love these.) Or why you get a little thrill of anticipation when you check your Instagram after posting a cool photo? Each of these design techniques and many others like them—Snapchat's score, Bumble's 24-hour response window, push notifications—are all built to maximize engagement. And no one is more engaged than someone who is addicted.

Technology author and journalist Simon Parkin has described Facebook as an empire built on a molecule, in reference to the dopamine high that social media relies on to keep its captives—I mean, customers—coming back for more.[47] In order to appreciate how well dopamine works in this capacity, it's helpful to understand the science behind it all.

Dopamine is little molecule (is there another kind?) known as a neurotransmitter. We have lots of neurotransmitters, which are like the messengers of the nervous system, each of which has a different job. Dopamine functions to serve as an indicator of reward and pleasure, which, from an evolutionary perspective, is incredibly adaptive. Dopamine helps motivate us to set and achieve goals and reminds us to eat, drink, and reproduce. When we get a hit of dopamine, we're flooded with pleasurable sensations that reinforce whatever behavior caused them (for example, having an orgasm, completing a marathon, or finishing a degree or project). Dopamine is the most addictive molecule running around our system, and while it can help make us more productive, organized, and motivated, it can also lead to anxiety, reward-seeking behavior, and—especially—addiction. Over time, we can become hooked on the little hits of dopamine we receive and, consequently, less able to control our impulses to indulge in them.

In addition to dopamine, it's useful to understand a few of the other chemicals that influence our mood and behaviors: endorphins, serotonin, oxytocin, and cortisol. Endorphins help us to rise above perceptions of pain or danger, like when we push through the final set of a workout or run away from a bear. Serotonin is the chemical that gives us feelings of recognition, contentment, and confidence, particularly within a group. Simon Sinek calls serotonin the "leadership chemical," as it encourages acting on behalf of or with others and creates group cohesion. Oxytocin is the feeling of true love, trust, and safety. A good example is the love and protection a mom shows her child, but it can also be the intimacy of any strong relationship. Finally, cortisol is released in response to stress.

Unsurprisingly, perhaps, dopamine is the chemical of choice of both social media and the tech industry more broadly. The exploitation of reward-seeking dopamine-driven psychological processes is the single biggest reason we have collectively become so consumed with technology. Many early investors, founders, and former employees at Facebook, such as Sean Parker, Chamath Palihapitiya, Antonio García Martínez, Justin Rosenstein, and Sandy Parakilas, now publicly condemn the addictive nature and mental health effects of the attention economy they helped build at the company. While many cite their own immaturity[48] or ignorance, others, such as former Facebook exec Chamath Palihapitiya and former Facebook president Sean Parker, have acknowledged that they knowingly and purposefully exploited human psychology for the purposes of growth, engagement, and profit.

> How do we consume as much of your time and conscious attention as possible? That means that we needed to sort of give you a little dopamine hit every once in a while because someone liked or commented on a photo or a post or whatever and that's gonna get you to contribute more content …

It's a social validation feedback loop … It's exactly the kind of thing that a hacker like myself would come up with, because you're exploiting a vulnerability in human psychology … The inventors… understood this, consciously, and we did it anyway.[49]

The fact that we continually anticipate mini "rewards" from our phones and social media platforms (not only likes and comments, but emails, follows, or any other type of engagement) keeps us coming back for more in anticipation of what might be there.

The dopamine-fueled feedback loop Parker describes relies heavily on triggers and variable rewards. These concepts are taught, not on the dark web or in the back alleys of tech campuses, but in the heart of Silicon Valley, at Stanford's Persuasive Technology Lab. The lab, which is run by behavioral psychologist B.J. Fogg, boasts of its capacity to program "machines designed to change humans,"[50] and employs Fogg's own model to teach students how to build persuasive design into technology, such as digital machines, video games, and apps. Fogg's model has three components: motivation, ability, and trigger. *Motivation* is the drive to use a product, which Fogg explains is rooted in the need for sensation, anticipation, or belonging. *Ability* relates to how easy or "user-friendly" the product is: in other words, it has to be easy enough to use in order for it to stick. *Trigger* refers to what keeps you coming back for more, which could be a signal indicating someone is typing a message, a reward for increased time spent on a platform, or notifications that remind you something is waiting that needs to be checked or actioned. Thousands of students have taken Fogg's class, among them some of Silicon Valley's most prominent engineers and founders, including Nir Eyal, Ed Baker, Kevin Systrom, Mike Krieger, and countless others who would go on to work at Facebook, Google, Uber, and some of the Bay Area's most prestigious companies. In one of his classes, students practiced putting Fogg's model to work; in just over two months, the result was a series of apps with over 16 million users, which generated $1,000,000 in advertising revenue.[51]

The key to designing for addiction lies in offering variable rewards that eventually become so engrained they become second-nature to our daily functioning. Nir Eyal, an expert of persuasive design and habits, explains that in order to achieve this, tech companies employ the Hook Model. The Hook Model "goes beyond reinforcing behaviour" and instead "creates habits, spurring users to act on their own, without the need for expensive external stimuli like advertising."

> The Hook Model is at the heart of many of today's most habit-forming technologies. Social media, online games, and even good ol' email utilize the Hook Model to compel us to use them. At the heart of the Hook Model is a powerful cognitive quirk described by B.F. Skinner in the 1950s, called a variable schedule of rewards. Skinner observed that lab mice responded most voraciously to random rewards. The mice would press a lever and sometimes they'd get a small treat, other times a large treat, and other times nothing at all. Unlike the mice that received the same treat every time, the mice that received variable rewards seemed to press the lever compulsively. Humans, like the mice in Skinner's box, crave predictability and struggle to find patterns, even when none exist. Variability is the brain's cognitive nemesis and our minds make deduction of cause and effect a priority over other functions like self-control and moderation.[52]

The anticipation of an unknown reward, then, like a potentially important email or a pull-to-refresh newsfeed, is likely to draw us in on a much deeper, more reactive level. This is particularly true when rewards are combined with a little bit of cortisol, which is released when we hear or see a notification. This creates just enough stress for us to experience what neuroscientist Ramsay Brown, co-founder of Dopamine Labs, describes as an "emotional need to go resolve it, to get the red away."[53] Eventually, as Jory McKay explains, the habits associated with variable rewards and triggers become internalized, and we act instinctively, without thought.

> It's not just these notifications that drive our app and phone usage. After being triggered to use a product enough times, the trigger becomes internalized. All of a sudden, we don't need a reminder to check Facebook, but instead are driven by some emotional cue (like loneliness or a need for connection).[54]

The true genius of social media is to connect variable rewards with our most deeply held psychological needs: social validation, love, and belonging.

Facebook, Twitter, and Instagram have recognized and capitalized on these desires: we may very well check our phones hundreds of times per day in anticipation of feeling connected, seen, and praised.

Happiness vs. Pleasure

The modern world has gone to great lengths to convince us that what we seek is pleasure. (Or perhaps, more accurately, that pleasure is happiness.) The dopamine-filled experiences and objectives that advertising promotes in our culture are predominantly extrinsic goals, which center on consumerist, material, and wealth-focused aims. Buying something, drinking something, smoking something, playing something, scrolling through something, buying more somethings. All associated with dopamine. Unfortunately, while dopamine can give us a lovely little short-lived high, it is not related in any way to either contentment or happiness. Samantha Lee and Hilary Brueck provide a helpful breakdown of the key differences between dopamine and serotonin.

> [D]opamine, associated with reward and motivation, is very different from serotonin, associated with contentment and true happiness. You can't get contentment from an app or from a purchase, but you *can* click or buy your way to a whole lot of reward and pleasure.[55]

Dopamine is addictive, short-term, visceral (meaning it's felt in the body), self-perpetuating, and is generally a solitary experience. Perhaps the most important feature of dopamine is that it always makes us want more dopamine. Serotonin, by contrast, is non-addictive, long-term, ethereal (meaning it's experienced in the mind, not the body), is generally a shared experience, inspires leadership and generosity, and is associated with contentment. Serotonin also has five times the number of receptors in the brain, which scientists think may be the reason it is responsible for a wider variety of experiences.[56] Not having enough of this important chemical in our system can lead to depression.

In his book *Sapiens*, Yuval Harari argues that "[m]ost current ideologies and political programmes are based on rather flimsy ideas concerning the real source of human happiness,"[57] namely, the erroneous idea that happiness is correlated with economic prosperity and wealth.[58] Instead, Harari explains, strong families, supportive communities, and contentment with what we have are the strongest indicators of human happiness.[59] Rather than helping members of society grow and nurture true sources of contentment, like family, community, and self-actualization, Harari contends that the modern world instead cultivates unrealistic expectations of material wealth and possessions, which it constantly attempts to convince us will generate happiness. "If happiness is determined by expectations," Harari argues, "then two pillars of our society— mass media and the advertising industry—may unwittingly be depleting the globe's reservoirs of contentment."[60]

Johann Hari, author of *Lost Connections: Uncovering the Real Causes of Depression—and the Unexpected Solutions*, makes a similar case to Harari's. Hari believes mounting cultural anxiety and depression are the result of the way we live our lives in the modern world. Unhappiness and depression, he believes, "are caused, to an extent, by the same thing: disconnection from the things we need to be happy."[61] What at first sounds like a fairly obvious statement gets infinitely more interesting when we consider what science tells us it takes to be happy—"the need to belong in a group, the need to be valued by other people, the need to feel like we're good at something, and the need to feel like our future is secure"[62]—and contrast this to the world tech companies are shaping, in which we feel more isolated, unsure of ourselves, and insecure about the future. Hari's recommendations for a happier and more fulfilling life include thinking more about others and less about ourselves, making genuine connections in order to feel less isolated, and avoiding materialism, consumerism, advertising, and social media. Hari also suggests recognizing and aligning ourselves with our intrinsic values—the things we find truly meaningful and are passionate about—rather than the extrinsic values imposed on us by the expectations of others or society.[63]

Hari and Harari's arguments on happiness don't just make logical sense, they stand up scientifically as well. Wilkinson and Pickett have found that those who are most engaged with and reliant on consumer culture "are the least happy, the most insecure and often suffer poor mental health,"[64] while Twenge's research suggests that "screen activities are linked to less happiness" and "nonscreen activities are linked to more happiness."[65] The Health Foundation summarizes the most essential elements of health as follows:

> a healthy person is someone with the opportunity for meaningful work, secure housing, stable relationships, high self-esteem and healthy behaviours.... People who are more socially connected to family, friends or their community are happier and live longer, healthier lives with fewer physical and mental health problems than people who are less well connected.[66]

Emotionally, this includes a well-connected and positive family life, "supportive relationships," the ability to "develop intellectual, social and emotional skills," and "take part in community life," each of which protect health and wellbeing.[67] The displacement of the true foundations of human happiness with watered-down, modern material alternatives is a moral failing, both on the part of the technology companies who propagate advertising and consumer culture and the hypercapitalist economic system that encourages them to do so.

Tech's failure to promote happiness centers on its elevation of the individual, a concept woven deeply into both Silicon Valley's psychology and the internet itself. The industry's libertarian ideals promote the importance of personal satisfaction, personal opinions, and personal happiness, which as Jessi Hempel observes, "elevates individuals while deprecating institutions."[68] The primacy of individual needs is embedded not only in the mantras of individual tech companies (Broadcast yourself!, Give everyone a voice!, Tweet til your fingers fall off! Post pictures of every meal you eat!), but in the very DNA of the industry, which promotes messages of individualism and self-interest. The priorities adopted by many prominent tech companies aren't that surprising when we consider the origins of one of most dominant moral philosophies that guides the industry: objectivism. In a Vanity Fair article on Silicon Valley's obsession with Ayn Rand's theory of objectivism, Nick Bilton writes:

> [Steve] Jobs's co-founder, Steve Wozniak, has suggested that *Atlas Shrugged* was one of Jobs's "guides in life." For a time, [Travis] Kalanick's Twitter avatar featured the cover of *The Fountainhead*. Peter Thiel, whose

dissatisfaction with a Gawker story led him to underwrite a lawsuit that eventually killed off the site, and who made the outré decision to publicly support Donald Trump, is also a self-described Rand devotee. At their core, Rand's philosophies suggest that it's O.K. to be selfish, greedy, and self-interested, especially in business, and that a win-at-all-costs mentality is just the price of changing the norms of society. As one start-up founder recently told me, "They should retitle her books *It's O.K. to Be a Sociopath!*" And yet most tech entrepreneurs and engineers appear to live by one of Rand's defining mantras: The question isn't who is going to let me; it's who is going to stop me.[69]

The theory of objectivism posits that a moral life is centered on pursuing one's own happiness and individual success. (According to Rand, the system most consistent with her vision of morality, in which individual rights were respected above all else, was laissez-faire capitalism.) The prominence of such ideas in Silicon Valley is intimately tied not only to a troubling lack of concern for civic and social institutions, but a denigration of the very ingredients of true happiness: relationships, service, and human connection.

The Input-Output Problem

The sheer amount of information on the internet is enough to do your head in. Mitch Kapor, co-founder of the Electronic Frontier Foundation, has compared getting information on the internet to "taking a drink from a fire hydrant." We have, at a rather impressive speed, compiled the world's available information in a single place, to which we all have equal access. We have failed, however, not only to provision how we would identify, promote, or remove information based on its basis in fact and reality, but also to consider what so much information would do to us emotionally and mentally. In providing every type and flavor of information we could have asked for, the internet has also thrown in the cognitive equivalents of soda, cocaine, and arsenic, alongside genuine, accurate knowledge, with no indication of which is which and no plan to help us manage it. In addition to the mental health effects of technology, we are now beginning to witness a variety of cognitive impacts with equally dire consequences.

Larry Rosen, a professor of psychology at California State University, Dominguez Hills and co-author of *The Distracted Mind: Ancient Brains in a High-Tech World*, has spent his career studying the psychological impacts of technology. Rosen is particularly interested in the addictive qualities of tech and the effects these have on us cognitively, emotionally, and physically. According to Rosen's research, the effects of technology range from lack of sleep and increased anxiety, to less focus and a diminished capacity to tolerate boredom. Rosen's latest book argues that this is due, in part, to what he calls the "information foraging model," or the tendency of the human mind to seek out information. We're programmed "to maximize exposure and consumption of new information,"[70] Rosen explains, but often "don't have the metacognition to realize it's not good for us."[71] This leaves us constantly on alert, suffering from heightened cortisol levels, and feeling increasingly overstimulated, anxious, and distracted.

Both the pace of change and the amount of information we receive is problematic for our brains, which are not in any way adapted for a digital world that "produces as much information in two days as it did in all of pre-digital history."[72] Feeling the need to take in, classify, and understand the reams of information we are inundated with becomes not only impossible, it actually leaves us at risk of understanding less, rather than more.

> [T]oday our knowledge is increasing at breakneck speed, and theoretically we should understand the world better and better. But the very opposite is happening. Our newfound knowledge leads to faster economic, social and political changes; in an attempt to understand what is happening, we accelerate the accumulation of knowledge, which leads only to faster and greater upheavals. Consequently we are less and less able to make sense of the present or forecast the future.[73]

Harari equates this to a new form of information suppression, in which there is simply so much for us to process that we cannot reasonably make sense of it all.

> Humans are relinquishing authority to the free market, to crowd wisdom and to external algorithms partly because we cannot deal with the deluge of data. In the past, censorship worked by blocking the flow of information. In the twenty-first century censorship works by flooding people with

irrelevant information. We just don't know what to pay attention to, and often spend our time investigating and debating side issues. In ancient times having power meant having access to data. Today having power means knowing what to ignore.[74]

The capacity to shut off the flow of information and selectively determine what is worthy of our attention is hugely at odds with our more innate information-gathering instincts, described by Rosen. Information discretion is both a critical and necessary modern skill, which, if it was taught, we might apply to our news diet, advertising intake, and political conversations.

Such mammoth flows of information require a quick turnaround. That is, once we take in information, we must act quickly in order to process it and move on to the next item of interest. Susan Greenfield suggests that this dynamic has led to a phenomenon in which we go immediately from input (information) to output (response) without any meaningful cognitive or emotional processing in between. Examples include reading articles (or worse, article headlines) and re-posting them without verifying their accuracy; forming snap decisions without stopping to consider multiple perspectives; and the endless marvel of otherwise sane people screaming into the void of Twitter. The lack of time and consideration we allow ourselves when it comes to processing information not only has cultural implications, such as increased hostility online and a more polarized, less informed electorate, but, as Greenfield explains, impinges upon our individuality and intellectual autonomy.

> What is the real you if all you are is an output machine that's responding to inputs? It's so important to have something that goes on in the middle between the input and the output. It saddens me and worries me.[75]

When we attempt to tackle unrealistic amounts of information, we fail to give ourselves the time we truly need to process, make sense, and derive knowledge or wisdom from it. Understanding the difference between information, knowledge, and wisdom is paramount to appreciating the importance of how technology impacts our cognitive processes. Where previously individuals were able to "distil data into information, information into knowledge, and knowledge into wisdom," Harari states, "humans can no longer cope with the immense flows of data, hence they cannot distil data into information, let alone into knowledge or wisdom."[76] Instead, we have collectively shifted our emphasis to observations and perceptions, which do not necessarily constitute either knowledge or wisdom.[77]

Researchers who study digital addiction outline the consequences of sustained technology use, which include decreased focus and impaired cognitive ability.

> Being plugged in and connected limits the time for reflection and regeneration. Unprogrammed time allows new ideas and concepts to emerge, giving time to assess your own and other people's actions from a distant perspective. It offers the pause that refreshes and allows time for neural regeneration. Our nervous system, just like our muscular system, grows when there is enough time to regenerate after being stressed. Ongoing stress or stimulation without time to regenerate leads to illness and neural death.[78]

The relationship between excessive screen time and neural degeneration has also been demonstrated in childhood development studies, which show that more screen time is associated with poorer cognitive performance and a decrease in kids hitting development milestones.[79] These statistics have also been born out in U.K. figures on early childhood reading and speaking skills, which show that over a quarter of four- and five-year-olds starting primary school do not meet literacy levels and are unable to communicate in full sentences. Information overload also impacts the capacity for sustained attention in both adults and children. According to Gloria Mark, a researcher at the University of California, Irvine, our ability to stay focused on a task decreased from 3 minutes in 2004 to 1 minute 15 seconds in 2012.[80]

The idea that we are increasingly less adept at deep and considered thought is recognized both within and outside of Silicon Valley. In her book, *How to Break Up with Your Phone*, Catherine Price examines the ways in which the use of technology rewires our brains, such that "they are less organised for deep thought."[81] This correlation is directly related to the time we spend consuming disparate, low-quality information, which both decreases the quality of information we take in and leaves us less time for high-quality, evidenced-based facts and arguments. Writer Charles Chu points out that in the time we currently dedicate to social media, the average person sacrifices reading between 200–300 books each year, a habit research suggests improves the quality of white matter in our brains, where information is processed,[82] and also builds skills such as patience, perseverance, and emotional intelligence. One employee at a popular San Francisco company put it to me a slightly different way over coffee: "we're constantly consuming, constantly reading, constantly—there's no reflection. It's like mind control."

Relationships

There is a beautiful study, called the Harvard Study on Adult Development, that has focused on a single question over the past 80 years: what makes human beings happy and healthy? Starting in 1938, the study has followed three cohorts over the course of their lifetimes, making it one of the world's longest research projects on adult development in human history. The single most significant finding of the study has been, in the words of its current director, Robert Waldinger, that "good relationships keep us happier and healthier. Period."[83] While other factors, such as genetics, smoking, and drinking influence our health, the single biggest predictor of longevity and happiness is the quality of our close relationships.

I have a unique ability to reference this study in nearly any context, perhaps because its implications relate to topics that mean a lot to me, or perhaps because I just like its conclusion: that the people in one's life matter more than anything else, and that our satisfaction with our relationships will, in the end, be the marker of whether we consider our life happy and well-lived. Susan Pinker, a psychologist and author of *The Village Effect: How Face-to-Face Contact Can Make Us Healthier and Happier*, had similar findings after researching the habits and culture of Sardinia, a place with more centenarians (people over 100-years-old) than anywhere in the world. Pinker discovered that the key to longevity in Sardinia is highly correlated to the close relationships and regular face-to-face interactions they enjoy.[84] Countless other studies have reported similar findings around the connection between our health and our relationships. As social beings, the benefits of deep supportive relationships are paramount, not only when it comes to happiness, longevity, and life satisfaction, but to everyday mental health as well.[85,86,87,88]

What allows us, then, to develop the deep, meaningful, connected relationships that are so good for our longevity, life satisfaction, and mental wellbeing? And is our hyper-connected digital world enabling the connection we need, or changing our interactions in a way we need to think about and provision solutions for? Answering the first question is relatively easy, if slightly more difficult to practice. In order to have mature, psychologically healthy relationships, psychologists point to a variety of factors that influence the health of our interactions. Dr. John Gottman, executive director of the Relationship Research Institute, explains that characteristics like open communication, emotional intelligence, authenticity, intimacy, respect, trust, the ability to listen, the ability to be present, a tolerance for individual differences, and a caring, appreciative approach to others are central to the health of our relationships.[89] To answer the second question, we must determine if the technology in our lives enables or hinders these markers of healthy relationships.

The way technology affects our relationships is a big question, which many researchers have spent many years trying to answer. So far, the answer is a resounding... it's complicated. There are certainly social and relational benefits to social media specifically and technology more broadly—the diversity of our networks, for instance, increases substantially when we have the opportunity to connect to everyone else on the internet. Old friends, family who live across the country, and people with similar interests around the globe are only a click or two away. Research has shown increased social media use is positively correlated with the size of our network and number of interactions we have.[90] While the merits of social media and technology are appreciable, the drawbacks also come in heavy. The most commonly cited outcomes of increasing our use of digital technologies include a decrease in the depth of our connections, increased loneliness, and the divisive properties of technology when used in the company of others.

Teddy Wayne, a journalist and award-winning author, refers to the first of these problems as the issue of friendship "thickness." Wayne argues that while the quantity of our interactions has increased over the past decade, the quality of those interactions has diminished. This is because, while "[s]ocial media and smartphones spread affection around more easily," the quality and depth—or thickness—of those interactions tend to be less pronounced.[91] Many researchers, psychologists, and social media experts agree with Wayne's estimation, citing the difficulty of connecting in a deep or meaningful way in a digital environment. The predominance of digital interaction in our lives—from emails, texts, group chats, and Messenger, to Whatsapp, chat rooms, comment sections, and tweets—has shifted a good proportion of our interactions with others online, to a space where both the behavioral norms and the health benefits of social interactions do not necessarily apply. A 2003 study on the differences between online and in-person interactions found that those assigned to a face-to-face group had a more meaningful conversation, "felt more satisfied with the experience and experienced a higher degree of closeness and self-disclosure with their partner,"[92] than those in a control group who did not meet in person. Another study performed two separate experiments, both of which confirmed that communicating via technology "can have negative effects on closeness, connection, and conversation quality. These results demonstrate that the presence of mobile phones can interfere with human relationships, an effect that is most clear when individuals are discussing personally meaningful topics."[93]

The increase in the quantity of our interactions is perhaps most notable in the world of dating and romantic relationships. The rise of dating apps like Tinder, Grindr, Bumble, and their many spin-offs has had a curious effect on the love lives of young people in particular, who are free to swipe their way through hundreds of romantic matches in a matter of minutes. As with other online relationships, our dating circles have expanded exponentially, meaning we are more likely to meet people we otherwise wouldn't in our day-to-day lives. The downsides of our increased choice, however, are palpable to many, who cite the lack of romance, manners, and empathy on dating apps; the gamification of relationships; and the rise of acts such as "benching," "ghosting," "submarining," and "breadcrumbing."[94] Others are quick to point out the mental health impacts of these and other elements of online dating. In a 2019 BBC documentary, one man described how the app he used had, over time, become a barometer of his self-esteem and a form of validation, which resulted in an addiction to the platform. Another described his perception of what seemed an endless availability of potential mates, which he believed discouraged him from committing to one partner. The experiences these daters describe have become familiar to many, according to London-based psychotherapist Denise Dunne, who notes that while dating apps provide an effective way to meet lots of different people, the price of that convenience can be considerable. Apps like Tinder are instinctively compelling; swiping not only fuels a dopamine-driven feedback loop, but also has the capacity to sooth anxiety. Given the visual, transient aesthetic of most dating apps, there is also a tendency, Dunne explains, for increased focus on less substantive qualities, like looks and snappy bios, and a flattening or wholesale abandonment of social etiquette.[95]

*   *   *

If online interaction was merely a supplement to our existing relationships, interactions, and conversations, its widespread use and our increased reliance on it might be less problematic. The more time we devote to online interactions, however, the less we tend to spend engaged in face-to-face conversations. Researchers Norman Nie and Lutz Erbring found that

> [T]he more time people spend using the Internet, the more they lose contact with their social environment. This effect is noticeable even with just 2–5 Internet hours per week, and it rises substantially for those spending more than 10 hours per week.[96]

Nie and Erbring's findings were released at a time when 10 hours a week online was considered substantial. Today, according to the 2019 Digital Trends report, the average person worldwide spends 6 hours and 42 minutes per day,[97] or 47 hours per week online, nearly five times what Nie and Erbring's study considered substantial use. Countless studies point to the fact that social media makes us lonely,[98] while others have found that, more generally, time spent at home on internet activities "is positively related to loneliness and negatively related to life satisfaction."[99]

As we are encouraged to spend an increasing amount of our time online, our mental health continues to decline. While there is nothing wrong with spending time alone, the effects of moving our relationships and conversations to a digital environment come at a profound cost to our individual and collective mental health. Human beings are social creatures who have evolved to spend time together; as we continue to divert our interactions from face-to-face to online environments, our friendships flatten, our conversations become less deeply engaged, and our relationships become mere connections. The General Social Survey, which measures American society across a vast number of measures, reported that between 1985 and 2004, the average number of confidants, or extremely close friendships, dropped from 2.94 to 2.08, while the number of people reporting there was no one they felt they could discuss important issues with tripled.[100] The depletion of close relationships in the U.S., decreased social interaction, and increased isolation have deep consequences: numerous studies have linked isolation and loneliness to both physical and mental ill-health,[101,102,103,104] while others have found that a lack of social relationships influence the risk of mortality.[105] Former U.S. Surgeon General Vivek Murphy has warned that technology is contributing to what he calls a "loneliness epidemic,"[106] wherein 40 percent of American adults report feeling alone and without someone they can turn to in times of need.

The effects of technology on our social relationships extend beyond the use of phones and devices when we're alone. In one study, 70 percent of couples said that their cell phones had interfered in their interactions with their partners.[107] A separate survey of American adults found that 82 percent believed using their phone during a social gathering damaged the quality of the interaction, but in the same cohort, 89 percent admitted to using their phone during their last social activity.[108] The presence of a phone, even if it is not used or touched, has the capacity to diminish the quality of an interaction, according to researchers. A 2014 study at Virginia Tech observed conversations among 100 pairs of participants, half of whom had a phone on the table. The presence of the phone, which was untouched and unused for the duration of the experiment, decreased not only the perceived quality of the conversation, but also the level of empathy experienced among participants.[109] The presence of technology can also impact our friendliness towards strangers; a 2019 study found that, when participants were carrying a smartphone, they were significantly less likely to smile at others.[110]

The importance of our psychosocial needs and the role technology plays in shaping our new relational paradigms cannot be overstated. As we mediate our connections through quick, crafted messages, emojis, and a multitude of screens, the ways we connect with each other have shifted dramatically in an exceptionally short period of time. Our new methods of communication, however, are not in line with the evolution of human connection and relationships, which are predicated on our ability to be present, both physically and emotionally, in our interpersonal interactions. The more we prioritize online communication, the more likely we are to sacrifice face-to-face interactions, increase rates of loneliness and depression, and diminish both the number and quality of our relationships. We would benefit from recognizing that devices can be highly divisive; that tech-free face-to-face interactions are central to our health, wellbeing, and the quality of our relationships; and that we collectively must take steps to redress the imbalance that technology has caused in our relational and social lives.

Notes

1. Ratnayake, K., Payton, J. L., Lakmal, O. H., & Karunarathne, A. (2018). Blue Light Excited Retinal Intercepts Cellular Signaling. *Scientific Reports, 8*(1), 10207. https://doi.org/10.1038/s41598-018-28254-8

2. Loughran, S. P., Wood, A. W., Barton, J. M., Croft, R. J., Thompson, B., & Stough, C. (2005). The Effect of Electromagnetic Fields Emitted by Mobile Phones on Human Sleep. *NeuroReport, 16*(17), 1973. https://doi.org/10.1097/01.wnr.0000186593.79705.3c

3. Borbély, A. A., Huber, R., Graf, T., Fuchs, B., Gallmann, E., & Achermann, P. (1999). Pulsed High-Frequency Electromagnetic Field Affects Human Sleep and Sleep Electroencephalogram. *Neuroscience Letters, 275*(3), 207–210. https://doi.org/10.1016/S0304-3940(99)00770-3

4. Vernon, L., Modecki, K. L., & Barber, B. L. (2018). Mobile Phones in the Bedroom: Trajectories of Sleep Habits and Subsequent Adolescent Psychosocial Development. *Child Development, 89*(1), 66–77. https://doi.org/10.1111/cdev.12836

5. Johnson, D. A., Billings, M. E., & Hale, L. (2018). Environmental Determinants of Insufficient Sleep and Sleep Disorders: Implications for Population Health. *Current Epidemiology Reports, 5*(2), 61–69. https://doi.org/10.1007/s40471-018-0139-y

6. Cellular Phones. (2018, November 5). Retrieved June 14, 2019, from American Cancer Society website: https://www.cancer.org/cancer/cancer-causes/radiation-exposure/cellular-phones.html

7. Wyde, M., Cesta, M., Blystone, C., Elmore, S., Foster, P., Hooth, M., … Bucher, J. (2018). Report of Partial Findings from the National Toxicology Program Carcinogenesis Studies of Cell Phone Radiofrequency Radiation in Hsd: Sprague Dawley SD Rats (Whole Body Exposure). *BioRxiv, Working Paper.* https://doi.org/10.1101/055699

8. Carlo, G. (1999, October 7). *Letter to AT&T Chairman* [Letter to Michael Armstrong]. Retrieved from http://www.goaegis.com/articles/gcarlo_100799.html

9. Hertsgaard, M., & Dowie, M. (2018, July 14). The Inconvenient Truth about Cancer and Mobile Phones. *The Observer.* Retrieved from https://www.theguardian.com/technology/2018/jul/14/mobile-phones-cancer-inconvenient-truths

10. Sandler, N. (1994, December 13). *Motorola, Microwaves and DNA Breaks: "War-Gaming" the Lai-Singh Experiments.* Retrieved from https://www.rfsafe.com/wp-content/uploads/2014/06/cell-phone-radiation-war-gaming-memo.pdf

11. Hertsgaard, M., & Dowie, M. (2018, July 14). The Inconvenient Truth about Cancer and Mobile Phones. *The Observer.* Retrieved from https://www.theguardian.com/technology/2018/jul/14/mobile-phones-cancer-inconvenient-truths

12. A less well-known but equally abhorrent example is the food industry's annihilation of John Yudkin, a Cambridge-educated researcher who, in 1972, published a book exposing the dangers of a high-sugar diet. The industry promptly vilified Yudkin and special interest groups spent decades promoting research that touted the benefits of a low-fat, high-carbohydrate diet.

13. Electromagnetic fields and public health: Mobile phones. (2014, October 8). Retrieved June 11, 2019, from https://www.who.int/newsroom/fact-sheets/detail/electromagnetic-fields-and-public-health-mobile-phones

14. Kraut, R. E., Patterson, M., Lundmark, V., Kiesler, S., Mukopadhyay, T., & Scherlis, W. L. (1998). Internet Paradox: A Social Technology That Reduces Social Involvement and Psychological Well-being? *American Psychologist, 53*(9), 1017–1031.

15. Shakya, H. B., & Christakis, N. A. (2017). Association of Facebook Use with Compromised Well-being: A Longitudinal Study | American Journal of Epidemiology | Oxford Academic. *American Journal of Epidemiology, 185*(3), 203–211.

16. Tromholt, M. (2016). The Facebook Experiment: Quitting Facebook Leads to Higher Levels of Well-being. *Cyberpsychology, Behavior, and Social Networking, 19*(11), 661–666. https://doi.org/10.1089/cyber.2016.0259

17. Kross, E., Verduyn, P., Demiralp, E., Park, J., Lee, D. S., Lin, N., ... Ybarra, O. (2013). Facebook Use Predicts Declines in Subjective Well-being in Young Adults. *PLOS ONE, 8*(8), e69841. https://doi.org/10.1371/journal.pone.0069841

18. Chou, H.-T. G., & Edge, N. (2011). "They are Happier and Having Better Lives than I Am": The Impact of Using Facebook on Perceptions of Others' Lives. *Cyberpsychology, Behavior, and Social Networking, 15*(2), 117–121. https://doi.org/10.1089/cyber.2011.0324

19. Tromholt, M. (2016). The Facebook Experiment: Quitting Facebook Leads to Higher Levels of Well-being. *Cyberpsychology, Behavior, and Social Networking, 19*(11), 661–666. https://doi.org/10.1089/cyber.2016.0259

20. Griffith, E. (2018, May 8). Facebook's New Focus on "Community" Might Actually Depress You. *Wired*. Retrieved from https://www.wired.com/story/facebooks-new-focus-on-community-might-actually-depress-you/

21. Lin, L. Y., Sidani, J. E., Shensa, A., Radovic, A., Miller, E., Colditz, J. B., ... Primack, B. A. (2016). Association between Social Media Use and Depression among U.S. Young Adults. *Depression and Anxiety, 33*(4), 323–331. https://doi.org/10.1002/da.22466

22. Kross, E., Verduyn, P., Demiralp, E., Park, J., Lee, D. S., Lin, N., ... Ybarra, O. (2013). Facebook Use Predicts Declines in Subjective Well-being in Young Adults. *PLOS ONE, 8*(8), e69841. https://doi.org/10.1371/journal.pone.0069841

23. Leung, L., & Lee, P. S. N. (2005). Multiple Determinants of Life Quality: The Roles of Internet Activities, Use of New Media, Social Support, and Leisure Activities. *Telematics and Informatics, 22*(3), 161–180. https://doi.org/10.1016/j.tele.2004.04.003

24. Teo, A. R., Choi, H., Andrea, S. B., Valenstein, M., Newsom, J. T., Dobscha, S. K., & Zivin, K. (2015). Does Mode of Contact with Different Types of Social Relationships Predict Depression in Older Adults? Evidence from a Nationally Representative Survey. *Journal of the American Geriatrics Society, 63*(10), 2014–2022. https://doi.org/10.1111/jgs.13667

25. Kraut, R. E., Patterson, M., Lundmark, V., Kiesler, S., Mukopadhyay, T., & Scherlis, W. L. (1998). "Internet Paradox: A Social Technology that Reduces Social Involvement and Psychological Well-being?" *American Psychologist, 53*(9), 1017–1031.

26. Kraut, R., Kiesler, S., Boneva, B., Cummings, J., Helgeson, V., & Crawford, A. (2002). Internet Paradox Revisited. *Journal of Social Issues, 58*(1), 49–74. https://doi.org/10.1111/1540-4560.00248

27. Sandstrom, G. M., & Dunn, E. W. (2014). Social Interactions and Well-being: The Surprising Power of Weak Ties. *Personality and Social Psychology Bulletin, 40*(7), 910–922. https://doi.org/10.1177/0146167214529799

28. Twenge, J. M., Joiner, T. E., Rogers, M. L., & Martin, G. N. (2018). Increases in Depressive Symptoms, Suicide-Related Outcomes, and Suicide Rates among U.S. Adolescents after 2010 and Links to Increased New Media Screen Time. *Clinical Psychological Science, 6*(1), 3–17. https://doi.org/10.1177/2167702617723376

29. Twenge, J. (2017, November 14). With Teen Mental Health Deteriorating over Five Years, There's a Likely Culprit. Retrieved September 8, 2018, from The *Conversation* website: http://theconversation.com/with-teen-mental-health-deteriorating-over-five-years-theres-a-likely-culprit-86996

30. Plemmons, G., Hall, M., & Browning, W. (2017). Trends in Suicidality and Serious Self-harm for Children 5–17 Years at 32 US Children's Hospitals, 2008–2015. *Pediatric Academic Societies Meeting*, 6–9.

31. Curtin, S. C., Warner, M., & Hedegaard, H. (2016). *Increase in Suicide in the United States, 1999–2014* (National Center for Health Statistics Data Brief No. 241). Retrieved from Center for Disease Control website: https://www.cdc.gov/nchs/products/databriefs/db241.htm

32. Noble, S. U. (2018, March 4). Social Inequality will Not be Solved by an App. *Wired*. Retrieved from https://www.wired.com/story/social-inequality-will-not-be-solved-by-an-app/

33. Shorter, E. (2016, August 8). Why Have We Become so Anxious? Retrieved September 2, 2018, from *Psychology Today* website: https://www.psychologytoday.com/blog/how-everyone-became-depressed/201608/why-have-we-become-so-anxious

34. Dunant, S., & Porter, R. (1996). *The Age of Anxiety* (p. xi). New York: Virago Press.

35. Thompson, D. (2017, April 17). More Americans Suffering from Stress, Anxiety and Depression, Study Finds. Retrieved September 1, 2018, from *CBS News* website: https://www.cbsnews.com/news/stress-anxiety-depression-mental-illness-increases-study-finds/

36. Twenge, J. M., Gentile, B., DeWall, C. N., Ma, D., Lacefield, K., & Schurtz, D. R. (2010). Birth Cohort Increases in Psychopathology among Young Americans, 1938–2007: A Cross-temporal Meta-analysis of the MMPI. *Clinical Psychology Review, 30*(2), 145–154. https://doi.org/10.1016/j.cpr.2009.10.005

37. Gray, P. (2017, October 3). The Decline of Play and Rise in Children's Mental Disorders. Retrieved September 19, 2018, from *Medium* website: https://medium.com/the-mission/the-decline-of-play-and-rise-in-childrens-mental-disorders-7cc348ee8529

38. Ibid.

39. Greenfield, S. (2017, June 15). *Interview with Susan Greenfield* (K. Cook, Interviewer).

40. Gray, P. (2017, October 3). The Decline of Play and Rise in Children's Mental Disorders. Retrieved September 19, 2018, from *Medium* website: https://medium.com/the-mission/the-decline-of-play-and-rise-in-childrens-mental-disorders-7cc348ee8529

41. Feinstein, B. A., Hershenberg, R., Bhatia, V., Latack, J. A., Meuwly, N., & Davila, J. (2013). Negative Social Comparison on Facebook and Depressive Symptoms: Rumination as a Mechanism. *Psychology of Popular Media Culture, 2*, 161–170. https://doi.org/10.1037/a0033111

42. Wilkinson, R., & Pickett, K. (2018, June 10). Inequality Breeds Stress and Anxiety. No Wonder so Many Britons are Suffering. *The Guardian*. Retrieved from https://www.theguardian.com/commentisfree/2018/jun/10/inequality-stress-anxiety-britons

43. Ibid.

44. Ibid.
45. Botton, A. D. (2008). *Status Anxiety*. New York City: Knopf Doubleday Publishing Group.
46. Meyer, M. N. (2014, June 30). Everything You Need to Know about Facebook's Controversial Emotion Experiment. *Wired*. Retrieved from https://www.wired.com/2014/06/everything-you-need-to-know-about-facebooks-manipulative-experiment/
47. Parkin, S. (2018, March 4). Has Dopamine Got Us Hooked on Tech? *The Observer*. Retrieved from https://www.theguardian.com/technology/2018/mar/04/has-dopamine-got-us-hooked-on-tech-facebook-apps-addiction
48. Lewis, P. (2017, October 6). "Our Minds can be Hijacked": The Tech Insiders Who Fear a Smartphone Dystopia. *The Guardian*. Retrieved from https://www.theguardian.com/technology/2017/oct/05/smartphone-addiction-silicon-valley-dystopia
49. Parker, S. (2017, November 9). *Facebook was Designed to Exploit Human "Vulnerability"* [Axios]. Retrieved from https://www.axios.com/sean-parker-facebook-was-designed-to-exploit-human-vulnerability-1513306782-6d18fa32-5438-4e60-af71-13d126b58e41.html
50. Freed, R. (2018, March 12). The Tech Industry's Psychological War on Kids. Retrieved September 8, 2018, from Richard Freed website: https://medium.com/@richardnfreed/the-tech-industrys-psychological-war-on-kids-c452870464ce
51. McKay, J. (2018, February 13). Here's Why You Can't (or Won't) Delete Distracting Apps from Your Phone. Retrieved September 8, 2018, from *RescueTime Blog* website: https://blog.rescuetime.com/delete-distracting-apps-find-focus/
52. Eyal, N. (2012, March 27). Variable Rewards: Want to Hook Users? Drive them Crazy. Retrieved January 31, 2019, from *Nir and Far* website: https://www.nirandfar.com/2012/03/want-to-hook-your-users-drive-them-crazy.html
53. Reevell, J. (2018). *Tricks That Keep You Hooked on Your Phone*. Retrieved from https://www.bbc.com/news/av/uk-43758910/the-design-tricks-that-get-you-hooked-on-your-phone
54. McKay, J. (2018, February 13). Here's Why You Can't (or Won't) Delete Distracting Apps from Your Phone. Retrieved September 8, 2018, from *RescueTime Blog* website: https://blog.rescuetime.com/delete-distracting-apps-find-focus/

55. Brueck, H., & Lee, S. (2018, March 24). This is Why Our Phones are Making Us Miserable: Happiness Isn't the Same Thing as Pleasure, and Our Brain Knows It. Retrieved September 8, 2018, from *Business Insider* website: http://uk.businessinsider.com/why-our-phones-are-making-us-miserable-pleasure-isnt-happiness-2018-3

56. Ibid.

57. Harari, Y. N. (2014). *Sapiens: A Brief History of Humankind* (p. 422). London: Vintage.

58. Ibid., p. 425.

59. Ibid., p. 429.

60. Ibid., p. 430.

61. Schiller, B. (2018, February 16). Everyone is Miserable: Here's What We can Do about It. Retrieved September 7, 2018, from *Fast Company* website: https://www.fastcompany.com/40527184/everyones-miserable-heres-why-and-what-we-can-do-about-it

62. Ibid.

63. Ibid.

64. Wilkinson, R., & Pickett, K. (2018, June 10). Inequality Breeds Stress and Anxiety. No Wonder so Many Britons are Suffering. *The Guardian*. Retrieved from https://www.theguardian.com/commentisfree/2018/jun/10/inequality-stress-anxiety-britons

65. Huffington, A. (2018, February 28). The Great Awakening. Retrieved August 18, 2018, from *Thrive Global* website: https://medium.com/thrive-global/the-great-awakening-8bf08fa95eda

66. The Health Foundation. (2018). *What Makes Us Healthy?: An Introduction to the Social Determinants of Health* (pp. 1–33). Retrieved from https://www.health.org.uk/sites/health/files/What-makes-us-healthy-quick-guide.pdf

67. Ibid.

68. Hempel, J. (2018, March 21). The Irreversible Damage of Mark Zuckerberg's Silence. *Wired*. Retrieved from https://www.wired.com/story/mark-zuckerberg-trust-in-facebook/

69. Bilton, N. (2016, November). Silicon Valley's Most Disturbing Obsession. *The Hive*. Retrieved from https://www.vanityfair.com/news/2016/10/silicon-valley-ayn-rand-obsession

70. Gazzaley, A., & Rosen, L. D. (2016). *The Distracted Mind: Ancient Brains in a High-Tech World* (p. 14). MIT Press.

71. Rosen, L. (2016, July 6). *Interview with Larry Rosen* (K. Cook, Interviewer).

72. *Brain Overload.* (2016). Retrieved from https://curiositystream.com/ video/1660/brain-overload

73. Harari, Y. N. (2017). *Homo Deus: A Brief History of Tomorrow* (p. 67). London: Vintage.

74. Ibid., p. 462.

75. Greenfield, S. (2017, June 15). *Interview with Susan Greenfield* (K. Cook, Interviewer).

76. Harari, Y. N. (2017). *Homo Deus: A Brief History of Tomorrow* (p. 429). London: Vintage.

77. Harari, Y. N. (2014). *Sapiens: A Brief History of Humankind* (p. 283). London: Vintage.

78. Peper, E., & Harvey, R. (2018). Digital Addiction: Increased Loneliness, Anxiety, and Depression. *NeuroRegulation, 5*(1), 3. https://doi.org/10.15540/nr.5.1.3

79. Madigan, S., Browne, D., Racine, N., Mori, C., & Tough, S. (2019). Association between Screen Time and Children's Performance on a Developmental Screening Test. *JAMA Pediatrics.* https://doi.org/10.1001/jamapediatrics.2018.5056

80. *Brain Overload.* (2016). Retrieved from https://curiositystream.com/ video/1660/brain-overload

81. Samadder, R. (2018, March 11). Breaking Up (with My Smartphone) is Hard to Do. *The Guardian.* Retrieved from https://www.theguardian.com/commentisfree/2018/mar/11/breaking-up-with-my-smartphone-is-hard-to-do

82. Yeatman, J. D., Dougherty, R. F., Ben-Shachar, M., & Wandell, B. A. (2012). Development of White Matter and Reading Skills. *Proceedings of the National Academy of Sciences, 109*(44), E3045–E3053. https://doi.org/10.1073/pnas.1206792109

83. Waldinger, R. (2016). *What Makes a Good Life? Lessons from the Longest Study on Happiness.* Retrieved from https://www.youtube.com/watch?time_continue=26&v=8KkKuTCFvzI

84. Pinker, S. (2015). *The Village Effect: How Face-to-Face Contact can Make Us Healthier and Happier.* Random House of Canada.

85. Wallis, C. (2005, January). The New Science of Happiness. *Time Magazine*, p. 22.

86. Jackson, T., Soderlind, A., & Weiss, K. E. (2000). Personality Traits and Quality of Relationships as Predictors of Future Loneliness among American College Students. *Social Behavior and Personality: An*

International Journal, 28(5), 463–470. https://doi.org/10.2224/sbp.2000.28.5.463

87. Horesh, N., & Apter, A. (2006). Self-disclosure, Depression, Anxiety, and Suicidal behavior in Adolescent Psychiatric Inpatients. *Crisis, 27*(2), 66–71. https://doi.org/10.1027/0227-5910.27.2.66

88. House, J. S., Landis, K. R., & Umberson, D. (1988). Social Relationships and Health. *Science, 241*(4865), 540–545. https://doi.org/10.1126/science.3399889

89. Coutu, D. (2007, December 1). Making Relationships Work. *Harvard Business Review*. Retrieved from https://hbr.org/2007/12/making-relationships-work

90. Hampton, K. N., Sessions, L. F., & Her, E. J. (2011). Core Networks, Social Isolation and New Media: How Internet and Mobile Phone Use is Related to Network Size and Diversity. *Information, Communication & Society, 14*(1), 130–155.

91. Wayne, T. (2018, May 12). Are My Friends Really My Friends? *The New York Times*. Retrieved from https://www.nytimes.com/2018/05/12/style/who-are-my-real-friends.html

92. Mallen, M. J., Day, S. X., & Green, M. A. (2003). Online Versus Face-to-face Conversation: An Examination of Relational and Discourse Variables. *Psychotherapy: Theory, Research, Practice, Training, 40*(1–2), 155–163. https://doi.org/10.1037/0033-3204.40.1-2.155

93. Przybylski, A. K., & Weinstein, N. (2013). Can You Connect with Me Now? How the Presence of Mobile Communication Technology Influences Face-to-face Conversation Quality. *Journal of Social and Personal Relationships, 30*(3), 237–246. https://doi.org/10.1177/0265407512453827

94. Benching is the act of keeping a previous date in a human "maybe" category while looking for better options; ghosting refers to cutting someone off with no warning or explanation; submarining is the phenomenon of ghosting someone and reappearing after an extended period of time; and breadcrumbing is the act of talking to or flirting with someone online (often for attention) without the intent to meet them in real life.

95. Ingram, L. (2019). *Are Dating Apps Messing with Our Heads?* Retrieved from https://www.bbc.com/news/av/stories-46836938/dating-apps-what-are-they-doing-to-our-mental-health

96. Nie, N. H., & Erbring, L. (2002). Internet and Society: A Preliminary Report. *IT & Society, 1*(1), 275–283.

97. Kemp, S. (2019, January 30). Digital Trends 2019: Every Single Stat You Need to Know about the Internet. Retrieved February 11, 2019, from *The Next Web* website: https://thenextweb.com/contributors/2019/01/30/digital-trends-2019-every-single-stat-you-need-to-know-about-the-internet/

98. Song, H., Zmyslinski-Seelig, A., Kim, J., Drent, A., Victor, A., Omori, K., & Allen, M. (2014). Does Facebook Make You Lonely?: A Meta Analysis. *Computers in Human Behavior, 36*, 446–452. https://doi.org/10.1016/j.chb.2014.04.011

99. Stepanikova, I., Nie, N. H., & He, X. (2010). Time on the Internet at Home, Loneliness, and Life Satisfaction: Evidence from Panel Time-Diary Data. *Computers in Human Behavior, 26*(3), 329–338. https://doi.org/10.1016/j.chb.2009.11.002

100. McPherson, M., Smith-Lovin, L., & Brashears, M. E. (2006). Social Isolation in America: Changes in Core Discussion Networks over Two Decades. *American Sociological Review, 71*(3), 353–375. https://doi.org/10.1177/000312240607100301

101. Ibid.

102. Cacioppo, J. T., Fowler, J. H., & Christakis, N. A. (2009). Alone in the Crowd: The Structure and Spread of Loneliness in a Large Social Network. *Journal of Personality and Social Psychology, 97*(6), 977–991. https://doi.org/10.1037/a0016076

103. Cornwell, E. Y., & Waite, L. J. (2009). Social Disconnectedness, Perceived Isolation, and Health among Older Adults. *Journal of Health and Social Behavior, 50*(1), 31–48. https://doi.org/10.1177/002214650905000103

104. Winch, G. (2014, May 14). Why We Need All the Acquaintances We can Get. Retrieved August 28, 2018, from *Psychology Today* website: http://www.psychologytoday.com/blog/the-squeaky-wheel/201405/why-we-need-all-the-acquaintances-we-can-get

105. Holt-Lunstad, J., Smith, T. B., & Layton, J. B. (2010). Social Relationships and Mortality Risk: A Meta-analytic Review. *PLOS Medicine, 7*(7), e1000316. https://doi.org/10.1371/journal.pmed.1000316

106. Former surgeon general sounds the alarm on the loneliness epidemic. (2017, October 19). Retrieved February 11, 2019, from *CBS News* website: https://www.cbsnews.com/news/loneliness-epidemic-former-surgeon-general-dr-vivek-murthy/

107. Roberts, J. A., & David, M. E. (2016). My Life has become a Major Distraction from My Cell Phone: Partner Phubbing and Relationship Satisfaction among Romantic Partners. *Computers in Human Behavior*, *54*, 134–141. https://doi.org/10.1016/j.chb.2015.07.058

108. Rainie, L., & Zickuhr, K. (2015, August 26). Americans' Views on Mobile Etiquette. Retrieved August 18, 2018, from Pew Research Center: Internet, Science & Tech website: http://www.pewinternet.org/2015/08/26/americans-views-on-mobile-etiquette/

109. Misra, S., Cheng, L., Genevie, J., & Yuan, M. (2016). The iPhone Effect: The Quality of In-person Social Interactions in the Presence of Mobile Devices. *Environment and Behavior*, *48*(2), 275–298. https://doi.org/10.1177/0013916514539755

110. Kushlev, K., Hunter, J. F., Proulx, J., Pressman, S. D., & Dunn, E. (2019). Smartphones Reduce Smiles between Strangers. *Computers in Human Behavior*, *91*, 12–16. https://doi.org/10.1016/j.chb.2018.09.023

Part III

Next Steps

9

A Way Forward

Scientific progress makes moral progress a necessity; for if man's power is increased, the checks that restrain him from abusing it must be strengthened.
—Madame de Stael

Given what has been explored in the preceding chapters, your first instinct may be to panic. I would encourage you not to; at least, not yet. There's a lot we can do to shift the course of history and therefore a lot of cause for hope. If we panic, hope and excitement get lost in the shuffle of fear, chaos, and cortisol, which makes it much harder to thoughtfully and meaningfully take action. So let's take a big relaxing breath and remember, as eBay founder Pierre Omidyar is fond of saying, "while change is certain, the direction is not."[1] It is completely reasonable to believe we can still chart a new course and steer the tech industry, and the market forces that direct it, in a more socially conscious direction.

It has long been my contention that a lack of emotional intelligence is at the heart of the vast majority of Silicon Valley's problems. A lack of emotional intelligence is not a diagnosable problem. You will never go to rehab, have an intervention, or present at the emergency room for being

© The Author(s) 2020
K. Cook, *The Psychology of Silicon Valley*,
https://doi.org/10.1007/978-3-030-27364-4_9

emotionally unintelligent. That's not to say, however, that emotional unintelligence can't affect your life in profound ways. Emotional unintelligence may mean you find yourself unable to connect with or understand others, control your emotions, retain employees, or have lasting and emotionally fulfilling relationships. A focus on developing what we might think of as more traditional markers of intelligence—rationality, problem-solving, analytical reasoning—often neglects more emotional and social types of intelligence. This type of thinking is particularly prominent in tech and has caused the industry to elevate the perceived importance of certain characteristics and skills while ignoring others. While the industry is not psychologically unwell, per se, it is profoundly lopsided.

Have you ever counted the number of times Zuckerberg says "I think" in an interview? Speaking from personal experience, and many hours in front of YouTube tallying Zuck's "thinks" and "feels," I can confirm it's a lot—enough to both ensure an excellent drinking game and make you question if the Facebook CEO ever gets the feels. In 2018, Kara Swisher, founder of Recode, interviewed Zuckerberg about how his company's many controversies, particularly around privacy and the mishandling of data, had affected him personally.

> *Kara Swisher*: Can I ask you that, specifically about Myanmar? How did you feel about those killings and the blame that some people put on Facebook? Do you feel responsible for those deaths?
>
> *Mark Zuckerberg*: I think that we have a responsibility to be doing more there.
>
> *Kara Swisher*: I want to know how you felt.
>
> *Mark Zuckerberg*: Yes, I think that there's a terrible situation where there's underlying sectarian violence and intention. It is clearly the responsibility of all of the players who were involved there. So, the government, civil society, the different folks who were involved, and I think that we have an important role, given the platform, that we play, so we need to make sure that we do what we need to.

Whenever Swisher asks a question about how he feels, even when she presses repeatedly and explicitly asks him to identify a feeling, Zuckerberg invariably answers in terms of what he thinks. She tries again later in the interview, this time in the context of Facebook's social responsibility, Zuckerberg's leadership role, and the lack of awareness plaguing the industry.

> *Kara Swisher*: An issue I've talked about a lot is Silicon Valley's responsibility, and taking responsibility. And taking responsibility of your dark things, and not being quite as optimistic, and a lot of people here have a problem with looking at that. How do you look at your responsibility, as a leader? As a leader of a massive company with enormous power?
>
> *Mark Zuckerberg*: I think we have a responsibility to build the things that give people a voice and help people connect and help people build community, I think we also have a responsibility to recognize that the tools won't always be used for good things and we need to be there and be ready to mitigate all the negative uses....
>
> *Kara Swisher*: Yeah. How does that feel personally?
>
> *Mark Zuckerberg*: I mean, personally, my take on this is that for the last 10 or 15 years, we have gotten mostly glowing and adoring attention from people, and if people wanna focus on some real issues for a couple of years, I'm fine with it.[2]

In the course of the interview, which lasts over 80 minutes, Swisher says "feel" four times and "think" twice; Zuckerberg says "feel" once and "think" 28 times.[3] Zuckerberg's tendency to prioritize thinking over feeling is indicative of a larger pattern of reasoning and deduction that demonstrates the cognitive lopsidedness of the tech industry. What began as a questionable pronouncement about the skills necessary for engineering gave us an industry flush with a single, circumscribed type of Zuckerberg-esque intelligence. By shaping the narrative that successful engineers like puzzles but not people, psychologists William Cannon and Dallis Perry laid the foundations for an industry that would, decades later, find itself profoundly unbalanced and psychologically bankrupt in terms of its emotional intelligence.

The products, priorities, and behaviors of many companies and individuals within the tech community are indicative of an industry that does not understand the importance of emotional intelligence—or perhaps does not even understand the concept itself. Where IQ represents one's intelligence in terms of reasoning ability (as measured by problem-solving tests), one's EQ, or emotional quotient, measures the capacity for emotional intelligence. Emotional intelligence is defined as "the capacity to be aware of, control, and express one's emotions, and to handle interpersonal relationships judiciously and empathetically."[4] According to expert Daniel Goleman, emotional intelligence can be broken down into five core skillsets: self-awareness, emotional control, self-motivation, empathy and relationship skills.[5] While no one could accuse Silicon Valley of lacking self-motivation (albeit, at times, motivation of a morally questionable variety), industry execs' capacity for self-awareness, emotional control, empathy, and social skills leave a lot to be desired. This widespread lack of emotional intelligence in Silicon Valley has precluded a more holistic and sophisticated cognitive approach that embraces both rational and emotional skillsets, the effects of which have begun to materialize.

Self-awareness

James Hollis, a rather brilliant psychoanalyst, once wrote that "no prisons are more confining than the ones of which we are unaware."[6] The first step to shift either a personal or cultural narrative in a more positive direction is to grow our awareness. Self-awareness can be broken down into two categories: internal self-awareness, which "represents how clearly we see our own values, passions, aspirations, fit with our environment, reactions (including thoughts, feelings, behaviors, strengths, and weaknesses), and impact on others;" and external self-awareness, which demonstrates an understanding of "how other people view us, in terms of those same factors listed above."[7] Research has shown that increasing awareness of ourselves and others can increase empathy, creativity, and self-control, and can help us navigate the world in a more informed and conscious way.[8] A 2015 study found that self-awareness is also associated with improved communication, better leadership, and a greater appreciation of diversity[9]—all of which could stand to be disrupted in the tech industry.

M.G. Siegler has lamented what he describes as a "complete and utter lack of self-awareness" demonstrated throughout the industry, and by many of the industry's most prominent leaders, which Siegler argues are indicative of a larger pattern of obliviousness in Silicon Valley characterized by arrogance, insularity, and an abdication of responsibility.[10] Nick Thompson and Fred Vogelstein explain how Facebook's handling of the Cambridge Analytica scandal, for example, in which Zuckerberg denied and downplayed the situation, was rooted in an ignorance of the company's true impacts, combined with a rejection of any liability: "Mark Zuckerberg's initial reaction to Trump's victory, and Facebook's possible role in it, was one of peevish dismissal.... Zuckerberg's comments did not go over well, even inside Facebook. They seemed clueless and selfabsorbed."[11] This example illustrates a profound lack of both selfawareness and cultural awareness on Zuckerberg's part, as well as an abdication of responsibility, the combination of which proved disastrous to Facebook's public image. What began as a multi-year apology tour has devolved into congressional and parliamentary hearings, wherein Zuckerberg and Sandberg have been forced to assume responsibility for the company's actions and awkwardly and vaguely promise to do better. Facebook is not the only company that has failed to maintain a modicum of awareness. Twitter and Google have come under increasing scrutiny for their handling of customer data, anti-competitive practices, and effects on users' wellbeing; Amazon and Tesla have been forced to acknowledge their substandard treatment of employees; and the industry as a whole has been forced to reckon with its lack of diversity and inclusion. Despite the difference in the nature of these transgressions, the psychological quality that connects them is the same. A lack of understanding, or perhaps a wilful ignorance of the emerging issues and challenges created by their products, services, and business practices have rendered the industry increasingly unaccountable, untrustworthy, and profoundly unaware.

What, then, is the answer to increased awareness in Silicon Valley? How do we begin to even out the mental lopsidedness of the tech mindset before the industry implodes into a fire of arrogance and socially unaware, morally reprehensible behaviors? According to Ted Chiang, the answer is the same as it would be for anyone seeking psychological growth: we increase the capacity and capability for psychological insights. Chiang explains that,

> [i]n psychology, the term insight is used to describe a recognition of one's own condition, such as when a person with mental illness is aware of their illness. More broadly, it describes the ability to recognize patterns in one's own behavior. It's an example of metacognition, or thinking about one's own thinking.[12]

Increasing one's sophistication of thought to include self-reflection is a relatively straightforward process. It is not, however, easy, particularly when the insights one is forced to reckon with include the propagation of economic inequality, job displacement, the undermining of democracy, the rise of misinformation, and, in the case of Facebook, the fact "that the machine [they've] built to bring people together is being used to tear them apart."[13]

Self-reflection and insights are, more often than not, a result of our experience with others. We have evolved to be highly social creatures, and our capacity to change is a highly collaborative process, often derived from our interaction with others, either in the form of feedback, criticism, or disagreement.

> Sometimes insight arises spontaneously, but many times it doesn't. People often get carried away in pursuit of some goal, and they may not realize it until it's pointed out to them, either by their friends and family or by their therapists. Listening to wake-up calls of this sort is considered a sign of mental health.[14]

A barrier to this process that often arises in Silicon Valley, particularly around executives with high degrees of power, is an insularity of thought and resistance to feedback. James O'Toole, a business professor at the University of Denver, who specializes in leadership, ethics, and corporate culture, relates this back to the paradox of power: as an individual's power grows, his willingness to listen and capacity for empathy shrink, problematizing the feedback loop and the cultivation of self-awareness.[15] At Facebook, for example, tech journalist Salvador Rodriguez interviewed over a dozen former employees, who said the environment was one in which they were discouraged from speaking up, which caused the problems they saw to go unchecked and proliferate. Some employees likened the company to a "bubble" and a "cult" and said there was no option for employees other than to pretend they loved working there.[16] Not surprisingly, employee confidence fell over 30 percentage points between 2017 and 2018, according to internal employee surveys.[17]

In the short-term, then, we cannot put the onus of responsibility solely on tech companies and executives, many of whom will lack the toolkit to look either inwardly or critically. Growing the qualities necessary to enrich the industry's self-awareness will require building a culture of continual self-improvement and prioritizing qualities such as humility, collaboration, and reflection. Simultaneously, the public, government, journalists, and academics alike must point to the behaviors and norms of tech companies that fail to meet either the ethical or legal standards expected of them. As technology moves forward and the stakes become higher—highly capable AI, cyber warfare, deepfakes, mass automation, DNA modification—a willingness to learn about, draw attention to, and engage creatively with threats and social challenges, such that potential risks are mitigated in advance rather than rectified and apologized for after the fact, will hinge on improving our collective awareness, both within and outside of the tech community.

Emotional Control

Closely related to the subject of self-awareness is the concept of emotional control. Emotional control is a marker of emotional intelligence which is demonstrated by the capacity for self-discipline in relation to one's words and actions. While Silicon Valley's lack of emotional control doesn't manifest as overtly as its systematic lack of self-awareness, the industry's failure to self-regulate is hugely problematic. This can be seen in the behaviors of companies and executives who repeatedly fail, according to author Ted Chiang, to "tak[e] a step back and [ask] whether their current course of action is really a good idea."[18] We may not be sensible all the time, but being able to exercise impulse control is a hugely useful quality, which a subset of tech executives appear to lack.

There is no shortage of examples in Silicon Valley of what can happen when one's ego is disproportional to one's capacity for self-control. A series of cultural missteps, imprudent business decisions, impulsive emails, and shouting matches, eventually cost Uber CEO Travis Kalanick control of the company he built. Elon Musk's lack of self-control has been similarly visible, primarily in his endless string of bizarre and seemingly spontaneous tweets, which range from calling British rescue worker Vern Unsworth a pedophile, to claiming Tesla was going private, a false statement that resulted in Musk stepping down as chairman of the company and a lawsuit from the S.E.C. accusing Musk and Tesla of securities fraud. Kalanick and Musk are bold thinkers who took on important social problems, such as transportation, electronic banking, and reducing carbon emissions; however, they have also demonstrated an inability to self-regulate. Executives of any company in any industry would do well to remember the importance of understanding and mediating one's emotional reactions.

> Personality has three main parts: (1) the receiving portion (receptors) that looks out on stimuli (attention and appreciation are its great functions); (2) a responding side (effectors) that looks toward behavior or response; and (3) that which lies between stimulus and response whose function is to correlate and adjust behavior to stimulus. This third region is where our real personal values lie. This is where we grow most.[19]

Emotional control is a marker of both psychological maturity and emotional sophistication. In a time where the industry is having difficulty comporting itself appropriately, it would behoove Silicon Valley to encourage self-awareness and emotional regulation, particularly among its leadership.

Social Skills

In addition to self-awareness and emotional control, two final components of Goelman's model of emotional intelligence include social skills and empathy. Social skills are relatively self-explanatory: our interactions with others are marked by both verbal communication and non-verbal forms of communication, which can either facilitate connection or inhibit it. Verbal communication includes things like our tone, words, and pace of speech, while non-verbal communications includes things like our body language, gestures, and eye contact. Both verbal and non-verbal communication include acts of reinforcement, such as nodding, "mmm-hmm-ing," and warm facial expressions, which serve as an acknowledgement of others and build rapport by facilitating a sense of reciprocity in conversation. Individuals with good social skills are often adept at mirroring others, active listening, and adjusting their actions and words in relation to others; their conversations are more likely to flow and they are more likely to instill a sense of connection in their interactions. Those with fewer social skills are more likely to be experienced as awkward and may leave those they speak to feeling confused, unheard, or frustrated.

The tech industry is many things, but socially gifted is not one of them. Indeed, the awkwardness of the industry is as intrinsic to its identity as its ability to code, love of scooters and hoodies, and proclivity for delivery apps of all kinds. Women who date in the Bay Area, where there are a comparatively high number of single men, have a saying that captures the tech demographic, which comprises a substantial part of the dating pool: "the odds are good, but the goods are odd." While there are plenty of lovely, warm people in tech, the awkwardness that plagues a large subset of the industry tends to be constellated around a lack of social, interpersonal, and relational skills. This may manifest in an inability to communicate in a socially normative way (lack of active listening or talking too much or too little), missing social cues, or a lack of interpersonal gestures of recognition (eye contact, nodding, etc.).

While some (including yours truly) find this quality of Silicon Valley by turns endearing, amusing, and weirdly attractive, the ability to competently understand and communicate with others has important implications not only for our relationships, but also for society more broadly. Social skills encourage strong relationships, facilitate learning, build trust, compassion, collaboration, and a sense of mutuality between oneself and others. Social intelligence, aside from making our lives easier when it comes to interacting with others, enables us to consider the implications of our actions and make better, more socially-minded decisions.

Empathy

Empathy is a more specific type of interpersonal skill. Where sympathy is a feeling of pity or sorrow for someone's circumstances or misfortune, empathy is the capacity to understand and share someone's feelings by entering imaginatively into their experience.[20] Perhaps more than any other type of emotional competence, empathy helps us form bonds and positive relationships by allowing us to better appreciate the experiences, emotions, and perspectives of others.[21]

Two experts on the subject of empathy, Peter Bazalgette and Simon Baron-Cohen, suggest this particular emotional skill may have even more pronounced and extensive impacts than more general social competence. Bazalgette calls empathy "a fundamental human attribute, without with mutually cooperative societies cannot function,"[22] while Baron-Cohen argues empathy is "the most valuable resource in our world."[23] Bazalgette and Baron-Cohen's arguments are supported by dozens of studies that illustrate the extent and range of positive impacts of empathy on society, including a 2011 study linking empathy to prosocial behaviors.[24] A separate study published the same year linked the neurobiological mechanism of empathetic behavior to human evolution, suggesting we have evolved to be empathetic creatures.[25] It is not an exaggeration to say that empathy and social perceptiveness are highly correlated to our success as a species.

The years I've spent studying the tech industry have proven, again and again, how exceptionally talented the men and women who work in Silicon Valley are. Entrepreneurs envision solutions to problems most of us don't even know exist, like identifying homoglyphs or cryptographic signing of software; engineers consistently build technically beautiful products, underpinned by elegant code that makes everything from thermostats to email to electric vehicles function seamlessly and securely. It is a place populated by truly intelligent people, who happen to conceptualize intelligence in a very specific way: as a blend of cognitive skills that center predominantly on logic, inference, and problem-solving. While these skills are practically useful, particularly in engineering and entrepreneurship, they do not capture the full range of human mental abilities, including those rooted in social and emotional competence.

In a 2016 article for *The New Yorker*, Om Malik argued that "Silicon Valley's biggest failing is not poor marketing of its products, or follow-through on promises, but, rather, the distinct lack of empathy for those whose lives are disturbed by its technological wizardry."[26] While technological change is typically associated with progress, Malik points out that new technology also represents the displacement of jobs and the destruction of legacy industries, on which many people rely for both their livelihoods and their identity. The lack of empathy for the disruption its own progress causes normal people is central to what Malik views as the industry's biggest problem of emotional unintelligence.

> My hope is that we in the technology industry will … try to understand the impact of whiplashing change on a generation of our fellow-citizens who feel hopeless and left behind…. when you are a data-driven oligarchy like Facebook, Google, Amazon, or Uber, you can't really wash your hands of the impact of your algorithms and your ability to shape popular sentiment in our society. We are not just talking about the ability to influence voters with fake news. If you are Amazon, you have to acknowledge that you are slowly corroding the retail sector, which employs many people in this country.[27]

For many, the increasing speed of technology changes the fabric of the world they know and understand, leading them to feel not only that they are being left behind, but that their identity no longer has meaning.

> It is time for our industry to pause and take a moment to think: as technology finds its way into our daily existence in new and previously unimagined ways, we need to learn about those who are threatened by it. Empathy is not a buzzword but something to be practiced.[28]

Malik believes it is important the tech industry acknowledges the role it has played in leaving a large segment of the population both economically and ideologically behind. A failure to do so, he warns, will leave Silicon Valley "an even bigger villain in the popular imagination, much like its East Coast counterpart, Wall Street."[29]

There are many theories as to why Silicon Valley might lack empathy, which include the financial success, insularity, and hierarchical nature of tech companies. Malik suggests that the industry's focus on profits, growth, and engagement have decreased the likelihood that they will pause to consider the social effects their products, services, and business models have on their customers or society. Another factor that may feed Silicon Valley's empathy deficit is its well-documented insularity. Those who work in tech's homogenous culture, Malik explains, may "lack the texture of reality outside the technology bubble."[30] In a workforce that lacks diversity, there are simply fewer divergent perspectives available, which means the industry as a whole may lack the requisite range of experience not only to solve the problems it faces, but also to creatively address the issues that require more developed emotional awareness. Studies have repeatedly shown that a lack of diversity leads to decreased cognitive flexibility and diminished creativity, while exposure to different types of people and experiences lead to creativity, more sophisticated thinking, and increased levels of empathy.[31,32] A final barrier to the industry's empathy problem, according to Ben Tarnoff, is the hierarchical management arrangement of many Silicon Valley tech companies. Even if individuals do express empathy for their end users, Tarnoff explains, a majority of tech corporations are arranged in such a way that there is often "no mechanism by which they can really act on it. There are severe limitations on what an individual worker can do in these firms."[33] The systematic repression of employee feedback in certain Silicon Valley companies complicates the problem of emotional intelligence in tech by cutting off a potentially vital line of insight into product design, making it more difficult to effectively mitigate against unempathetic practices, products, and outcomes. Whatever the reason, many within the industry have begun to recognize and lobby for increased empathy, including engineers Clementine Pirlot and April Wensel, who have made compelling arguments for instilling more compassion, empathy, and emotional intelligence in tech.[34]

Leadership

Changes to the industry's cultural priorities will not be realized without the guidance of exceptionally competent, courageous, and emotionally intelligent leadership. The current climate of cultural uncertainty and chaos, of being unmoored from a world order whose trajectory only a decade ago felt largely predictable, requires leaders who are not only visionaries but also take the more nuanced responsibilities of leadership seriously. Successful leaders help people feel more hopeful, secure, and cared for, and also more "anchored, resilient, and propelled" into a better future, according to author and journalist Thomas Friedman.[35] A leader, according to Umair Haque, "is someone who takes people, and the world, forward, inward, and upward—not backward."[36] Good leaders are consistent, honest, and responsible; they demonstrate transparency and integrity; show up; and define the environment and priorities of their company or industry.

While there are certainly glimpses of inspiration to be found among Silicon Valley's leaders—Jaron Lanier, Dave Coplin, Tim Berners-Lee, Reed Hoffman, Tim Cook, and Marc Benioff, to name a few—much of Silicon Valley appears to be experiencing a leadership drought. While a subset of leaders aim to uphold the original intentions of the tech industry, which focused on openness, sharing, and advancing a shared humanist vision, a competing set of more corporate priorities have consumed the attention of many Silicon Valley execs. As these priorities—profit, market dominance, and shareholder maximization—have woven their way into the collective psyche of the tech industry, the original values that defined this inspired, intelligent, and irreverent community have been overshadowed by more pressing financial objectives, and in many organizations have vanished entirely. Facebook co-founder Chris Hughes explains that the influences of the technocapitalist objective in Silicon Valley will almost always trump the social aims and values its leaders profess. Hughes has been dismayed to find that the leaders of most tech companies "prefer to focus on the bottom lines of their companies rather than also talk about their companies' relationship to their workers and society."[37] Herein lies the problem with entrusting the future to the current leaders of Silicon Valley: the values of technocapitalism are not the values that will make the world a better place; they are the values that will line the pockets of those who hold the most stock in the biggest companies.

Matt Rosoff, the editorial director of technology at CNBC, traces Facebook's current existential and PR crises back to the troubling lack of leadership displayed by Zuckerberg and Sandberg. Rather than honestly and openly addressing the very real problems on the platform, the company's "top execs are selling, spinning and staying silent. That's not leadership. And when leaders fail to lead, companies fail."[38] Frederic Filloux, a professor of journalism at the Paris Institute of Political Studies, has compared the leadership at Facebook to an authoritarian system, noting the company shares the same building blocks as a dictatorship, including strong ideology, hyper-centralized leadership, a cult-like environment, a desire to control all aspects of society, and little tolerance for dissenting opinions. Filloux explains these qualities inhibit Facebook from effectively addressing problems like misinformation, as its true motivations are financially driven and its leadership remains centralized with Zuckerberg. "Facebook's DNA is based on the unchallenged power of an exceptional but morally flawed—or at least dangerously immature—leader who sees the world as a gigantic monetization playground."[39] Filloux's point was illustrated at Facebook's 2019 annual shareholder meeting, wherein 68% of external shareholders voted to fire Zuckerberg from the company's board and hire an external chairperson. As Zuckerberg holds approximately 60% of the voting power at Facebook, however, no one but Zuckerberg can move to vote Zuckerberg out.[40]

Rosoff argues that, while Zuckerberg and Sandberg have been given multiple opportunities to course-correct and assume accountability for their actions, at every turn they have failed to own their responsibility, demonstrate humility, and instill better values in their organization.

> Facebook is facing an existential test, and its leadership is failing to address it. Good leaders admit mistakes, apologize quickly, show up where they're needed and show their belief in the company by keeping skin in the game. Facebook executives, in contrast, react to negative news with spin and attempts to bury it. Throughout the last year, every time bad news has broken, executives have downplayed its significance. Look at its public statements last year about how many people had seen Russian-bought election ads—first it was 10 million, then it was 126 million.[41]

Despite changing their unofficial motto, Zuckerberg's company has continued to move fast and break things in the interests of growth and profits. The company's most recent promise—to orient its platform around privacy—has been lauded by some and derided by others, who question how privacy can co-exist with Facebook's business model. Some propose Zuckerberg's pivot is yet another PR spin, or an attempt to enmesh Facebook's services such that they cannot be dismantled by forthcoming antitrust laws. Like so many CEOs who purport to be leaders, Zuckerberg has underestimated the correlation between mature, socially responsible leadership, and the long-term success of his company.

The failure of leadership that plagues much of Silicon Valley rests on a fundamental misunderstanding of what leadership actually entails, and how to do it. Leadership author and expert Max De Pree describes the simple (but by no means easy) art of leadership as follows:

> The first responsibility of a leader is to define reality. The last is to say thank you. In between the two, the leader must become a servant and a debtor. That sums up the progress of an artful leader.... The art of leadership requires us to think about the leader-as-steward in terms of relationships... of momentum and effectiveness, of civility and values.[42]

Tech execs tend to excel at the first of De Pree's standards: defining reality. Have you ever watched clips of Steve Jobs showing off the first iPhone, read excerpts from Tim Berners-Lee on reinventing the web, or heard Elon Musk paint a picture of a carbon-neutral future? It takes an exceptionally visionary and brilliant mind to get hundreds of thousands of people excited about solar panels and batteries, yet Musk repeatedly demonstrates the hugely effective and ambitious reality-setting skills that have made him the visionary leader of not one but multiple companies, including PayPal, Tesla, SpaceX, and the Boring Company. No one could level a complaint that tech execs lack vision—what they could perhaps stand to develop are the qualities required of successful leaders once they have defined their vision: self-awareness, emotional intelligence, and values that seek to address real-world problems.

One of the problems facing Silicon Valley founders is that the skills needed to be an effective entrepreneur are entirely different to those needed to be an effective leader of a multi-national corporation. Derek Lidow, author of *Building on Bedrock* and *Startup Leadership*, explains that the transition from one role to the other can be tricky when entrepreneurs fail to recognize and develop the qualities demanded by their new role as a business leader, which rest on an underlying capacity for self-knowledge. "To lead others, you must first lead yourself, and leading yourself requires that you must realistically understand your capabilities—both strengths and weaknesses."[43] Lidow makes a compelling case for mastering the skills of self-awareness and relationship building, as well as the necessity of understanding one's own motivations, in order to be an effective entrepreneurial leader.

Values

The lack of emotional intelligence in Silicon Valley is underscored by a scarcity of the type of values that would make the world a more equitable, safe, and sustainable place. A conversation has begun to emerge recently about the role of ethics in technology—how important they are, how we might go about defining ethical frameworks for tech products, and how to enforce and achieve them. It has become increasingly accepted that ethics are desperately needed in everything from computer science classrooms to leadership training.[44] Illah Nourbakhsh, a professor of robotics at Carnegie Mellon University, explains that engineers, "designers, computer scientists and CTOs all need to understand the ethical implications of" the technology they create if they are to effectively mitigate the negative impacts of their products and services.[45] A 2018 study published in *Science* similarly concluded that ethical frameworks were central to the development of future AI technology:

> Artificial intelligence (AI) is not just a new technology that requires regulation. It is a powerful force that is reshaping daily practices, personal and professional interactions, and environments. For the well-being of humanity it is crucial that this power is used as a force of good. Ethics plays a key role in this process by ensuring that regulations of AI harness its potential while mitigating its risks.[46]

A deeper awareness of ethical concerns within Silicon Valley would not only help direct technology in a more prosocial direction, but could mitigate many of the threats we currently face, such as job displacement, economic inequality, and election interference.

What conversations about ethics tend to miss is the role values play in informing ethical frameworks. (There is also a tendency to conflate the two, though they are importantly different). According to the Oxford English Dictionary, ethics are defined as "a set of moral principles, especially ones relating to or affirming a specified group, field, or form of conduct," where values are "the regard that something is held to deserve; the importance, worth, or usefulness of something." Where ethics and morality are systems—codes, principles, standards of conduct—values are our judgments of what is worthy or important in life. What we value informs our ethics; without understanding what we value, it is impossible to advocate for any particular set of ethics that might meaningfully direct corporate behavior in one way or another. The primary ethical threat posed by Silicon Valley is that it is utterly unaware of its values.

In order to understand what we value, we need to understand what drives and motivates us. According to Bay Area psychotherapist Brooke Dougherty, our values are a facet of our psychology, in that how we are shaped informs what we come to value, which in turn affects what we believe and how we act. Not all values are virtuous, nor are they necessarily conscious, but they are all part of who we are. As outlined in Chap. 5, the primary motivation of the industry is profit, specifically, a kind of profit that values shareholder maximization above all else, the effects of which are economically unsustainable. The value that underlies this motivation is money. Other values core to Silicon Valley and its corporations more broadly include innovation, creativity, convenience, problem-solving, work ethic, growth, speed, and disruption. Individually, these are neither negative nor particularly problematic. Naturally an industry wants to grow, naturally it cares about profit. Taken together, however, they represent a troubling dynamic, in which the most influential industry in the world is organized around speed rather than reflection and planning, convenience over connection, and individualism above social good.

In addition to more openly discussing the stated values and practiced values of Silicon Valley, we might also pause to reassess our broader social and cultural values. The mores that govern technological development will ideally represent the needs and values of everyone who uses technology, rather than the small subset of those who design, deploy, and profit from it. To do this effectively, it is useful to understand what it is we place value on collectively, and how we would like to see the world progress. While I'm not a fan of fearmongering, this is a conversation we might want to sit down and have sooner rather than later. Professors Evan Selinger and Brett Frischmann remind us that if we fail to address "critical social policy questions... proactively while systems are being designed, built, and tested," we run the risk that unhealthy values will become "entrenched as they're embedded in the technology."[47]

Following a rather impressive string of missteps, breaches of public trust, and apology tours, can we reasonably trust the industry to regulate itself, create a system of ethics, and act in accordance with its stated values? I would argue we cannot. Fool us once, shame on you; fool us hundreds of times, still shame on you, but also, really, what the hell were we thinking letting you blatantly flout the law, ignore the needs of your users, and repeatedly break your promises, all while paying relatively no corporate tax and buying up all your competition? Can big tech be trusted? If we are to base our response on the data associated with its patterns of behavior, the answer is no. This is not to say that the industry cannot change, merely that it needs some assistance to do so. What happens in the next five years will irreversibly affect what happens in the next fifty. Whether technology serves humanity in a positive way or continues to concentrate wealth in the hands of an elite few individuals, leave workers behind, and undermine democracy are all questions that will be answered in the next several years. Such problems are simply far too important to leave in the hands of the people who created them.

Why Tech Can't Fix Itself

There are many reasons the tech industry is not in a position to remedy the problems it has brought about, several of which stand out as particularly problematic. First, there is a tendency among those in tech to address the flaws of their technology with more technology. Eugyny Morozov refers to this as technological solutionism, an ideology that imagines engineering better algorithms can effectively answer all problems, including those caused by engineering and algorithms. The second is that taking the steps necessary to truly fix many of the tech industry's problems, particularly those perpetuated by the attention economy and advertising business model, is at odds with how most companies generate growth and revenue. The final complication of self-regulation is the problem of perpetuating the thinking engrained in tech and assuming those who got the industry into its current predicament can be entrusted to get it out.

Employing technology to fix technology is the kind of approach one might expect from an industry known for its insularity and a somewhat blinkered approach to problem-solving. The notion that more tech is the answer to bad tech is psychologically curious at best, irrational and self-serving at worst; and yet it happens constantly, not only within the tech industry, but throughout society. Our increased reliance on technical solutions is rooted in a cultural narrative that purports the boundless power of science and technology—we put a man on the moon; we put a communication device in the hands of nearly every human on the planet; we recently put a second case of HIV into remission; we made cars that can drive themselves. The reason the narrative exists is that, to a degree, it's true. We have accomplished extraordinary things in the fields of science and technology, of which we should be exceedingly proud. The effect of these accomplishments, however, particularly as they stack up in greater numbers and at a dizzying pace, is the false assumption that science and technology can solve all our problems. Thanks to recent advancements in science, many of which we previously considered "unsolvable," Yuval Harari explains that many people have come to believe all problems can be solved by the right application of science, engineering, or technology.[48] Technologists, in particular, have become fond of the idea "that science and technology hold the answers to all our problems,"[49] including those created by technology.

As convenient as that narrative would be, the truth is that not all problems can be coded away. How we relate to one another online should not simply be a matter of automatically flagging harmful content, but of setting and enforcing communication standards across all social platforms. Offering online education is not a commensurate solution to the elimination of whole sectors of middle-class jobs. Removing the Facebook pages of Russian-based propaganda organizations does not address the existential catastrophe of misinformation. Relying on code and algorithms to fix the problems caused by code and algorithms is a deeply flawed approach that misses the issue—and the irony—of trying to engineer away social, political, and human problems. Harari explains that while scientific knowledge has "led to astounding breakthroughs in astronomy, physics, medicine and multiple other disciplines," it has one central drawback, in that science cannot "deal with questions of value and meaning."[50] There is simply no purely technical solution to questions about how to handle wealth concentration, body shaming, or the proliferation of misinformation. These each require pluralistic moral discussions, not updated codes and algorithms.

Immature Silicon Valley organizations are famous for relying on data in order to make significant and sweeping decisions about policy, practice, and standards, seemingly operating under the belief that no problem is too big, complicated, or human to be solved with some combination of 1s and 0s. This misplaced confidence was at the heart of a 2018 controversy, in which YouTube came under fire for its practices around automatic content moderation. Jacob J. Hutt, a fellow at ACLU's Speech, Privacy, and Technology Project, concluded that YouTube's technical solution to what is essentially a human problem was insufficient at best, solutionist at worst.

> YouTube's new report, while an important step toward greater transparency, doesn't resolve those concerns. First, while it assures that a human reviews content flagged by artificial intelligence, it neither describes the standards for this review process nor reveals how frequently human reviewers reject the machine's initial flag. This is especially concerning for content flagged as "violent extremist content." In the last quarter of 2017, a staggering 98 percent of content removed for reflecting violent extremism was flagged by machine, which raises the concern that YouTube may be relying almost exclusively on automated tools to flag content in the first instance.[51]

Hutt continued,

> YouTube's transparency report raises other questions about the role of machine learning in content takedowns.... Under what circumstances does

YouTube's machine-learning algorithm automatically remove videos flagged as potentially inappropriate? And how many videos have been removed without a human ever having reviewed them? ... If machines are learning from human decisions, how are the companies ensuring that the machines do not reproduce, or even exacerbate, human biases?[52]

Hutt's argument against over-engineering YouTube's problem of violent and extremist content draws attention to a one-dimensional approach that tech companies often employ to police their platforms and rectify their misconduct. Implementing a technological solution may indeed be compulsory, but it should be both preceded and followed by a comprehensive evaluation and analysis of the factors contributing to the problem that could be solved with policy or human input.

This example illustrates not only the difficulty of self-regulation, but also the unlikelihood of prioritizing morally right alternatives over and above an organization's economic interests. The vast majority of efforts to police social media platforms across a range of issues—including everything from instructions for self-harm and suicide, to Holocaust denial, white supremacy channels, and anti-Semitic content—typically amount to little more than a distraction. Professor and author John Naughton of the Open University in London has argued that the fundamental issue preventing platforms from acting responsibly "is that social media platforms cannot solve the societal problems they have created—because, ultimately, doing so will hurt their revenues and growth."

This is the unpalatable truth they are all squirming to avoid. And in doing so they're really just confirming HL Mencken's observation about the impossibility of getting someone to understand a proposition if his income depends on not understanding it. It's not that the companies don't get it, just that they cannot afford to admit that they do.[53]

Naughton cites YouTube's misled attempt to mitigate conspiracy theory videos on its platform by showing factual information alongside them, which CEO Susan Wojcicki indicated would be sourced from Wikipedia. A conspiracy video about flat-earth theories, for example, might be paired with information from third-party sources about the moon landing or a space station. YouTube's proposed technical solution to the cultural problem of misinformation leads Naughton to conclude one of two possibilities: either that Wojcicki and her colleagues do not understand conspiracy theories and the "current crisis of disinformation and computational propaganda" on the internet or, that they understand both perfectly well, but are unwilling to admit the scale or severity of the problem if it means inhibiting the company's growth or revenue.

Another well-documented instance of willful blindness is Facebook's attempt to ignore the threat of bad actors on its platform. In 2011 and 2012, Sandy Parakilas led the team at Facebook tasked with overseeing policy and privacy issues for the site's developer platform. Four years before Brexit and the U.S. election debacle, Parakilas warned Facebook's executives of the risk of foreign interference on the platform.

> [I]n mid-2012, I drew up a map of data vulnerabilities facing the company and its users. I included a list of bad actors who could abuse Facebook's data for nefarious ends, and included foreign governments as one possible category. I shared the document with senior executives, but the company didn't prioritize building features to solve the problem. As someone working on user protection, it was difficult to get any engineering resources assigned to build or even maintain critical features, while the growth and ads teams were showered with engineers. Those teams were working on the things the company cared about: getting more users and making more money.

Parakilas notes that he was not the only person to raise questions about misuse of the platform.

> During the 2016 election, early Facebook investor Roger McNamee presented evidence of malicious activity on the company's platform to both Mark Zuckerberg and Sheryl Sandberg. Again, the company did nothing. After the election it was also widely reported that fake news, much of it from Russia, had been a significant problem, and that Russian agents had been involved in various schemes to influence the outcome. Despite these warnings, it took at least six months after the election for anyone to investigate deeply enough to uncover Russian propaganda efforts, and ten months for the company to admit that half of the US population had seen propaganda on its platform designed to interfere in our democracy. That response is totally unacceptable given the level of risk to society.[54]

Parakilas's account illustrates the dilemma companies face when their financial priorities come into conflict with social responsibility. At some point in the industry's past, a responsibility to users may have trumped financial incentives; today, however, values appear not only to have taken a backseat to profit, but have been relegated to a different vehicle entirely.

Some companies seem genuinely concerned with fighting the unintended impacts their products and services have contributed to (others, not so much). One proposal that has been floated and, in several cases, implemented has been the addition of Chief Ethics and Culture Officers, as well as ethical oversight boards. Shannon Vallor was recently appointed as a consulting ethicist at Google Cloud; in 2018, Uber hired a Chief Compliance and Ethics Officer, Scott Schools; and, in late 2018, Salesforce hired Paula Goldman as its first Chief Ethics and Humane Use Officer. Microsoft set up an internal ethics board in 2016, as did Google, in order to oversee its AI branch, Deepmind (very little is known about the current state of the Deepmind oversight committee). A separate group, the Advanced Technology External Advisory Council, which was launched in 2019 to oversee Google's AI efforts more broadly, was shut down after less than two weeks. Such appointments and initiatives are a step in the right direction and any company making an attempt to improve compliance and ethics should be applauded for their effort. Anna Lauren Hoffman suggests, however, the well-meaning act of establishing these positions will never sufficiently address the complex moral issues tech companies face.

> [O]ne individual (or team or council or department) is not a panacea for all possible ethical problems.... The solution is not to corporatize ethics internally—it's to bring greater external pressure and accountability. Rather than position the problem as one of "bringing" ethics to companies like Facebook via a high-powered, executive hire, we should position it as challenging the structures that prevent already existing collaborations and ethically sound ideas from having a transformative effect.[55]

The greatest ethicist on earth, or a board of the smartest and most well-meaning people, would ultimately do very little to combat the tsunami of ethical issues tech companies face. One voice, or a handful of voices, particularly when they operate internally, will not be able to change the moral direction of companies like Facebook and Google if those voices are at odds with the financial interests of the company.

A final problem that precludes the tech industry's ability to effectively police itself are the behavioral qualities and characteristics that dominate the tech landscape, which collectively make it extremely unlikely Silicon Valley would prove capable of course-correcting on its own. Journalist Stephen Johnson cites the Audre Lorde maxim that "the master's tools will never dismantle the master's house," noting that we will not fix the problems of technology with the same thinking that created them. Instead, Johnson suggests, we will "need forces outside the domain of software and servers to break up cartels with this much power."[56] Vivek Wadhwa, a professor at Carnegie Mellon's School of Engineering and author of *Your Happiness Was Hacked*, argues that successfully "tackling today's biggest social and technological challenges requires the ability to think critically about their human context,"[57] rather than simply engineer solutions.

Experts have suggested we might look to philosophers, ethicists, and academics in the humanities to help supplement and rebalance the tech industry's ethics and copious errors in judgment. AI safety researchers Geoffrey Irving and Amanda Askell at OpenAI argue that the act of aligning technology with human values will be paramount in ensuring future technologies serve rather than undermine human progress. Meeting this need, and resolving the "many uncertainties related to the psychology of human rationality, emotion, and biases" embedded in tech's products and services, they explain, will require extensive and enduring collaborations between social scientists and technologists.[58] Richard Freed, author of *Wired Child*, suggests that psychologists, in particular, will be uniquely positioned to understand human nature, ethics, and the longer-term implications of the industry's practices.[59]

Power to the People

As we begin to re-envision a future unmarred by the corrupting influences of targeted advertising, technocapitalism, and outdated values, it's worth mentioning—clearly and unequivocally—that we can. The power of a few billionaires is nothing compared to the power of billions of people, and the idea that a handful of obscenely rich men control the future is both laughable and patently false. They know this, and so do we. The system as it stands is unsustainable and will soon change; the only question that remains is what shape that will take and the methods by which it will occur. The first line of defense in guarding the future against the often morally questionable behaviors of the tech industry is the very people upon whose data it has built its fortune. Recognizing the power we hold as consumers and the ways in which we can stand up to the unprincipled behaviors that emerge from Silicon Valley is our most immediate source of influence.

When companies promote misinformation, disregard privacy, and neglect mental health, it is our responsibility to express our disapproval, not only in principle, but also in practice. Every time we visit a website, platform, or app, we are communicating to the executives and stockholders of that company that its services are a valuable use of our time. John Montgomery, Executive Vice President for brand safety at GroupM, and Brian Wieser, a media analyst at Pivotal Research, explain that the number one means of immobilizing companies like Facebook is to diminish their user base.[60] The number one way to do that is to delete, deactivate, or simply not use services like Facebook until they meet certain ethical standards. As Taipei-based tech writer and former Apple and Microsoft engineer Ben Thompson has argued, the best place to look for weakness in any tech company "is not in the supplier base or distribution or even regulation: it is with the end users."[61] When we continue to engage with companies who have abused our trust, we condone the mishandling of private information, disruption of our democracy, and knowing assault on our wellbeing.

In a 2017 talk at Stanford's Graduate School of Business, former Facebook executive Chamath Palihapitiya discussed the significance of using data-driven social media platforms like Facebook.

> If you feed the beast, that beast will destroy you; if you push back on it, we have a chance to control it and rein it in… it is a point in time where people need to hard break from some of these tools… The things that you rely on the short-term—dopamine driven feedback loops that we have cre-

ated—are destroying how society works. No civil discourse, no cooperation, misinformation, mis-truth. And it's not an American problem—this
is not about Russian ads—this is a global problem.... You don't realize it,
but you are being programmed. It was unintentional, but now you got to
decide how much you're willing to give up, how much of your intellectual
independence [you are willing to sacrifice].[62]

If you live in the U.S. or Europe, your decision to disengage from companies whose behaviors or business practices you object to holds more
weight in terms of the advertising dollars your Western eyeballs generate.

Part of the business concern over the current scandal is that Facebook
would lose its most valuable users if there's an exodus of Western users. The
global average revenue per user is around $6 per quarter, but for users based
in North America, it's nearly $27 per quarter. In the developing world,
where many of Facebook's newer users are found, Facebook generates
significantly less revenue: Outside of Europe, Asia, and North America, the
average revenue per user is just $2 per quarter.[63]

Until such time when governments are able to hold tech companies to
account for their actions, it is up to users to say what they will and will
not stand for. To consciously use platforms and products whose behaviors
and impacts are aligned with our values is the least we can do to ensure
that, as they build their presence across the globe, companies learn from
their mistakes and recognize they cannot sacrifice ethics without also sacrificing their user base.

Agents of Change

A second group that wields immense power and has the capacity to shift
the direction of the industry's values is its own workforce. Employees at
top tech companies have increasingly vocalized their concerns, disappointment, and even outrage at the morally questionable actions of their
employers, which has led, in many cases, to measurable and immediate
change. In an article titled "Inside Google's Civil War," journalist Beth

Kowitt observes that "[n]o one is closer to tech's growing might, as well as its ethical quandaries, than the employees who help create it."[64] Kowitt's thoughtful and revealing article explores a growing defiance among Silicon Valley employees who refuse to be complicit or sit idly by while their company engages in morally questionable behavior, ranging from sexual harassment to workers' rights to projects that threaten democracy and human rights.

One key area of discontent among workers has centered on the treatment and working conditions of tech staff themselves. Exacerbated by the disintegration of unions, there have been resounding calls for change from employees at companies such as Amazon, Uber, and Tesla, which have drawn attention to everything from working conditions and safety concerns, to transparency and fair pay. A spate of employee complaints against Amazon, for example, garnered international media attention, a flurry of undercover reporting and investigations, and calls from top public officials to increase pay to a living wage.

Employees have also been increasingly outspoken about the morally questionable uses of the products their companies design, the projects in which they involve themselves, and the broader ethical decisions executives make. In 2018, Microsoft employees protested the company's $19.4 million contract with the U.S. Immigration, Customs and Enforcement Agency (ICE), who was using the company's deep learning facial recognition and identification software to detain individuals at the U.S. border. The U.S. government's increased reliance on ICE detention centers and the inhumane treatment of migrants in custody has resulted in calls for reform and increased oversight of the 200-plus detention centers across the country. In the past two years alone (2016–2018), 22 immigrants have died in ICE custody.[65] The letter from employees to Microsoft's CEO Satya Nadella openly questioned Microsoft's involvement with ICE and the decisions to put company profits over human rights.

> We believe that Microsoft must take an ethical stand, and put children and families above profits. Therefore, we ask that Microsoft cancel its contracts with US Immigration and Customs Enforcement (ICE) immediately, including contracts with clients who support ICE. We also call on Microsoft to draft, publicize and enforce a clear policy stating that neither Microsoft

nor its contractors will work with clients who violate international human rights law. We were dismayed to learn that Microsoft has a standing $19.4M contract with ICE. In a clear abdication of ethical responsibility, Microsoft went as far as boasting that its services "support the core [ICE] agency functions" and enable ICE agents to "process data on edge devices" and "utilize deep learning capabilities to accelerate facial recognition and identification." These are powerful capabilities, in the hands of an agency that has shown repeated willingness to enact inhumane and cruel policies. In response to questions, Brad Smith published a statement saying that Microsoft is "not aware of Azure products or services being used for the purpose of separating families." This does not go far enough. We are providing the technical undergirding in support of an agency that is actively enforcing this inhumane policy. We request that Microsoft cancel its contracts with ICE, and with other clients who directly enable ICE. As the people who build the technologies that Microsoft profits from, we refuse to be complicit. We are part of a growing movement, comprised of many across the industry who recognize the grave responsibility that those creating powerful technology have to ensure what they build is used for good, and not for harm.[66]

The letter ends with a request that the company cancel the existing government contract immediately, draft a policy stating that Microsoft will not be affiliated "with clients who violate international human rights law," and commit to transparency between any contracts the company enters into with foreign or domestic governments. In June 2018, Amazon CEO Jeff Bezos received similar requests from shareholders, consumers, and over 40 advocacy groups in regard to the use of Amazon's facial recognition software, Rekognition. Critics of the contract, such as the ACLU, called the product "perhaps the most dangerous surveillance technology ever developed,"[67] while others expressed their fear that the software, which has been marketed to police and government offices as a surveillance tool, could be used to disproportionately target immigrants and people of color.[68]

When it comes to the ethical trajectory of tech companies, Google employees have been some of the most vocal. Protests, public letters, and leaked memos have attracted considerable attention as employees demand explanation, transparency, and change, both in regard to internal behaviors and corporate projects. One of the most controversial projects at the company is Project Maven, a contract with the U.S. Department of Defense that used Google's artificial intelligence for "algorithmic warfare" to improve drone targeting.[69] Once employees became aware of the contract, over 3,000 staff signed a letter to CEO Sundar Pichai expressing disapproval of the project and demanding the contract be cancelled. The letter highlights both the potential for reputational damage and the discrepancy between Google's actions and its stated values.

> We cannot outsource the moral responsibility of our technologies to third parties. Google's stated values make this clear: Every one of our users is trusting us. Never jeopardize that. Ever. This contract puts Google's reputation at risk and stands in direct opposition to our core values. Building this technology to assist the US Government in military surveillance—and potentially lethal outcomes—is not acceptable. Recognizing Google's moral and ethical responsibility, and the threat to Google's reputation, we request that you: 1. Cancel this project immediately 2. Draft, publicize, and enforce a clear policy stating that neither Google nor its contractors will ever build warfare technology.[70]

The following month, the International Committee for Robot Arms Control sent a follow-up letter signed by academics and scholars, including founder Larry Page's PhD advisor Terry Winograd, in support of ending Project Maven.[71] By June, Pichai announced that Google would not renew the contract when it expired, but made clear it would continue to work "with governments and the military in many other areas."[72]

The trend of tech inserting itself into defense projects is an uncomfortable turn for many employees, who signed up to work at companies for a multitude of reasons that likely did not include improving surveillance systems or the "lethality" and "readiness" of war tools.[73] Even for those who do not work directly on the projects in question, journalists Scott Shane and Daisuke Wakabayashi point out that the budding Silicon Valley-Department of Defense relationship "underscor[es] the difficulty of separating software, cloud and related services from the actual business of war."[74] For Google employees, in particular, who joined a company that explicitly claimed to not be evil, reconciling these PR promises with the company's actions—as well as employees' individual ethics—can become a difficult moral situation that leaves many disillusioned with their organization's priorities.

When the tension between personal and corporate ethics is felt to be too incompatible, resignation is a common form of escape. While some high-profile exits are shrouded behind PR stories of new ventures or of execs getting back to their coding roots, others are more conspicuous. Former Facebook CSO Alex Stamos, who clashed with Mark Zuckerberg and Sheryl Sandberg over Russian interference on the platform, left the company following the Cambridge Analytica scandal to work as a professor at Stanford. Whatsapp founders Jan Koum and Brian Acton, both critics of digital advertising, also left Facebook over a difference of opinion about encryption and ads, sacrificing stock worth $1.3 billion.[75] The founders of Instagram, Kevin Systrom and Mike Krieger, recently left Facebook as well, as did Chief Product Officer Chris Cox and Whatsapp Vice President Chris Daniels. While the specific reasons for departures vary, the commonality for many who choose to leave appears to be an inability to work for a company that centralizes power and compromises morality for profit.

In early 2019, site reliability engineer Liz Fong-Jones quit her job at Google, citing patterns of behavior that she believed impinged on diversity, human rights, and equality. During her 11 years at the company, Fong-Jones stood up to Google's management on a number of issues she believed the company was getting wrong, including growth hacking, harassment, and Google's work in China. Early in her career, Fong-Jones was instrumental in the decision to overturn a policy that required people share their real name on Google+, which she and others recognized was a risk to vulnerable users such as teachers, therapists, and members of the LGBTQ community who might need anonymity for safety reasons. Though Fong-Jones and her colleagues eventually prevailed, subsequent attempts to change the culture proved "less effective as leadership repeatedly stonewall[ed] employees who privately raise[d] concerns."[76] After over a decade at the company, Fong-Jones resigned, saying she wanted to devote her career to "creating a more just world rather than exacerbating inequalities" and would be moving to a company with "a more diverse and fair working environment and a firm commitment to ethical computing."

Central to this decision was Fong-Jones's concern about the priorities and decisions at Google, particularly those related to the strategic and moral directions of the company.

> I have grave concerns about how strategic decisions are made at Google today, and who is missing a seat at the bargaining table. Google bears the responsibility of being one of the most influential companies in the world, but it has misused its power to place profits above the well-being of people. Executives seem to have forgotten the ethos of the company's earliest employees—"don't be evil"—and ethical stances, such as pulling out of China over censorship concerns in 2010, have been supplanted by shadowy efforts to appease the country's government at the expense of human rights.[77]

Fong-Jones's article covers some of the most disturbing incidents at the company during her tenure, including Google's failure "to implement an ethics review process for government contracts that would automate surveillance and targeting of civilians in the Middle East" and the company's foray into the Chinese search market. (Although Google abandoned plans to move into the Chinese market in 2010 due to concerns over censorship and security, it is again rumored to be building a censored version of its search engine for China, nicknamed Project Dragonfly, which would reportedly block any information related to democracy, human rights, religion, and peaceful protests.) In addition to their work in China and the Middle East, Fong-Jones also cites a breakdown of internal dialogue and a sharp increase in internal harassment of the company's most marginalized and vulnerable employees, which began as "trolling and rapidly escalated to leaks of the names, photos, and posts of LGBT+ employees to white supremacist sites." When employees complained or raised concerns, Fong-Jones explains, they were "ignored, stonewalled, or even punished for doing so."

The discriminatory issues Fong-Jones raises have also come to light in public demonstrations and lawsuits that highlight Google's tolerance of harassment. In 2018, the New York Times published an editorial detailing how the company had protected multiple men accused of sexual misconduct, including Andy Rubin, creator of the company's Android mobile software. Rubin was reportedly asked to resign in 2014 after multiple allegations of misconduct against him had been filed; when he finally left, he was given an exit package of $90 million. In 2016, Google paid Amit Singhal upwards of $45 million when he resigned after accusations surfaced that he had groped a fellow employee.[78] Following the revelations of sexual misconduct and multi-million dollar exit packages, James Martin, one of Google's shareholders, filed a lawsuit in early 2019, charging the company with "breach of fiduciary duty, unjust enrichment, abuse of power, and corporate waste."[79] Fong-Jones said the payouts "utterly shattered employees' trust and goodwill in management" and subsequently led over 20,000 Google employees (about a fifth of its workforce) to walk out in protest in late 2018.

> Employees had been complaining about pay inequity, mistreatment of contractors, and other forms of discrimination for years. To see how the company handled an executive harassment case revealed the utter lack of scruples among management. Employees walked out en masse, holding signs reading: "I reported, he got promoted," and "Will leave for $90M, no harassment needed." More than 20 percent of full-time employees joined the protest along with a large number of contractors who faced even greater risks of retaliation from their superiors.

Dr. Cameron Sepah has argued a company's culture is defined by whom it hires, fires, and promotes.[80] By offering excessive payouts to those accused of discrimination and harassment, companies may, perhaps unintentionally, send a culturally confusing message to their staff that such behavior is not only tolerated, but also financially rewarded.

In addition to protests and employee-led accountability movements, Silicon Valley has also seen the rise of tech humanism, led by the Center for Humane Technology and its many allies. The group, which is comprised primarily of former industry employees, has taken on the design mistakes and ethical transgressions of the industry. In a 2018 article, Ben Tarnoff and Moira Weigel describe the movement's focus on addressing the social problems that have arisen from unethical technology design, which include distraction, disconnection, mental health, and the erosion of information and democracy. Tarnoff and Weigel report that, like other employee-led movements, Silicon Valley has taken notice of the charges leveled against them by tech humanists, noting that industry leaders "are starting to speak its idiom." Snap CEO Evan Spiegel has "warned about social media's role in encouraging 'mindless scrambles for friends or unworthy distractions,'" Twitter's Jack Dorsey "recently claimed he wants to improve the platform's 'conversational health,'" and Mark Zuckerberg co-opted the Center for Humane Technology's language that engaging with digital devices should be "time well spent."[81]

As tech companies continue to test the waters (and profitability) of veering into the muddy territory of human rights violations, surveillance, and war, scrutiny from employees at all levels will be vital to help hold them to account. Thankfully, there appears to be a healthy scepticism within Silicon Valley's workforce that continues to grapple with and, when necessary, actively resist the morally questionable corporate decisions and priorities of their employers.

~~Winter~~ Regulation is Coming

I've never been a big fan of rules. That said, I appreciate the ones that serve an obvious, constructive purpose, hold society together, and generally keep us from doing vile things to each other. Rules become particularly useful, I find, when a given situation cannot be controlled by those involved in or responsible for its outcome. Such is the case in Silicon Valley, where an inability to self-regulate or maintain acceptable ethical standards have ensured that, like it or not, regulation is coming for the tech industry.

If social responsibility includes both consumers and employees standing up and demanding better from big tech, regulation sits squarely in the government's realm of responsibility. Which might worry anyone who saw the 2018 congressional hearings with Facebook, Twitter, and Google execs, in which a number of elected officials displayed a concerning lack of awareness about the basic ins and outs of platform governance, security, and the implications of an advertising-centered business model. The first regulatory problem, according to Devon Maloney, is not a matter of regulation at all, but a basic assumption that elected officials should understand the implications and issues associated with big tech.

> Within a few decades, our elected officials will all be from a generation that understands a lot more about technology than this one. Whether those representatives will understand the ins and outs of our digital world remains to be seen; it's possible many of them will remain willfully in the dark. But wouldn't you rather vote for someone who took the time to understand the threats to their constituents' well-being, and to democracy itself, however complicated those threats may be?[82]

The complexity and range of the issues Maloney refers to, which include changes to employment, the economy, health, cognition, security, existential threats, privacy, and human rights, will shape our future, for better or worse. Journalist Amy Zegart and U.S. Air Force Lieutenant Colonel Kevin Childs have deemed closing the government-tech divide a "national-security imperative" and have argued that the gulf between the two could prove catastrophic across a number of ethical and security fronts.[83] Should we fail to elect politicians who understand these problems, and who are willing to proactively address them and envision intelligent solutions, we risk allowing legislative officials into office who are out of touch with some of the most urgent problems in our world.

Tim Berners-Lee's internet began as and has continued to be borderless, without relevant social or legal frameworks to direct our behaviour. The speed at which the tech industry has grown has allowed it to remain largely lawless and get ahead of any regulation that may have meaningfully addressed some of its more nefarious actions. The pace of the industry, combined with the myth of the well-meaning, prosocial company out to save the world, has repeatedly allowed tech giants to evade regulation despite a growing number of offences. Facebook still contends, for example, that it is a platform and not a media company, which protects Facebook from taking responsibility for the content on Facebook. For years, big tech was able to convince both an adoring public and (a largely digitally confused) government that their interests were different from other for-profit corporations. Roger McNamee explains that,

[t]hanks to the U.S. government's laissez-faire approach to regulation, the internet platforms were able to pursue business strategies that would not have been allowed in prior decades. No one stopped them from using free products to centralize the internet and then replace its core functions. No one stopped them from siphoning off the profits of content creators. No one stopped them from gathering data on every aspect of every user's internet life. No one stopped them from amassing market share not seen since the days of Standard Oil. No one stopped them from running massive social and psychological experiments on their users. No one demanded that they police their platforms. It has been a sweet deal.[84]

McNamee, a mentor of Zuckerberg and an early investor in Facebook, contends that companies like "Facebook and Google are now so large that traditional tools of regulation may no longer be effective," citing a lack of relevant legal frameworks and fines commensurate with the scale of abuse.[85] McNamee suggests that any lasting and effective change must be the product of both a shift in the approach and strategies of legislation.

Like any comprehensive and successful change program, the legal arm of responsibility will be a cocktail of both reactive and proactive approaches, including investigations, legislation, and frameworks that address the liability, abuse, and responsibility of tech companies and their leadership. Investigations are, by their nature, reactive, and offer a means of systemic inquiry into actions that may have breached existing laws or standards of conduct. There are simply too many current and past investigations into the conduct of big tech corporations to take inventory; such a list would make our heads spin and put me well over my allotted word count. It is worth briefly delving into the types of lawsuits and investigations that have been brought against big tech, as well as where they originated and how they might inform future policy decisions. Some of the most recent and significant instances include:

- A US lawsuit filed against Google for illegally tracking its customers' movements, even when users had enabled a privacy setting to prevent tracking.[86]
- A class-action lawsuit against Facebook for logging users' text messages and phone calls without their consent.[87]

- A UK investigation, stemming from the Cambridge Analytica scandal, into the use of data analytics in political campaigns, which found that Facebook had breached the Data Protection Act, as users were not made aware that their data could be utilized and shared with political parties. This resulted in a £500,000 fine against the company, the maximum allowed for violating the 1998 Data Protection Act.
- Google is currently being sued for £3.2bn in the UK for tracking and collating the personal information of 4.4 million iPhone users illegally.
- In 2012, Google was fined $22.5m in the US by the FTC for similar practices around user data.
- In 2019, EU regulators fined Google €1.5bn for blocking rival advertisers and stifling competition.
- The EU fined Facebook £94m for providing misleading information over its technical capabilities in terms of sharing user data prior to its acquisition of Whatsapp in 2014.
- And speaking of Whatsapp, in 2016, the EU asked the company to stop sharing data with its parent company, Facebook. In 2017, the latter was fined €3 million by Italy's Antitrust Regulator, AGCM. In 2018, the U.K.'s Information Commissioner's Office determined that WhatsApp had "not identified a lawful basis of processing for any such sharing of personal data" and that "if they had shared the data, they would have been in contravention of the first and second data protection principles of the Data Protection Act."[88]
- Google was fined a record €4.34bn—the largest ever handed down by the European Commission—for anti-competitive practices that included abusing its dominance on Android products and squashing competition.[89]
- The Federal Trade Commission is expected to levy an approximately $5 billion dollar fine against Facebook for violating user privacy, which will be the largest ever issued against a tech company by the FTC.[90] The FTC is also considering whether to hold Zuckerberg personally accountable for the company's privacy failures.

Several conclusions can be drawn from the above information: first, with the exception of the European Commission's historic €4.34bn fine, the financial punishments against big tech are not commensurate with the scale and illegality of their actions. A fine of £500,000 to atone for the chaos and global political ramifications of the Cambridge Analytica scandal is preposterous and in no way serves as a deterrent for a company like Facebook, which takes in the same amount in revenue every five-and-a-half minutes.[91] Both Brian Barrett and McNamee have argued that retroactive fines, while well-intentioned, are simply ineffective.[92][93] New laws, steeper fines, and harsher punishments are rumored to be on the horizon as legislators appear poised to take on the behaviors of big tech. In the weeks following the live-streaming of the Christchurch massacre on Facebook, for example, the EU approved a proposal to impose a 4% fine of total global turnover on tech companies who fail to remove terrorist content on their platforms within one hour.

A second lesson we can take away from the number, scale, and financial penalties of the above investigations are the vast differences between the countries who levy them. Both the EU and individual European countries have implemented far more aggressive regulation than the United States. In Germany, for example, legislators have little tolerance for propaganda, consumer privacy violations, and assaults on democratic processes, and thus have some of the strongest local regulations around hate speech and misinformation. Once implemented, Germany's standards led to a 100% increase in Facebook's performance of removing hate speech.[94] Other countries, such as Finland, rely on a "strong public education system and a coordinated government response... to stave off Russia's propaganda."[95] The U.S., by comparison, has more lenient laws when it comes to policing tech giants, including section 230 of the Communications Decency Act, which protects platforms from being liable for the content on their site.[96] (Nearly all experts in the U.S. agree removing or amending section 230 of the Communications Decency Act is necessary to ensure platforms bear some form of responsibility for what occurs on their platforms.) Barrett suggests that efforts in the EU and Germany "offer something like an outline, if not an outright blueprint" for the U.S. as it moves to increase legislative action.[97]

A final inference we can draw from the above fines and investigations is that the current laws governing the business practices of tech corporations are not fit for purpose. Barrett points out that while the "FTC has a modicum of authority, and has used it when companies grossly overreach—as it did against Facebook in 2011, when the company failed to keep its promises regarding how it treated their data," the agency "can only work with the legislative tools it's given."[98] Based on previous and ongoing investigations, it stands to reason that new, more specific laws are necessary, specifically around data privacy, advertising, hate speech, harassment, and anti-competitive practices. Forward-thinking lawmakers should also consider policies and mitigating strategies to combat developing problems such as misinformation, corporate transparency, and ethical standard for developing AI.

New Laws: Coming Soon to a Platform Near You

While investigations have been fairly plentiful, new laws and policies limiting the power and conduct of tech giants have been stagnant, particularly in the U.S. Historically, Scott Galloway points out that Americans tend to have an aversion to regulation.[99] When it comes to the tech industry, however, there appears to be a growing appetite among Americans for some semblance of law and order. Olivia Solon reports that 83% of people polled in the Tech Media Telecom Pulse Survey support more penalties and laws around data privacy, while 84% say they believe tech companies "should be legally responsible for the content they carry on their systems."[100] Because Silicon Valley companies have failed so spectacularly at self-regulation, Brian Barrett notes "regulation seems not only plausible but imminent," in order to combat the growing number of data breaches and repeated moral lapses from "all corners of Silicon Valley."[101]

In the coming decades, a range of new laws, policies and frameworks will be needed; which issues we prioritize and how we go about drafting and enforcing regulations, however, are yet to be determined. According to Paul Laudicina, chairman of the Global Business Policy Council, forthcoming laws and policies will center around issues of digital content, user privacy, and antitrust legislation.[102] Stanford PhD candidate Melody Guan has argued that a natural place to start is with data privacy, owing to the fact that while big tech prolifically abuses its vast troves of user data, little has been done to combat the harvesting and monetization of that information, particularly in the U.S.

> The poor regard for personal protection and rights in the current unregulated state of affairs shows us that we cannot simply rely on the goodwill of tech companies. Indeed, the nature of corporations themselves may expose them to lawsuits if they fail to prioritize the interests of their shareholders over debatable moral concerns. We need a citizen-centric government to shepherd the ethical and fair use of technology.[103]

In 2018, the EU passed the General Data Protection Regulation (GDPR), which regulates the collection, storage, and use of personal data throughout the 28 member states of the EU. A 2019 report by the U.K.'s Information Commissioner's Office (ICO) suggested that a significant portion of information used for targeted advertising relies on sensitive data, or "special category data," much of which is collected and used without consent. The report suggests that, at least within the EU, less "mature" segments of the adtech industry may be in violation of various elements of GDPR, which prohibits profiling users without consent and requires data to be collected transparently, stored securely, utilized for a lawful basis.[104]

In 2020, California will implement the most comprehensive data privacy law in the U.S., which is modeled to resemble GPDR. Though similar laws have been scarce as of yet in the U.S., some meaningful policies have been implemented, including various cybersecurity bills, revenge porn prevention laws, and the Honest Ads Act, which aims to regulate U.S. political advertising online, similar to how political ads must adhere to specific rules on TV, radio, and in print media.

A second likely area of policy development is antitrust reform; a third is more sensible taxation. Questions around fair competition in tech have already begun to drop, like big fat legislative bombs, onto the likes of Google, Facebook, and Amazon. While Zuckerberg has carefully avoided questions about Facebook's status as a monopoly and has, thus far, avoided legislative action, in 2019, the U.S. Justice Department reportedly began preparing an antitrust investigation of Google,[105] while the

FTC is said to have increased its anticompetitive oversight of Amazon.[106] In 2017, the EU ruled Google had abused its powers by "unfairly favouring its own services and products over others."[107] In an article for MIT Technology Review, Mariana Mazzucato explains that the difficulty of regulating tech companies as monopolies comes back to a perception that the industry is somehow distinct from other corporations, which has allowed tech companies, in particular those providing free services, to sidestep questions about competition and consumer harm.

> Historically, industries naturally prone to monopoly—like railways and water—have been heavily regulated to protect the public against abuses of corporate power such as price gouging. But monopolistic online platforms remain largely unregulated, which means the firms that are first to establish market control can reap extraordinary rewards.[108]

Central to the question of how to impose anti-trust regulation on "free" services is the historical association of antitrust with price setting. Silicon Valley Congressman Ro Khanna has suggested that a new understanding of digital monopolies and antitrust legislation must be adopted which frames the antitrust argument in terms of the broader impacts of monopolies. Khanna has suggested this might include the suppression of innovation, a more nuanced definition of customer harm, and the effects of tech monopolies on wages and job loss.[109] The suppression on innovation can be seen clearly in the acquisition patterns of big tech companies. Between 2007 and 2019, Google acquired over 270 companies, 171 of which were competitive acquisitions. In the same timeframe, Facebook acquired 92 companies, 46 of which were competitors, almost all of which were purchased and then immediately shut down.[110]

As tech corporations operate globally, so too does their money flow freely around the world, ending up increasingly in places like Ireland, which has an extremely low corporate tax, and Bermuda, which has a corporate tax rate of zero. BBC reports that the latter is where Google keeps all of its non-US generated profits. Apple, too, keeps "their profits in the parts of the world that charge the least—if any—tax."[111] Even in the U.S., where most tech companies are based, corporate tax rates can leave the average person both incensed and confused. For the second year in a row in 2018, Amazon paid zero federal taxes in the U.S., despite being valued at close to a trillion dollars and generating profits of $5.6 billion and $11.2 billion in 2017 and 2018, respectively.[112] The Institute on Taxation and Economic Policy reports that Netflix also saw its largest ever profits in 2018, in excess of $800 million, and similarly paid no federal income tax in the U.S. Mariana Mazzucato has argued that the low tax rates tech companies enjoy are "perverse," particularly "given that their success was built on technologies funded and developed by high-risk public investments: if anything, companies that owe their fortunes to taxpayer-funded investments should be repaying the taxpayer, not seeking tax breaks."[113]

Regulating tech companies begins with a better understanding of their business model, social impacts, and corresponding responsibilities. Jessi Hempel has observed that because new businesses "powered by the rise of the internet.... operate differently from those in more traditional industries, they must be regulated differently."[114] Congress and lawmakers, however, have not sufficiently understood the impacts of the tech industry thoroughly enough to effectively regulate them. This trend appears, thankfully, to be changing, as Democratic presidential candidates such as Elizabeth Warren and Amy Klobuchar draw attention to the need for regulation of big tech. Ensuring all members involved in policy decisions are educated about the regulatory differences and impending impacts of the digital economy is paramount to ensuring these are formulated in a way that benefits society at large and addresses both the short- and long-term impacts of technology.

> [We] need the government to assume its rightful role in protecting personal privacy and rights in the AI era. The government needs to step in and use its resources and powers of legislation and coordination to provide the structure for industry and research to develop and utilize AI without compromising civil rights and liberties, and do so soon. What is at issue is unprecedented assault to personal data and behavior; what is at stake is personal safety, privacy, dignity, autonomy, and democracy.[115]

Relevant and meaningful legislation will ultimately be the result of more awareness, knowledge, and wisdom—both on the part of consumers and lawmakers—alongside "smart, well-designed technology"[116] on the part of tech companies.

You Say You Want a Revolution

The emergence of "smart, well-designed technology" will depend on the simultaneous convergence of several crucial changes from within the tech community. These improvements—which include increased awareness, better values, and emotionally intelligent leadership—will challenge the core psychology, and with it the normalized behaviors, of many of the tech industry's most prominent organizations. While these changes are relatively straightforward, they are by no means simple. Changing the culture of an organization can take many years, changing the culture of an entire industry is infinitely more difficult. Working to reform the values and psychological norms of the tech industry, however, will ultimately provide the most comprehensive mitigation of Silicon Valley's most pressing problems. Unless the social values and collective psychology of the tech industry changes at a systemic level, the institutions and products it produces will not.

Notes

1. Kubzansky, M. (2019, February 11). How is Omidyar Network Evolving to Meet Today's Challenges? Retrieved February 12, 2019, from Omidyar Network website: https://www.omidyar.com/spotlight/how-omidyar-network-evolving-meet-todays-challenges
2. Zuckerberg, M. (2018, July 18). *Zuckerberg: The Recode Interview* (K. Swisher, Interviewer). Retrieved from https://www.recode.net/2018/7/18/17575156/mark-zuckerberg-interview-facebook-recode-kara-swisher
3. Ibid.
4. Thakrar, M. (2018, December 19). Political Savvy and Emotional Intelligence. Retrieved April 25, 2019, from *Forbes* website: https://www.forbes.com/sites/forbescoachescouncil/2018/12/19/political-savvy-and-emotional-intelligence/

5. Goleman, D. (2006). *Working with Emotional Intelligence* (p. 318). New York: Bantam Dell.
6. Hollis, J. (2002). *The Archetypal Imagination* (New ed., p. 39). College Station: Texas A&M University Press.
7. Eurich, T. (2018, January 4). What Self-awareness Really is (and How to Cultivate It). Retrieved September 1, 2018, from *Harvard Business Review* website: https://hbr.org/2018/01/what-self-awareness-really-is-and-how-to-cultivate-it
8. Silvia, P. J., & O'Brien, M. E. (2004). Self-awareness and Constructive Functioning: Revisiting "the Human Dilemma." *Journal of Social and Clinical Psychology, 23*(4), 475–489. https://doi.org/10.1521/jscp.23.4.475.40307
9. Sutton, A., Williams, H. M., & Allinson, C. W. (2015). A Longitudinal, Mixed Method Evaluation of Self-awareness Training in the Workplace. *European Journal of Training and Development.* https://doi.org/10.1108/EJTD-04-2015-0031
10. Siegler, M. G. (2018, April 18). Arrogance Peaks in Silicon Valley. Retrieved August 19, 2018, from *500ish Words* website: https://500ish.com/arrogance-peaks-in-silicon-valley-b3020f542e5e
11. Vogelstein, F., & Thompson, N. (2018, February 12). Inside Facebook's Two Years of Hell. *Wired.* Retrieved from https://www.wired.com/story/inside-facebook-mark-zuckerberg-2-years-of-hell/
12. Chiang, T. (2017, December 18). Silicon Valley is Turning into Its Own Worst Fear. Retrieved August 19, 2018, from *BuzzFeed News* website: https://www.buzzfeednews.com/article/tedchiang/the-real-danger-to-civilization-isnt-ai-its-runaway
13. Vogelstein, F., & Thompson, N. (2018, February 12). Inside Facebook's Two Years of Hell. *Wired.* Retrieved from https://www.wired.com/story/inside-facebook-mark-zuckerberg-2-years-of-hell/
14. Chiang, T. (2017, December 18). Silicon Valley is Turning into Its Own Worst Fear. Retrieved August 19, 2018, from *BuzzFeed News* website: https://www.buzzfeednews.com/article/tedchiang/the-real-danger-to-civilization-isnt-ai-its-runaway
15. Eurich, T. (2018, January 4). What Self-awareness Really is (and How to Cultivate It). Retrieved September 1, 2018, from *Harvard Business Review* website: https://hbr.org/2018/01/what-self-awareness-really-is-and-how-to-cultivate-it
16. Rodriguez, S. (2019). Facebook Culture Described as "Cult-like", Review Process Blamed. Retrieved February 18, 2019, from https://

www.cnbc.com/2019/01/08/facebook-culture-cult-performance-review-process-blamed.html

17. Read, M. (2018). The Decline and Fall of the Zuckerberg Empire. *Intelligencer*. Retrieved February 18, 2019, from http://nymag.com/intelligencer/2018/11/the-decline-and-fall-of-the-zuckerberg-empire.html

18. Chiang, T. (2017, December 18). Silicon Valley is Turning into Its Own Worst Fear. Retrieved August 19, 2018, from *BuzzFeed News* website: https://www.buzzfeednews.com/article/tedchiang/the-real-danger-to-civilization-isnt-ai-its-runaway

19. Galloway, T. W. (1917). Chapter 3: Some Essential Natural Elements in Education. In *The Use of Motives in Teaching Morals and Religion* (p. 40). Boston: The Pilgrim Press.

20. Bazalgette, P. (2017). *The Empathy Instinct: How to Create a More Civil Society* (pp. 3–4). London: John Murray.

21. Research shows that empathy is not only demonstrated in humans, but can also be observed across a range of other animal species, including orcas, dolphins, chimpanzees, bonobos, and even rodents, suggesting it may be a highly adaptable evolutionary trait.

22. Bazalgette, P. (2017). *The Empathy Instinct: How to Create a More Civil Society* (p. 3). London: John Murray.

23. Baron-Cohen, S. (2011). *Zero Degrees of Empathy: A New Theory of Human Cruelty* (p. 103). London: Allen Lane.

24. Bartal, I., Decety, J., & Mason, P. (2011). Helping a Cagemate in Need: Empathy and Pro-social Behavior in Rats. *Science, 334*(6061), 1427–1430. https://doi.org/10.1126/science.1210789

25. Decety, J. (2011). The Neuroevolution of Empathy. *Annals of the New York Academy of Sciences, 1231*(1), 35–45. https://doi.org/10.1111/j.1749-6632.2011.06027.x

26. Malik, O. (2016, November 28). Silicon Valley has an Empathy Vacuum. *The New Yorker*. Retrieved from https://www.newyorker.com/business/currency/silicon-valley-has-an-empathy-vacuum

27. Ibid.

28. Ibid.

29. Ibid.

30. Ibid.

31. Gocłowska, M. A., Crisp, R. J., & Labuschagne, K. (2013). Can Counter-Stereotypes Boost Flexible Thinking? *Group Processes &*

Intergroup Relations, 16(2), 217–231. https://doi.org/10.1177/1368430212445076

32. Maddux, W. W., & Galinsky, A. D. (2009). Cultural Borders and Mental Barriers: The Relationship between Living Abroad and Creativity. *Journal of Personality and Social Psychology, 96*(5), 1047. https://doi.org/10.1037/a0014861

33. Tarnoff, B. (2017, September 5). *Interview with Ben Tarnoff* (K. Cook, Interviewer).

34. Pirlot, C. (2019, February 22). Become a Better Developer by Increasing Your Empathy. Retrieved May 22, 2019, from *Welcome to the Jungle* website: https://www.welcometothejungle.co/fr/articles/better-developer-empathy

35. Friedman, T. L. (2016). *Thank You for Being Late: An Optimist's Guide to Thriving in the Age of Accelerations* (p. 202). New York: Farrar, Straus and Giroux.

36. Haque, U. (2018, March 16). Why Leadership Needs a Revolution. Retrieved August 31, 2018, from *Eudaimonia and Co* website: https://eand.co/its-making-us-bullies-or-wimps-leadership-needs-a-revolution-db10aff6dba3

37. Stan, A. (2018, July 1). Facebook Co-founder Chris Hughes is Fighting for Fairer Incomes. Retrieved September 12, 2018, from *Tech Crunch* website: http://social.techcrunch.com/2018/07/01/facebook-co-founder-chris-hughes-is-fighting-for-fairer-incomes/

38. Rosoff, M. (2018, March 18). Facebook Failing, Zuckerberg and Sandberg Absent. Retrieved August 31, 2018, from https://www.cnbc.com/2018/03/18/facebook-failing-zuckerberg-and-sandberg-absent-commentary.html

39. Filloux, F. (2018, August 20). Facebook's Flawed DNA Makes It Unable to Fight Misinformation. Retrieved September 6, 2018, from *Monday Note* website: https://mondaynote.com/facebooks-flawed-dna-makes-it-unable-to-fight-misinformation-3d0623282e79

40. Kanter, J. (2019, June 4). Facebook Shareholder Revolt Gets Bloody: Powerless Investors Vote Overwhelmingly to Oust Zuckerberg as Chairman. Retrieved June 12, 2019, from *Business Insider* website: https://www.businessinsider.com/facebook-investors-vote-to-fire-mark-zuckerberg-as-chairman-2019-6

41. Rosoff, M. (2018, March 18). Facebook Failing, Zuckerberg and Sandberg Absent. Retrieved August 31, 2018, from https://www.cnbc.

com/2018/03/18/facebook-failing-zuckerberg-and-sandberg-absent-commentary.html

42. De Pree, M. (1989). *Leadership is an Art* (Later Printing ed., pp. 11–13). New York: Doubleday Business.

43. Lidow, D. (2014). *Startup Leadership: How Savvy Entrepreneurs Turn Their Ideas into Successful Enterprises* (p. 9). John Wiley & Sons.

44. While ethics are part of professional education in many fields, such as medicine, aviation, and law, they have not been mandatory in computer science, AI, or related technology fields. Recently, some universities have started offering ethics as a part of their curriculum, these are typically theoretical rather than practical Universities, such as Harvard, MIT, Stanford, University of Texas at Austin have each developed new courses on ethics and AI regulation that examine the impacts of the technology that their students might go on to create. Recognizing their role in creating some of tech's most prominent founders and engineers, Stanford's course aims to more effectively train incoming engineers and covers topics such as AI, autonomous vehicles, privacy, and civil rights, as well as the ethics of existing platforms, like Facebook.

45. Kasriel, S. (2017, August 14). 6 Ways to Make Sure AI Creates Jobs for All and Not the Few. Retrieved September 19, 2018, from World Economic Forum website: https://www.weforum.org/agenda/2017/08/ways-to-ensure-ai-robots-create-jobs-for-all/

46. Taddeo, M., & Floridi, L. (2018). How AI can be a Force for Good. *Science, 361*(6404), 751–752. https://doi.org/10.1126/science.aat5991

47. Selinger, E., & Frischmann, B. (2018, March 23). How Self-driving Car Policy Will Determine Life, Death and Everything In-between. Retrieved September 17, 2018, from *Motherboard* website: https://motherboard.vice.com/en_us/article/j5a8d3/self-driving-car-policy-uber

48. Harari, Y. N. (2014). *Sapiens: A Brief History of Humankind* (p. 295). London: Vintage.

49. Ibid., p. 302.

50. Harari, Y. N. (2017). *Homo Deus: A Brief History of Tomorrow* (p. 277). London: Vintage.

51. Hutt, J. J. (2018, April 26). Why YouTube Shouldn't Over-Rely on Artificial Intelligence to Police Its Platform. Retrieved September 3, 2018, from American Civil Liberties Union website: https://www.aclu.org/blog/privacy-technology/internet-privacy/why-youtube-shouldnt-over-rely-artificial-intelligence

52. Ibid.

53. Naughton, J. (2018, March 18). Extremism Pays. That's Why Silicon Valley Isn't Shutting It Down. *The Guardian*. Retrieved from https://www.theguardian.com/commentisfree/2018/mar/18/extremism-pays-why-silicon-valley-not-shutting-it-down-youtube

54. Parakilas, S. (2018, January 30). Facebook Wants to Fix Itself. Here's a Better Solution. *Wired*. Retrieved from https://www.wired.com/story/facebook-wants-to-fix-itself-heres-a-better-solution/

55. Hoffmann, A. L. (2017, January 24). A Chief Ethics Officer Won't Fix Facebook's Problems. Retrieved February 17, 2019, from *Slate Magazine* website: https://slate.com/technology/2017/01/a-chief-ethics-officer-wont-fix-facebooks-problems.html

56. Johnson, S. (2018, January 16). Beyond the Bitcoin Bubble. *The New York Times*. Retrieved from https://www.nytimes.com/2018/01/16/magazine/beyond-the-bitcoin-bubble.html

57. Wadhwa, V. (2018, June 12). Why Liberal Arts and the Humanities are as Important as Engineering. *Washington Post*. Retrieved from https://www.washingtonpost.com/news/innovations/wp/2018/06/12/why-liberal-arts-and-the-humanities-are-as-important-as-engineering/

58. Irving, G., & Askell, A. (2019). AI Safety Needs Social Scientists. *Distill, 4*(2), e14. https://doi.org/10.23915/distill.00014

59. Freed, R. (2018, March 12). The Tech Industry's Psychological War on Kids. Retrieved September 8, 2018, from Richard Freed website: https://medium.com/@richardnfreed/the-tech-industrys-psychological-war-on-kids-c452870464ce

60. Maheshwari, S. (2018, April 18). Facebook's Current Status with Advertisers? It's Complicated. *The New York Times*. Retrieved from https://www.nytimes.com/2018/04/18/business/media/facebook-advertisers-privacy-data.html

61. Thompson, B. (2018, May 2). Divine Discontent: Disruption's Antidote. Retrieved August 27, 2018, from Stratechery by Ben Thompson website: https://stratechery.com/2018/divine-discontent-disruptions-antidote/

62. Palihapitiya, C. (2017, November 17). *Money as an Instrument of Change* (Stanford Graduate School of Business, Interviewer). Retrieved from https://www.youtube.com/watch?v=PMotykw0SIk&feature=youtu.be

63. Kozlowska, H., Murphy, M., Coren, M. J., & Rodriguez, A. (2018, March 25). Facebook is Too Big to Fail. Retrieved September 3, 2018, from *Quartz* website: https://qz.com/1236564/facebook-is-too-big-to-fail/

64. Kowitt, B. (2019, May 17). Inside Google's Civil War. Retrieved May 21, 2019, from *Fortune* website: http://fortune.com/longform/inside-googles-civil-war/

65. Rappleye, H., & Riordan Seville, L. (2019, June 9). 24 Immigrants have Died in ICE Custody During the Trump Administration. Retrieved June 14, 2019, from *NBC News* website: https://www.nbcnews.com/politics/immigration/24-immigrants-have-died-ice-custody-during-trump-administration-n1015291

66. Frenkel, S. (2018, June 20). Microsoft Employees Protest Work with ICE, as Tech Industry Mobilizes Over Immigration. *The New York Times*. Retrieved from https://www.nytimes.com/2018/06/19/technology/tech-companies-immigration-border.html

67. ACLU. (2019, May 22). Face Surveillance Arms Governments with Unprecedented Power to Track, Control, and Harm People. It is Perhaps the Most Dangerous Surveillance Technology Ever Developed, and It Needs to Come under Democratic Control. [Tweet]. Retrieved May 23, 2019, from @ACLU: https://twitter.com/ACLU/status/1131228523186802688

68. Tiku, N. (2018, June 19). Microsoft's Ethical Reckoning is Here. *Wired*. Retrieved from https://www.wired.com/story/microsofts-ethical-reckoning-is-here/

69. Fang, L. (2018, March 6). Google is Quietly Providing AI Technology for Drone Strike Targeting Project. Retrieved September 10, 2018, from *The Intercept* website: https://theintercept.com/2018/03/06/google-is-quietly-providing-ai-technology-for-drone-strike-targeting-project/

70. We Work for Google. It shouldn't be in the Business of War: Open Letter Signed by Google Employees. (2018, April 5). *The Guardian*. Retrieved from https://www.theguardian.com/commentisfree/2018/apr/04/google-ceo-drones-ai-war-surveillance

71. Godz, P. (2018, June 6). Tech Workers Versus the Pentagon. Retrieved August 31, 2018, from http://jacobinmag.com/2018/06/google-project-maven-military-tech-workers

72. Tiku, N. (2018, June 19). Microsoft's Ethical Reckoning is Here. *Wired*. Retrieved from https://www.wired.com/story/microsofts-ethical-reckoning-is-here/

73. Cronk, T. (2018, May 2). DoD Official: Lethality, Readiness Drive Acquisition and Sustainment Reform. *U.S. Department of Defense.* Retrieved from https://dod.defense.gov/News/Article/Article/1510642/dod-official-lethality-readiness-drive-acquisition-and-sustainment-reform/

74. Shane, S., & Wakabayashi, D. (2018, July 30). 'The Business of War': Google Employees Protest Work for the Pentagon. *The New York Times.* Retrieved from https://www.nytimes.com/2018/04/04/technology/google-letter-ceo-pentagon-project.html

75. Balakrishnan, A. (2018, June 5). WhatsApp's Co-founders Reportedly Gave Up $1.3 Billion as Facebook Merger Devolved to 'Low Class' Spat. *CNBC.* Retrieved from https://www.cnbc.com/2018/06/05/why-whatsapp-co-founders-koum-acton-left-facebook-wsj.html

76. Ibid.

77. Ibid.

78. Wakabayashi, D. (2019, March 12). Google Approved $45 Million Exit Package for Executive Accused of Misconduct. *The New York Times.* Retrieved from https://www.nytimes.com/2019/03/11/technology/google-misconduct-exit-package.html

79. Dwoskin, E. (2019, January 10). Google Shareholder Sues Company Board, Senior Managers for Allegedly Covering up Sexual Misconduct. *Washington Post.* Retrieved from https://beta.washingtonpost.com/business/economy/google-shareholder-sues-company-board-senior-managers-for-allegedly-covering-up-sexual-misconduct/2019/01/10/6226f36a-1519-11e9-90a8-136fa44b80ba_story.html?outputType=amp

80. Sepah, D. C. (2017, March 3). Your Company Culture is Who You Hire, Fire, and Promote. Retrieved May 22, 2019, from *Medium* website: https://medium.com/s/company-culture/your-companys-culture-is-who-you-hire-fire-and-promote-c69f84902983

81. Tarnoff, B., & Weigel, M. (2018, May 3). Why Silicon Valley Can't Fix Itself. *The Guardian.* Retrieved from https://www.theguardian.com/news/2018/may/03/why-silicon-valley-cant-fix-itself-tech-humanism

82. Maloney, D. (2018, April 26). Self-education is Our Best Bet in the Fight against the Panopticon. Retrieved September 1, 2018, from *Medium* website: https://medium.com/s/internet-law-and-ethics-101/self-education-is-our-best-bet-in-the-fight-against-the-panopticon-4584fe086066

83. Childs, A., & Zegart, K. (2018, December 13). The Divide between Silicon Valley and Washington is a National-Security Threat. Retrieved May 23, 2019, from *The Atlantic* website: https://www.theatlantic.com/ideas/archive/2018/12/growing-gulf-between-silicon-valley-and-washington/577963/

84. McNamee, R. (2018, January 7). How to Fix Facebook—Before It Fixes Us. *Washington Monthly, January/February/March 2018.* Retrieved from https://washingtonmonthly.com/magazine/january-february-march-2018/how-to-fix-facebook-before-it-fixes-us/

85. Ibid.

86. Stempel, J. (2018, August 20). Lawsuit Says Google Tracks Phone Users Regardless of Privacy Settings. *Reuters.* Retrieved from https://www.reuters.com/article/us-alphabet-google-privacy-lawsuit/lawsuit-says-google-tracks-phone-users-regardless-of-privacy-settings-idUSKCN1L51M3

87. Gibbs, S. (2018, May 11). Facebook Hit with Class Action Lawsuit over Collection of Texts and Call Logs. *The Guardian.* Retrieved from https://www.theguardian.com/technology/2018/may/11/facebook-class-action-lawsuit-collection-texts-call-logs

88. Gibbs, S. (2018, March 14). WhatsApp Sharing User Data with Facebook Would be Illegal, Rules ICO. *The Guardian.* Retrieved from https://www.theguardian.com/technology/2018/mar/14/whatsapp-sharing-user-data-facebook-illegal-ico-gdpr

89. Google hit with record €4.3bn Android fine. (2018, July 18). *BBC News.* Retrieved from https://www.bbc.com/news/technology-44858238

90. Romm, T. (2019, February 14). The U.S. Government and Facebook are Negotiating a Record, Multibillion-Dollar Fine for the Company's Privacy Lapses. *Washington Post.* Retrieved from https://www.washingtonpost.com/technology/2019/02/14/us-government-facebook-are-negotiating-record-multi-billion-dollar-fine-companys-privacy-lapses/

91. Hern, A., & Pegg, D. (2018, July 10). Facebook Fined for Data Breaches in Cambridge Analytica Scandal. *The Guardian.* Retrieved from http://www.theguardian.com/technology/2018/jul/11/facebook-fined-for-data-breaches-in-cambridge-analytica-scandal

92. Barrett, B. (2018, March 22). What Would Regulating Facebook Look Like? *Wired.* Retrieved from https://www.wired.com/story/what-would-regulating-facebook-look-like/

93. McNamee, R. (2018, January 7). How to Fix Facebook—Before It Fixes Us. *Washington Monthly, January/February/March 2018*. Retrieved from https://washingtonmonthly.com/magazine/january-february-march-2018/how-to-fix-facebook-before-it-fixes-us/

94. Bennhold, K. (2018, May 19). Germany Acts to Tame Facebook, Learning from Its Own History of Hate. *The New York Times*. Retrieved from https://www.nytimes.com/2018/05/19/technology/facebook-deletion-center-germany.html

95. Barrett, B. (2018, March 22). What Would Regulating Facebook Look Like? *Wired*. Retrieved from https://www.wired.com/story/what-would-regulating-facebook-look-like/

96. Solon, O. (2018, April 20). Americans Want Tougher Rules for Big Tech Amid Privacy Scandals, Poll Finds. *The Guardian*. Retrieved from http://www.theguardian.com/technology/2018/apr/20/facebook-tech-companies-us-privacy-poll

97. Barrett, B. (2018, March 22). What Would Regulating Facebook Look Like? *Wired*. Retrieved from https://www.wired.com/story/what-would-regulating-facebook-look-like/

98. Ibid.

99. Galloway, S. (2018, February 8). The Case for Breaking up Amazon, Apple, Facebook and Google. Retrieved August 31, 2018, from *Esquire* website: https://www.esquire.com/news-politics/a15895746/bust-big-tech-silicon-valley/

100. Solon, O. (2018, April 20). Americans Want Tougher Rules for Big Tech Amid Privacy Scandals, Poll Finds. *The Guardian*. Retrieved from http://www.theguardian.com/technology/2018/apr/20/facebook-tech-companies-us-privacy-poll

101. Barrett, B. (2018, March 22). What Would Regulating Facebook Look Like? *Wired*. Retrieved from https://www.wired.com/story/what-would-regulating-facebook-look-like/

102. Laudicina, P. (2018, March 12). This is the Future of the Internet. Retrieved September 18, 2018, from World Economic Forum website: https://www.weforum.org/agenda/2018/03/this-is-the-future-of-the-internet/

103. Guan, M. (2018, July 9). Regulating AI in the Era of Big Tech. Retrieved August 18, 2018, from *The Gradient* website: https://thegradient.pub/regulating-ai-in-the-era-of-big-tech/

104. Information Commissioner's Office. (2019). *Update Report into Adtech and Real Time Bidding.* Retrieved from https://ico.org.uk/media/about-the-ico/documents/2615156/adtech-real-time-bidding-report-201906.pdf
105. Kendall, B., & McKinnon, J. D. (2019, June 1). Justice Department is Preparing Antitrust Investigation of Google. *Wall Street Journal.* Retrieved from https://www.wsj.com/articles/justice-department-is-preparing-antitrust-investigation-of-google-11559348795
106. Romm, T. (2019, June 1). Amazon could Face Heightened Antitrust Scrutiny under a New Agreement between U.S. Regulators. *Washington Post.* Retrieved from https://www.washingtonpost.com/technology/2019/06/02/amazon-could-face-heightened-antitrust-scrutiny-under-new-agreement-between-us-regulators/
107. Laudicina, P. (2018, March 12). This is the Future of the Internet. Retrieved September 18, 2018, from World Economic Forum website: https://www.weforum.org/agenda/2018/03/this-is-the-future-of-the-internet/
108. Mazzucato, M. (2018, June 27). Let's Make Private Data into a Public Good. Retrieved September 5, 2018, from *MIT Technology Review* website: https://www.technologyreview.com/s/611489/lets-make-private-data-into-a-public-good/
109. Johnson, S. (2018, July 24). The Political Education of Silicon Valley. *Wired.* Retrieved from https://www.wired.com/story/political-education-silicon-valley/
110. Wu, T., & Thompson, S. A. (2019, June 7). The Roots of Big Tech Run Disturbingly Deep. *The New York Times.* Retrieved from https://www.nytimes.com/interactive/2019/06/07/opinion/google-facebook-mergers-acquisitions-antitrust.html?smid=nytcore-ios-share
111. Jack, S. (2017, November 21). Google—Powerful and Responsible? *BBC News.* Retrieved from https://www.bbc.com/news/business-42060091
112. Gardner, M. (2019). *Amazon in Its Prime: Doubles Profits, Pays $0 in Federal Income Taxes.* Retrieved from Institute on Taxation and Economic Policy website: https://itep.org/amazon-in-its-prime-doubles-profits-pays-0-in-federal-income-taxes/
113. Mazzucato, M. (2018, June 27). Let's make Private Data into a Public Good. Retrieved September 5, 2018, from *MIT Technology Review* website: https://www.technologyreview.com/s/611489/lets-make-private-data-into-a-public-good/

114. Hempel, J. (2018, April 16). What Tech's Insiders Think about Zuckerberg's Command Performance. *Wired*. Retrieved from https://www.wired.com/story/the-zuckerberg-hearings-were-silicon-valleys-ultimate-debut/
115. Guan, M. (2018, July 9). Regulating AI in the Era of Big Tech. Retrieved August 18, 2018, from *The Gradient* website: https://thegradient.pub/regulating-ai-in-the-era-of-big-tech/
116. Bazalgette, P. (2017). *The Empathy Instinct: How to Create a More Civil Society* (p. 130). London: John Murray.

10

Conclusion

There is a quote from Theodore Parker, often attributed to Martin Luther King Jr., which states, "the arc of the moral universe is long, but it bends towards justice."[1] Despite some evidence to the contrary, I tend to agree with Parker—perhaps because I have to; it would certainly be harder to get up in the morning if it seemed we were going backwards.

The rather solemn truth, which I know you can handle if you've read this far, is that this moment demands a great deal of us. We are in the midst of an unprecedented transition, standing at a crossroads, the stakes of which are incredibly high. Climate change, economic inequality, job displacement, civic unrest, and the corruption of truth and our social wellbeing each impel us to act, collectively and quickly, to avoid a range of potential catastrophes. Ady Barkan, a healthcare activist and Director of the Center for Popular Democracy's Fed Up Campaign, explains the significance of our historical moment:

> We will either become a society that works exclusively for the rich and powerful, or we will enact large-scale structural reforms that restore fairness to our economy and political system. Each of us is called to do everything we can to ensure our society winds up in the right place.... The wealthy and the powerful in this country want nothing more than for us to tune

© The Author(s) 2020
K. Cook, *The Psychology of Silicon Valley*,
https://doi.org/10.1007/978-3-030-27364-4_10

out.... get cynical and lose hope, because that only solidifies their grip on all of this. We need to fight that instinct, hold onto hope, and keep fighting for a better future.[2]

How do we follow Barkan's advice, hold onto hope, and fight for a better future in the face of such profound and sweeping change?

Before we run to act, it is worth pausing to acknowledge (or at least assume) that no one company or individual orchestrated the more nefarious impacts of technology knowingly. The negative consequences of technology are the result of the social and economic systems in which the tech industry operates and are unintended side effects of technological progress; it follows that these are also unplanned for. No one anticipated Facebook data could be weaponized to psychologically profile its users and incite white nationalism; YouTube would send whole cultures down rabbit holes of extreme and false information; or that a few, mostly white, mostly male billionaires would financially benefit from the digital revolution at the cost of economic stability and a bifurcated job market. It's understandable that we have yet to illustrate the playbook we use to set these and other problems right and it's worth reiterating that we're all in this together.

In order to address the consequences of the digital world we so enthusiastically adopted, we need to understand what went wrong in the first place. Carl Jung observed, of a different but equally perilous impending catastrophe, that "[i]t is not the bomb that is the danger, but the psychology of the men who control it."[3] Identifying the priorities, beliefs, and psychology of Silicon Valley that drive the problems created by tech is the first step to solving them.

Once we understand the psychology and values driving the industry, our responsibility rests on one simple thought: a belief that the world can be better than it currently is. This is our second, most difficult, and perhaps our most crucial task. Demanding a better future in the face of those that often seem to want nothing more than our fear, oppression, and complacency requires hope, resilience, and a shared reliance on each other for support.

Our third and final duty is to ensure the industry moves forward with better values and healthier psychological norms. This demands not only an awareness of the factors that have led us to this critical point, but also a collective re-envisioning of the tech industry's ethical foundations, such that we can proceed in the most appropriate and socially healthy way possible. The informational chaos of Facebook, Twitter, and YouTube; the bifurcation of the job market by Uber and others reliant on the gig economy; and the miserable working conditions in Amazon's factories share a central commonality, according to Ben Tarnoff and Moira Weigel: they "are profitable. If they were not, they would not exist. They are symptoms of a profound democratic deficit inflicted by a system that prioritises the wealth of the few over the needs and desires of the many."[4] The greed described by Tarnoff and Weigel, according to technology strategist and activist Andrew Rasiej, is one of the chief values in the industry we should aim to eliminate, along with speed and misogyny, while those we should attempt to instill include empathy, diversity, and equity.[5] To Rasiej's thoughtful list I would add the importance of collectively growing our emotional intelligence and awareness, which are the cornerstones of progress and psychological development.

In the same way positive thoughts can advance a prosocial agenda, negative thoughts can derail one. Our current political climate, combined with the ease of online outrage and a collective nervousness about the future, makes immobilizing our negative thoughts even harder than holding onto our positive ones. It's never been easier to backslide into feelings of fear and anger. It's worth bearing in mind, however, that panic and blame in particular "can distract us from looking at the whole system"[6] and taking meaningful action. As Hans Rosling explains, when we retreat to our respective corners, point fingers, and "identify the bad guy, we are done thinking. And it's almost always more complicated than that. It's almost always about multiple interacting causes—a system. If you really want to change the world, you have to understand [it]."[7] A more sophisticated method of thinking about how to improve technology demands not only emotional intelligence and psychological maturity, but, as Rosling outlines, perspective and the capacity to think systemically and across disciplines.

A revolution of systems and values may not sound as exciting as traditional social uprisings (unless you're me, who would consider a values reformation downright sexy). Such an evolution of thinking, behaviors, and ethics, however, could considerably mitigate the formidable task ahead of us, course-correct an unsustainable, hypercapitalist system, and help us to avoid actual, real-life, Age of Revolution-esque uprisings. Maintaining a functional, peaceful society lies in creating a safe, economically secure, equitable culture informed by prosocial values. Consider the impact, then, of reimagining the collective psychology of the world's most influential industry such that its values and behaviors were aligned with social good. Where priorities like privacy, facts, and wellbeing outweighed tracking, click-bait, and the exploitation of our attention. Where arrogance and insularity were supplanted by openness and collaboration, and pursuit of profits and power was replaced by a prioritization of ethics and emotional intelligence.

The creator of the World Wide Web, Tim Berners-Lee, has repeatedly expressed his dismay at the current state of his invention and a desire to restore the more prosocial foundations of the internet as he intended it to be. "I want to challenge us all to have greater ambitions for the web," Berners-Lee states, "I want the web to reflect our hopes and fulfil our dreams, rather than magnify our fears and deepen our divisions."[8] Berners-Lee is currently working on Solid, a decentralized online ecosystem that will give users power over their data and revive the peer-to-peer, open protocol on which the internet was originally developed. Solid is an example of technology built on the foundations of values and shared social good that gets us closer to the world as many of us imagine it could be—a world where we trust each other again, feel safe in our environments (both online and off), and use technology to create the best future for the greatest number of people, rather than an elite few. Are we up to the task? I believe we most certainly are. But only if we can appreciate how we got here, define a new narrative based on shared human values, and build up the parts of our psychology and humanity that will get us where we want to go.

Notes

1. Parker, T. (1918). Justice. In J. H. Holmes, H. D. Brown, H. E. Redding, & T. Goldsmith (Eds.), *Readings from Great Authors* (p. 18). New York: Dodd and Mead. (Martin Luther King, Jr., referenced Parker's quote in a 1958 article and again in a 1964 commencement ceremony.)

2. Favreau, J. (2019, May 2). *Pod Save America*. Retrieved from https://open.spotify.com/episode/02yFiyQATJQdnaCl9mKbEe?si=0-sMfVY9TBmVbVkD3i-jMA

3. Jung, C. G. (1970). *Mysterium Coniunctionis: An Inquiry into the Separation and Synthesis of Psychic Opposites in Alchemy* (H. Read, M. Fordham, & G. Adler, Eds., R. F. C. Hull, Trans., 2nd ed., p. XX). Princeton, NJ: Princeton University Press.

4. Tarnoff, B., & Weigel, M. (2018, May 3). Why Silicon Valley Can't Fix Itself. *The Guardian*. Retrieved from https://www.theguardian.com/news/2018/may/03/why-silicon-valley-cant-fix-itself-tech-humanism

5. Rasiej, A. (2018, September). *Interview with Andrew Rasiej* (K. Cook, Interviewer).

6. Rosling, H., Rosling, O., & Rosling Rönnlund, A. (2018). *Factfulness: Ten Reasons We're Wrong about the World—And Why Things are Better Than You Think* (p. 214). London: Sceptre.

7. Ibid., p. 221.

8. Berners-Lee, T. (2018, March 12). The Web is under Threat. Join Us and Fight for It. Retrieved August 18, 2018, from World Wide Web Foundation website: https://webfoundation.org/2018/03/web-birthday-29/

Index[1]

[1] Note: Page numbers followed by 'n' refer to notes.

CPSIA information can be obtained
at www.ICGtesting.com
Printed in the USA
LVHW081612061019

633339LV00001B/1/P

9 783030 273637